RAP-UP

★ THE ULTIMATE ★ GUIDE TO HIP-HOP AND R&B

CAMERON LAZERINE AND DEVIN LAZERINE

★ FOREWORD BY T.I. ★

GRAND CENTRAL
PUBLISHING

NEW YORK   BOSTON

Grand Central Publishing
Hachette Book Group USA
237 Park Avenue
New York, NY 10017

Visit our Web site at www.HachetteBookGroupUSA.com.

Printed in the United States of America

First Edition: February 2008

10 9 8 7 6 5 4 3 2 1

Grand Central Publishing is a division of Hachette Book Group USA, Inc. The Grand
Central Publishing name and logo is a trademark of Hachette Book Group USA, Inc.

Library of Congress Cataloging-in-Publication Data

Lazerine, Cameron.
    Rap-up : the ultimate guide to hip-hop and R&B / Cameron Lazerine & Devin Lazerine.
—1st ed.
        p.   cm.
    ISBN: 978-0-446-17820-4
    1. Rap (Music)—History and criticism. 2. Rhythm and blues music—History and
criticism. 3. Rap musicians—United States. 4. Rhythm and blues musicians—United
States. I. Lazerine, Devin. II. Title.
    ML3531.L39 2007
    782.421649—dc22

                                                                        2007015309

Author photography by Suzuki K.
Cover illustration by UPSO.org
Cover design and interior illustrations by Ian Lynam
Book design and text composition by Anne Ricigliano

This book is dedicated to Mom and Dad.
Thank you for your never-ending love and support.

CONTENTS

FOREWORD

By T.I.

I WAS BORN IN 1980, NOT LONG AFTER THE SUGARHILL GANG'S "Rapper's Delight" became the first hip-hop song to blow up nationally. So I guess you could say that hip-hop and I grew up together. As a kid I never imagined that the South would explode the way it has, but as an adult I've been fortunate enough to be part of hip-hop's evolution. It's exciting to think that kids today grow up listening to me the same way I grew up listening to Scarface, Master P, and Bun B.

Like pretty much everyone, I was into Run-D.M.C. How couldn't I be? The look, the songs, the attitude—what kid could resist? But the first joints I remember really, really getting into were N.W.A.'s *Straight Outta Compton* and LL Cool J's "I'm Bad." It's hard to say exactly what it was that struck me about either of these joints except that they felt really young and raw and dangerous. They moved me in a way nothing had really moved me before. They grabbed a hold of me and made me think, "Man, I wanna do this too."

So I started rapping along to all the songs I liked on the radio, but then around 1988 when I was seven or eight I started writing rhymes of my own. At first I rapped about typical kid shit—being the best rapper, having a good time, and taking pride in my 'hood. But I also rapped about the things my uncles used to be motivated by—nice cars, having lots of money.

As a kid it never occurred to me that people made money off of rap, let alone that I could pursue it as a career. Who thinks that far ahead? I was just having fun. Besides, hip-hop wasn't the big business it would become. It was more local and underground. Then the first acts from the South started to explode. You could hear the Geto Boys' "Mind Playing Tricks on Me" everywhere and not just in the South. Then Kris Kross came with "Jump" and I started to put two and two together and realize what hip-hop could do for people. Then OutKast came out.

Growing up, OutKast, Scarface, and UGK were the undisputed kings of the South. No question. They were the acts that held it down until the rest of the country was ready to hear different voices from the South, the Master Ps and Juveniles and T.I.'s.

People sometimes ask me what rappers I'm influenced by, and I've got to say I'm influenced by life more than anything else. When I'm writing rhymes I think about dealing drugs and people I know and shit that I've been through rather than another rapper's style. I didn't listen to Jay-Z's *Reasonable Doubt* over and over and over again so I could study his rhyme patterns or flow so I could imitate them. I didn't sound anything like Jay-Z back then. I did listen to *Reasonable Doubt* over and over and over again, but that didn't influence my style.

Jay-Z and I were worlds apart. I could relate to a lot of what he was rhyming about on *Reasonable Doubt* but there was a lot of shit on there I didn't really have knowledge about at the time, like Cristal. I didn't know what the fuck Cristal was—and Range Rovers. There were maybe four or five Range Rovers in Atlanta at the time. I couldn't really identify with a lot of what Jay was talking about, but I could recognize skill. With B.I.G. and the Coogi sweaters, I knew what that was all about. Jay went over my head at first with *Reasonable Doubt*. It took me a minute. But I did salute it. And I appreciated it.

When you show money and cars and the trappings of the good life to a kid who's never had anything, they're not really going to understand it all immediately. That's how it was for me with *Reasonable Doubt*. I was sixteen years old, man, a sixteen-year-old kid selling drugs, selling dope every day. I was listening to Master P at the time, 8Ball and MJG. Imagine listening to that every day and then coming to *Reasonable Doubt*. It's like, "Woah. This shit here is a world away from what I'm looking at."

Me and Jay-Z may have been rapping about the same thing but we did it differently. Back then when Jay rapped about vials, people in the South didn't know what he was talking about. I did because I'd come up North every summer, but down in the South we used different packaging and different marketing structures. So even though we were both selling drugs, we were doing it differently. There was a culture clash.

But if there was a culture clash there was also a cultural exchange. I learned about what life was like in New York from listening to Jay, just like folks can hopefully learn a little bit about where I'm from just by listening to my records.

Everything happens for a reason. So while I was disappointed that my first album, *I'm Serious*, didn't blow up, it just made me work harder on making my next album as strong as possible. I called it *Trap Muzik* because it's inspired by the Trap, that cornerstone of the underworld where drugs are sold and money is made. So many people have asked me why I wear rubber bands that I decided to put the explanation in a song ("Rubber Band Man"). I wore rubber bands when hustling drugs to symbolize the money I'd be making.

But when I made the song, it came to represent something else entirely. It symbolizes where I come from—the streets, the Trap, hustling—but also how far I've come. That's one of rap's greatest gifts to our country—it helps people transform something negative into something positive. That's why I think everyone has a responsibility to give back to their communities, not just rappers. There are no exceptions. That's why I'm involved in the Boys & Girls Clubs of America, King Foundation, and a bunch of other charities. I'm just happy to be able to help.

For me, the biggest problem in hip-hop today is oversaturation of the market. People have been burned by labels promising the latest hotness so often that they don't trust them anymore. The major labels are going to have to switch up their hustle if they're going to stay in business, but the music will always survive as long as it continues to speak to the everyday struggles of the hip-hop nation. A lot of people talk about hip-hop being dead, but I know that as long as I remain sincere and true to myself, then I'll be all right. And if hip-hop follows suit, it'll be straight as well.

RAP-UP

INTRODUCTION

IT WAS ALL A DREAM

The '70s were a time of great upheaval for New York, a funky-fresh decade of Studio 54, polyester suits, Reggie Jackson's booming bat, the Son of Sam's reign of terror, *Saturday Night Live*, and John Travolta disco-dancing up a storm. In the streets of New York throughout the '70s a revolution was brewing that would have profound ramifications for the decades to come, a musical and cultural upstart that began in noisy, disorganized park jams but went on to conquer the world. It was a revolution that flourished everywhere. There were black and white and Hispanic kids and Jews with kinky afros with too much time on their hands and not much in the way of money, resources, or parental supervision. It was an outlaw movement founded in the minor criminality of spray-painting graffiti (or bombing trains, to use the vernacular) and jacking public power sources to power up the turntables that got party people dancing.

1

HIP-HOP WASN'T JUST THE SOUNDS EMANATING FROM THE records of DJs and the microphones of rappers moving in unison. It was a lifestyle, culture, and philosophy that also entailed graffiti and break dancing, the raucous, aerobatic form of street dance that would become an ephemeral fad in the '80s but remains one of the immutable cornerstones of hip-hop culture.

Hip-hop was the first truly postmodern musical genre, an explosion of sound and attitude rooted immutably in the music of decades past. It was brand-new but it was also as reassuringly familiar as the hits it sampled. Hip-hop's roots can be found in the "toasting" of Jamaican DJs, a vastly influential practice where DJs would talk rhythmically over the music they were playing, often with the exaggerated braggadocio that would become synonymous with hip-hop.

Toasting played a key role in the development of hip-hop, as did the formidable legacies of George Clinton and James Brown, two of the most sampled artists in hip-hop history. Both artists helped pave the way for rap by experimenting constantly with the form, structure, and shape of black music. Brown seemed to shout and talk nearly as much as he sang, and his repetitive, groove-based sounds provided the sonic architecture for a huge cross section of golden age hip-hop. Indeed golden age hip-hop could loosely be defined as rappers rhyming over James Brown samples, especially "Funky Drummer," an endlessly recycled showcase for drummer Clyde Stubblefield.

Clinton's influence on hip-hop's development is equally crucial. Long before rappers gave themselves eighteen different names, Clinton created an endless string of increasingly outrageous alter egos for himself and his bandmates while simultaneously creating a P-funk movement that would morph into a G-funk movement under the direction of Dr. Dre, one of Clinton's most storied acolytes. OutKast, Digital Underground, and Afrika Bambaataa all owe Clinton's '70s work a huge debt. Clinton didn't just rewrite the black music rulebook. He threw that fucker away and began again from scratch with only one dictate: music was whatever the hell he wanted it to be, whether that meant endless stoned rambling or insane extraterrestrial concept albums.

Then again, Brown and Clinton worked with respected musicians like Bootsy Collins, Bernie Worrell, and the aforementioned Stubblefield, but the bored teenagers and casual revolutionaries who would create hip-hop out of little more than borrowed goods and ennui couldn't afford pianos or saxophones or elaborate drum sets, let alone lessons or studio time. But if DJs didn't have the time, money, and resources to play like the JBs, Brown's legendary backing band, they could at least spin a James Brown record and channel some of the Godfather of Soul's edgy funk. DJs like Kool Herc, a Jamaican-born innovator, found that by repeating and extending the breaks—generally the most rhythmic, percussion-heavy part of a song—in their favorite groove-heavy songs they could keep dancers on the floor longer. For DJs breaks were like orgasms—the visceral rush party people lived for—and by extending breaks they could consequently extend everybody's enjoyment.

Breaks could come from anywhere. James Brown's bountiful oeuvre was a treasure trove of dope breaks, but grooves could just as easily come from Krautrock pioneers like Kraftwerk—whose "Numbers" became a popular backdrop for break-dancers to strut their stuff—or even cheeseball arena rocker Billy Squier, whose "Big Beat" quickly made its way into the break-beat hall of fame. It didn't matter where the beat came from or what color its creator might be. All that mattered was that a break knocked, and dancers judged the relative dopeness of every break with their feet.

Grandmaster Flash improved on the groundwork laid by Kool Herc by adding "cutting," an innovation where DJs alternated between turntables playing two different copies of the same song so they could "cut" back and forth between them. Grand Wizard Theodore, meanwhile, invented "scratching," the intentional rubbing of vinyl records for percussive effect. DJs were acting as sonic mad scientists who divided songs and albums into their tastiest and most dance-friendly components. They kept the juiciest part of each song—the break—and discarded everything else.

ɔr DJs BREAKS WERE LIKE ORGASMS— THE VISCERAL RUSH PARTY PEOPLE LIVED FOR—AND BY EXTENDING BREAKS THEY COULD CONSEQUENTLY EXTEND EVERYBODY'S ENJOYMENT."

Old-school hip-hop made something out of nothing, transforming old records, turntables, a convenient electrical source, and the boundless nervous energy of an army of bored latchkey kids into a revolutionary indigenous American art form that would go on to change everything from presidential politics (who can forget John Kerry's hilarious comment about being "fascinated" by rap music or Wesley Clark's sad, perhaps disingenuous contention that Wyclef Jean was his favorite artist) to NBA dress codes.

DJs were and are the backbone of hip-hop culture but they're ultimately one component among many. They don't exist in a vacuum, after all. No, they exist to move asses and pump up parties, and the dancers who perfected their craft over the DJs' breaks became known as B-boys and B-girls and their flashy new form of dance became known as break dancing.

Like hip-hop DJing, break dancing evolved constantly with the never-ending addition of new and treacherous moves. It was intrinsically competitive. Break-dancers from one neighborhood would regularly square off against each other or crews from different neighborhoods. Even when no other break-dancers were involved, B-boys danced to improve their craft or impress girls.

A proto-break-dancing group called the Lockers, whose lineup at various times included Fred "Rerun" Berry of *What's Happening?* fame, one-hit wonder Toni Basil, and *Dance Fever* host Deney Terio, made noise and appeared on *Saturday Night Live* and *Soul Train* in the mid-'70s, but the first important break-dancing outfit was the Bronx's legendary Rock Steady Crew, the most respected group in break-dancing history.

In order to break into the Rock Steady Crew you had to defeat one of its members in a break-dancing battle, a demanding entry requirement that kept membership to a minimum. Nevertheless, a few expert B-boys managed to pass the test, most notably Richard "Crazy Legs" Colon, a graffiti writer who would acquire a curious notoriety as Jennifer Beals's dance double during the break-dance sequences of *Flashdance* after establishing a Manhattan branch of the Rock Steady Crew.

Break dancing was dismissed by some as a passing fad and demonized by hysterical parents convinced all that head-spinning and pop-locking would send their beloved babies to the emergency room with broken necks and cracked spines. But it was generally seen as harmless compared to an infinitely more controversial component of hip-hop culture: graffiti.

To its critics—and there are many—graffiti is nothing more than garden-variety vandalism glibly masquerading as self-expression. Like skateboarding, it is viewed by its practitioners as a lifestyle and an art form and denounced as a crime by its detractors. The rewards for enterprising graffiti writers in New York in the '70s were fleeting and ephemeral. Even if a graffiti writer succeeded in laying down a sweet-ass mural or insanely elaborate design on a sleeping subway train, chances were good their godlike work would be unceremoniously erased by the employees of the New York public transportation system or replaced by a rival graffiti writer's tag. To create a sense of permanence for this most ephemeral of pastimes, graffiti writers began photographing their work to document their youthful endeavors for posterity.

DJing transformed the music of the past into the soundtrack of the present and break dancing found vertical young hotshots dancing like no one had ever danced before, but graffiti was an art form that didn't just take from other art forms—it made destruction an essential component of its aesthetic. Graffiti writers were viewed by powerful people as hoodlums contributing to the ongoing desecration of one of the world's great cities. Not surprisingly, when politicians eventually cracked down on what they deemed "quality of life" offenses—relatively minor crimes sociologists feel contribute to a free-floating sense of lawlessness and contempt for authority—graffiti writers were one of the first groups they targeted.

Graffiti consequently became the official visual art form of hip-hop, just as break dancing became the nascent genre's dance of choice. We've already seen how DJs helped create hip-hop's musical aesthetic, which leaves us with arguably the final and most important component of hip-hop culture. No, not ringtones, snap music, or video skanks, though those are all fine guesses. We're talking about the MC, the master of ceremonies, rhymesayers, verse spitters, freestylers, and everyone else who makes music with the mouth, whether as a beatboxer or as a rapper.

Not surprisingly, in the heady early days of hip-hop there was a great deal of overlap between rappers, DJs, break-dancers, and graffiti writers. There still is. It wasn't at all unusual for an up-and-coming kid to start out exploring one element of hip-hop culture before trading it in for another or investigating a number of different elements at the same time as a graffiti writer/rapper/DJ. Hip-hop borrowed from punk rock the idea that enthusiasm and energy mattered more than craftsmanship and that anybody could be an artist, especially superfans. In hip-hop, as in punk, the line separating the audience from the performer was loose and slippery if not nonexistent.

Prominent early rappers include DJ Hollywood; the Herculoids, an influential group associated with DJ Kool Herc; the Furious Five, another influential group associated with Grandmaster Flash; and Kurtis Blow. In the prerecording days of hip-hop, MCs generally rapped for hours at a time with relatively simplistic rhymes aimed largely at keeping crowds moving. From the genre's very inception bragging has been an essential component of hip-hop. For kids growing up in a system that gave up on them before they were even grown, it was enormously empowering to get in front of a microphone at a street party and proclaim your godlike omnipotence and Shakespearean mastery of the English language. In its original form hip-hop was unashamedly party music. It wasn't until years later that people first began thinking of rap as something more than the soundtrack to illicit street parties.

In the late '70s standouts from New York's growing hip-hop community began recording singles. In late 1979 the funk group Fatback Band released the song "King Tim III (Personality Jock)," a track generally considered the first commercially released rap single. It arrived in stores just before the Sugarhill Gang's "Rapper's Delight" changed the sound and vibe of black music forever.

The Sugarhill Gang was essentially a prefabricated studio concoction of Sugar Hill Records founders Sylvia and Joe Robinson. The Robinsons heard the lusty sound of cash registers ka-chinging merrily in the impromptu street parties rocking New York, so they assembled a trio of relative novices (Wonder Mike, Master Gee, and Big Bank Hank) and a studio band that included future Living Colour bassist Doug Wimbish and had them record material that included "Rapper's Delight."

"Rapper's Delight" was founded on multiple acts of theft or "borrowing." For its melody the tune simply borrowed the unmistakable bass line of Chic's monster hit "Good Times," much to the horror of Chic bassist Nile Rodgers, who sued for royalties and songwriting credit and won. According to hip-hop legend, Big Bank Hank's lyrics on the track were "borrowed" from Grandmaster Caz of party-rap pioneers the Cold Crush Brothers, a well-respected figure within the rap community legendary for his live performances. Caz reportedly let nonprofessional Hank use his words with the understanding that Hank would in turn help Caz's career, only to be bitterly disappointed when Hank failed to reciprocate his generosity. Caz's mistreatment at the hands of rap's first hitmakers would become hip-hop's version of the original sin and has been referenced on songs from Brother Ali and Jay-Z.

Caz and other old-school pioneers were learning the undying truth of A Tribe Called Quest's Industry Rule Number 4080: record company people are shady. But it wasn't just record company people who behaved abhorrently throughout the early days of hip-hop. Rappers stole from each other even as they themselves were being horribly exploited by music industry sharks.

The Sugarhill Gang scored the first hit single in rap history, but they also became the genre's very first one-hit wonder when they were unable to capitalize on their breezy hit's runaway success. It took Kurtis Blow to prove to skeptics that the audience for hip-hop could be fans of artists as well as songs.

Like the Sugarhill Gang, Blow trafficked in goofy, lighthearted story songs about money, girls, and fame. A former break-dancer and DJ, Blow lucked out when he hooked up with manager Russell Simmons, the brother of Run-D.M.C. frontman Joseph "Run" Simmons and future founder of Def Jam and Phat Farm. Simmons saw in Blow a handsome, unthreatening, charismatic performer who would help break hip-hop for mainstream audiences.

In 1979 Blow released the classic single "Christmas Rappin'." A year later he became the first rapper to release a full-length album with his self-titled 1980 Mercury debut. In the late '70s the lines between downtown subcultures hip-hop, New Wave, and punk were porous, and intermingling between the genres was fairly common. For example, punk rock pioneers the Clash, a group legendary for their passion for black music and black culture, invited Blow to serve as their opening act, while Blondie introduced hip-hop to MTV audiences via Deborah Harry's painfully awkward rap in "Rapture," a hit whose video featured future *Yo! MTV Raps* host and all-around old-school tastemaker Fab Five Freddy.

Blow's hit singles helped pave the way for Run-D.M.C. Run of the group even DJed for Blow under the moniker "Kurtis Blow's Son." Run-D.M.C. and Blow would later appear alongside a veritable who's who of early hip-hop talent in 1985's *Krush Groove*, a fictionalized account of Def Jam's founding.

On the artier, spacier side of hip-hop, a former gangbanger was developing a musical movement to rival the Parliament-Funkadelic mythology erected by his hero George Clinton. As a teen, the man, who would grow up to be Afrika Bambaataa, ran with the Savage Seven and later the Black Spades, but a trip to Africa awakened a dormant social consciousness within the future icon.

Bambaataa founded an organization called Zulu Nation to uplift the black race. He began throwing huge parties and became famous as both a highly skilled DJ and a conceptual thinker. Where much of old-school hip-hop looked to the crowd-pleasing, dance-floor-friendly grooves of disco for inspiration, Bambaataa channeled the icy electro-funk of German weirdos Kraftwerk on his seminal 1982 single "Planet Rock." Bambaataa's icy technique still sounds sleek and futuristic today and would go on to influence everyone from Rick Rubin to Timbaland to Diddy's Hitmen squad. Bambaataa organized the first major European hip-hop tour and later engaged in seminal collaborations with Johnny Rotten and James Brown. He continues to tour and record and act as an unofficial hip-hop ambassador.

The year 1982 also saw the release of Grandmaster Flash and supergroup the Furious Five's "The Message," a grim bit of social commentary widely considered the first socially conscious hip-hop song. Where previous hip-hop hits trafficked in lighthearted escapism, "The Message" rubbed listeners' noses in the despair and desperation afflicting the underclass. By the time the track was released Flash was already regarded as one of rap's most respected and influential DJs, and his fame grew with the 1982 release of "Grandmaster Flash and the Wheels of Steel," a seven-minute-long showcase for Flash's turntable wizardry that would become a land-

"HIP-HOP WAS ALL ABOUT HAVING FUN AND PARTYING, NOT SOBERLY ADDRESSING SOCIETAL ILLS. THE ARRIVAL OF RUN-D.M.C. CHANGED ALL OF THAT."

mark in the burgeoning turntablist movement. Grandmaster Flash later served as the musical director for *The Chris Rock Show* and was recently inducted alongside the Furious Five into the Rock and Roll Hall of Fame.

Grandmaster Flash and Melle Mel of the Furious Five scored another classic early hip-hop message song in "White Lines," a jittery, paranoid anti-cocaine anthem built around a twitchy, disconcerting interpolation of Liquid, Liquid's "Cavern." But in the early days of hip-hop, dark, socially conscious songs like "White Lines" and "The Message" were the exceptions rather than the rule.

Most early rap stars trafficked in lighthearted escapism, like plus-sized wisenheimers the Fat Boys and disco hitmakers Whodini. Hip-hop was all about having fun and partying, not soberly addressing societal ills. The arrival of Run-D.M.C. changed all of that. Where "Rapper's Delight" borrowed its upbeat melody from Chic's "Good Times," Run-D.M.C. released a first single called "Hard Times" with a sound as dark, angry, and minimalist as the song's title.

The stripped-down beats of Def Jam founders Russell Simmons and Rick Rubin made the disco-based production of many old-school rappers suddenly seem corny and irrelevant. Just as New York history can be divided into the B.G. (Before Giuliani) and A.G. (After Giuliani) eras, hip-hop can pretty much be divided into the time before Run-D.M.C. (the old school) and post–Run-D.M.C. (the golden age and everything that followed). The concomitant rise of the Beastie Boys and LL Cool J, two other acts irrevocably associated with Russell Simmons and his fledgling Def Jam empire, helped further spur hip-hop's gradual shift away from airy escapism toward sparer, more minimalist sounds and sustained careers.

> **"IN SETTING OUT TO MAKE A NAME FOR THEMSELVES AND MAKE THEIR BLOCKS AND NEIGHBORHOODS PROUD, THESE LONG-FORGOTTEN RHYME SLINGERS NEVERTHELESS LAID THE FOUNDATION FOR ONE OF THE MOST INFLUENTIAL SOCIAL AND MUSICAL MOVEMENTS OF THE PAST CENTURY."**

The Def Jam/Run-D.M.C. contingent also helped kill talk about hip-hop being nothing more than a fad. For in the early to mid-'80s it sure seemed like everyone was out to exploit hip-hop. Break dancing found its way into commercials for breakfast cereal and inspired a string of dire exploitation movies like *Breakin' 2: Electric Boogaloo* that simply shoehorned gratuitous break-dancing scenes into hackneyed "urban" melodramas. Movies like the superb documentary *Style Wars* indelibly document the explosion of talent and energy erupting from the streets of New York throughout the late '70s and early '80s, but most "rap movies" disrespected the music and the culture they were ostensibly paying tribute to.

It's tempting to romanticize hip-hop's old school as a lost idyll of selflessness and cooperation, but it's important to remember that many of the icons who laid the foundation for hip-hop—people like Grandmaster Caz and Grand Wizard Theodore—were fucked over by record companies and peers alike. The music industry was just as shady then as it is today. Ego and competition have always been a part of hip-hop. True schoolers with a fuzzy sense of history and rose-colored glasses might insist that rappers in the old school were all about evolving the art form and uplifting the suffering masses, but you and I know they were out to get paid and out to get laid, just like every musician since the dawn of time.

In setting out to make a name for themselves and make their blocks and neighborhoods proud, these long-forgotten rhyme slingers nevertheless laid the foundation for one of the most influential social and musical movements of the past century. Perhaps Grand Puba said it best when he rapped, "What more can I say? I wouldn't be here today if the old school hadn't paved the way."

CHAPTER 1

BACK IN THE DAY:

'80s SOLO RAP

n a decade so closely associated with bad sitcoms, cocaine, terrible fashion, and the ever-present idiocy of the U.S. government, it's hard to believe that something good came out of the '80s. Dig a little deeper, though, and you'll find the debut records from some of the most classic MCs ever. Finally starting to come into its own, hip-hop in the '80s was still trying to find its footing, hence the varying (but all amazing) styles that came about: LL Cool J's ladies'-man persona, Biz Markie as the class clown, Slick Rick with his street tales and portable jewelry store . . . the list goes on and on. These men and women lived hip-hop before hip-hop was a lifestyle.

LL Cool J

Back in the day haters said rap music was a here today, gone tomorrow fad. Somebody forgot to tell LL Cool J. The veteran superstar has enjoyed the longest career in hip-hop, releasing CDs since the '80s and since then having hits in every decade.

Another Queens child who done real good, LL Cool J (government name James Todd Smith III; the nom de rap stands for "Ladies Love Cool James") started laying down raps as a kid. When he turned eleven, LL, who had been living with his grandparents since he was four (owing to a rocky, often violent home situation), got a DJ system from his grand-daddy. The budding B-boy started making tapes, one of which ended up at Def Jam's offices, specifically in the hands of Ad-Rock. The Beastie Boy hipped Def Jam's founders Rick Rubin and Russell Simmons, and in 1984 the upstart label signed young Mr. Smith. Def Jam released LL's "I Need a Beat" that same year. The sparse, hard-hitting 12-inch was not only LL's maiden vinyl experience, but also the first single to bear the Def Jam imprint. It would sell an impressive 100,000-plus copies and also put Def Jam, and of course LL Cool J, squarely on the map.

Encouraged by the almost immediate payoff, LL left school, entered the studio, and came out with 1985's *Radio*. Pushed by singles "I Can't Live Without My Radio" and "Rock the Bells," the album went platinum. In 1987 *Bigger and Deffer* went number three. Much of that success was because of the ballad "I Need Love," one of the first rap songs to cross over to pop and in addition the first rap love ballad. "I Need Love"'s sentimental, sweet lyrics appealed to the ladies and, along with his looks, helped make LL a heartthrob.

LL had proven that he had the smarts and songs to enjoy some pop love, but because of that some of the hardcore fans felt he was selling out. Although 1988's "Going Back to Cali" kept both camps happy, the hip-hop faithful gave an overall thumbs-down to '89s *Walking with a Panther*, which, even though it was top ten and contained the gold "I'm That Type of Guy," was dismissed by many as too soft. Another issue was rap's changing climate and sonics. With the more bombastic Public Enemy and the Native Tongues scene catching hold, LL's Kangol-rocking, sex-symbol, B-boy bragging was now bordering on outdated, so much so that at a show at Harlem's famed venue the Apollo, LL got booed. Understandably LL took the criticism hard, but it must have spurred him on because he came back harder—and swinging. His answer to his critics was 1990's *Mama Said Knock You Out*. Not only was the album the rawest and roughest LL had ever made, it entered the genius lyrical challenge "don't call it a comeback" into hip-hop's lexicon. Fierce LL brought his unrelenting album to television with a historic acoustic performance on *MTV Unplugged*, holding it down with deadly intent. Thanks to top ten R&B singles "The Boomin' System" and "Around the Way Girl" (number nine on pop and maybe one of LL's dopest cuts) and the hit title track, *Mama Said Knock You Out* was a triumph, the ultimate f-you and LL's biggest album. It also securely established him as a pop star, reestablished his status as a rap superstar, and shut down any and all beefin' from anyone. Speaking of beef, LL then took his newly pumped-up profile and body to the screen, appearing in forgettable flicks *The Hard Way* and *Toys*. His album *14 Shots to the Dome* came in 1993 and had a gangsta-esque street edge, something that LL didn't really do all that well. It sold nicely, debuted top ten, but was a bit of a letdown after *Mama* and yielded no major hit singles. In fact, *14 Shots* never went beyond gold and almost killed the love LL had recouped with his "comeback."

After *14 Shots*, LL went back to acting (the sitcom *In the House*) and then returned to making music with '95's *Mr. Smith*. Proving that he had more lives than a cat, *Mr. Smith* ended up being a big seller—going double platinum and delivering two of LL's biggest singles, the Boyz II Men duet "Hey Lover" and "Doin' It." At the close of 1996 came a greatest hits collection, which was followed by *Phenomenon* a year later. The CD's title was a significant hit, and while LL's importance might have faded a bit, he was still a player and more than capable of pulling a burner out of his hat. That point was proven when LL (no stranger to a good battle rap) took on then much-hyped rapper Canibus on "4, 3, 2, 1." After several verbal volleys, LL remained the champion. To kick off the Y2K, LL gave fans the modestly titled *G.O.A.T. (The Greatest of All Time)*. The egomania paid off and the CD hit the top spot. Two years later LL celebrated his tenth album, and by extension his sometimes contentious tenure with Def Jam (that sort of label longevity is unheard of in most music). That milestone featured The Neptunes-helmed "Luv U Better," one of LL's biggest singles in quite some time. Although Uncle L kept making CDs, he sure wasn't getting Snoop/Jay/50 numbers. Yet even so he was far from over. *The DEFinition* of 2004, boasting the Timbaland-produced "Headsprung," which found LL in sexy, party-hearty mode and featured a subtle shift in style, worked. To coincide with the album's release, LL, who had long been associated with the popular FUBU line, launched his own Todd Smith collection. Outside of its founder, not too many kids were seen rocking the clothes. But like the Energizer bunny, LL kept going. He was by now a cultural icon and talk show staple (the guy's got a winning way with words, and by hip-hop standards he's a brilliant public speaker). Yet for anyone thinking that this happily married father of four was looking to retire, "Control Myself" put that to rest. An all-out smash, the single, produced by Jermaine Dupri and featuring J.Lo, had a healthy sample of old-school jam "Looking for the Perfect Beat." The single was the lead in for '06's *Todd Smith* album. Despite that huge single, the CD didn't sell well and LL openly trashed Def Jam, going so far as to hang with crosstown rival 50 Cent at that year's MTV VMAs. As 2007 kicked off, LL was teaming up with 50 to executive produce his final album on Def Jam called *Exit 13* and was promoting a workout book. If you can't rhyme like the G.O.A.T., at least you can look like him.

POP QUIZ

What was the first single released by Def Jam Records?

a. Run-D.M.C.'s "It's Like That"/"Sucker MCs"

b. Beastie Boys' "Cooky Puss"

c. LL Cool J's "I Need a Beat"

d. Sugarhill Gang's "Rapper's Delight"

Big Daddy Kane

Big Daddy Kane (Antonio Hardy) was one of the major players in the late '80s, a.k.a. hip-hop's "golden age." He had a lover-man persona, complete with fly suits, gold jewelry, and a smooth vibe. But he could also drop serious science and preach conscious lyrics, all while being sexy. Kane never had that big crossover sensation, but he is widely seen as one of the best lyricists of his time and even today regularly gets name-checked by younger dudes.

> **"[BIG DADDY KANE]** HAD A LOVER-MAN PERSONA, COMPLETE WITH FLY SUITS, GOLD JEWELRY, AND A **SMOOTH VIBE."**

Born in Brooklyn, New York, Kane's moniker stood for King Asiatic Nobody's Equal. In 1984, he met another new jack, Biz Markie. Both eventually got down with the Juice Crew. That fam, based in the Queensbridge projects, home of Mobb Deep and Nas to name a few, was led by producer Marley Marl, who would famously be part of the legendary BDP/Juice Crew battle. Kane inked with Marley's Cold Chillin' label in '87, and came through with the single "Raw" the next year. The streets loved "Raw," and Kane's first LP, *Long Live the Kane*, was soon a reality, giving fans another favorite, "Ain't No Half Steppin'." Kane took it up a notch with 1989's *It's a Big Daddy Thing*, which featured the lover-man manifesto "Smooth Operator" and the Teddy Riley–produced "I Get the Job Done." The next joint was 1990's *Taste of Chocolate*. But on 1991's *Prince of Darkness*, which had a more laid-back vibe, Kane fell off a little. No worry. Kane kept it hot with his appearance in Madonna's notorious 1992 *Sex* book. After getting nekkid for Madge, Kane dropped 1993's *Looks Like a Job For . . .* The album sounded better, but hip-hop is fickle and trends change. Undeterred, Kane left for MCA and in '94 produced

Daddy's Home, which didn't do much of anything. Except for a few roles in totally who-cares flicks, Kane left the house. He resurfaced in 1998 with the indie CD *Veteranz Day*. Yet even though Kane doesn't make music, he still can move crowds. The still hot O.G. performs periodically at clubs and always does damage.

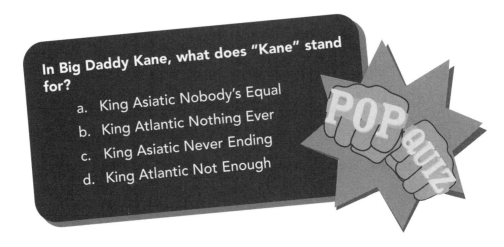

In Big Daddy Kane, what does "Kane" stand for?

a. King Asiatic Nobody's Equal
b. King Atlantic Nothing Ever
c. King Asiatic Never Ending
d. King Atlantic Not Enough

POP QUIZ

Biz Markie

Marcel Hall a.k.a. Biz Markie was a true original and funnier than all shit. He first got love rapping in New York in the early '80s, and met producer Marley Marl in 1985, who hired Biz to be a human beatbox for Marl's well-known acts MC Shan and Roxanne Shanté. With his infectious personality and massive mouth skills, Biz recorded demos and by '88 had signed with Cold Chillin'. That same year Biz released *Goin' Off*, which, thanks to the off-the-wall tracks "Vapors" and "Pickin' Boogers," became a sizable street hit. In 1989 Biz made the move to the mainstream with the outrageous "Just a Friend," which featured Biz half rapping and half "singing" like a cat being stepped on. The video starred Biz wearing an outlandish wig, which he rocked like Amadeus. The unbeatable fusion of humor and skills propelled "Just a Friend" into the top ten, and Biz's second album, *The Biz Never Sleeps*, went gold.

The Biz was living as large as his frame, but trouble lay ahead. Album number three, *I Need a Haircut*, wasn't selling as expected when Biz was slapped with a lawsuit from '70s singer/songwriter Gilbert O'Sullivan, who said that Biz's "Alone Again" contained an unauthorized sample of O'Sullivan's song "Alone Again (Naturally)." O'Sullivan was victorious and in the process changed the very way that hip-hop was created. The ruling by the courts stipulated that Biz's label, Warner Bros., had to yank *I Need a Haircut* off the shelves and out of circulation. Also, before any company or rapper could utilize a sample, that sample had to be cleared—i.e., signed off by the original artist. Biz fought back with 1993's *All Samples Cleared!*, but the damage had already helped to grind his career to a halt.

Throughout the '90s Biz kept it on the low, occasionally freestyling on other rappers' albums, most notably the Beastie Boys. Yet rather than return to rapping, Biz started DJing. He got some shine in 2002, when R&B singer Mario dropped his smash "Just a Friend," which was based on Biz's biggest hit and whose accompanying video had a Biz cameo. Biz returned to the studio with 2003's *Weekend Warrior* on Tommy Boy. Although he remains one of hip-hop's true characters, Biz sadly is best known to a new generation through his 2005 appearance on VH1's *Celebrity Fit Club.*

Slick Rick/Doug E. Fresh

Slick Rick didn't have many mainstream hits, but he did have one dope look. With his trademark eye patch, gold rope chain, and Kangol, he was a dazzling wordsmith and storyteller—even if those stories were often down and *very* dirty and not meant for kids' ears. Born to Jamaican parents in London, Ricky Walters was blinded in one eye by a freak accident as a kid—hence the eye patch. He came to the States in the mid-'70s and lived with his family in the Bronx. In high school Ricky became tight with Dana Dane, who would later have the hit "Nightmares." The two became the Kangol Crew and began performing at hip-hop battles around NYC.

At one such battle Ricky met Doug E. Fresh in the Bronx. Fresh (Doug E. Davis) was from Barbados, lived in Harlem, and by the time he and Ricky met had made quite the name for himself at local shows and parties as a human beatbox. In fact, he was the first human beatbox and to this day probably the best, using his mouth and a mic to create an amazing collection of drum-machine noises and sound effects. Basically, he was so dope that he could take the place of an actual drum machine. Doug went from the streets of Harlem to the studio with 1983's "Pass the Budda," with Spoonie Gee and DJ Spivey. But for most rap fans, Doug's debut was his mind-blowing appearance in the early hip-hop film *Beat Street*, where he backed up old-school faves the Treacherous Three. On his own, Doug threw down "Just Having Fun" and "Original Human Beatbox," both in 1984.

It was that same year that Doug met Ricky (who was then Ricky D.) and brought him into the Get Fresh Crew, which included Barry Bee and Chill Will. In 1985 they recorded "The Show/La Di Da Di," a mix of Doug's mouth music and Ricky's London-accented flow. The single exploded, went to number four on the R&B charts, and to this day is seen as one of the greatest moments in recorded rap history. Doug was now a major star. Throughout the '80s and into the '90s, he released a few albums, none of which enjoyed the across-the-board success or made the musical impact that "The Show" had. Yet even though he may have lacked in units moved, Doug remained a big draw. Along with popping up on Nas's "Virgo" (2004), Doug frequently served as an opening act for numerous rap acts, and, with his skills intact today, is a living, beatboxing embodiment of hip-hop's creativity.

As for Ricky D.? He went solo in 1987, renamed himself Slick Rick, and signed to Def Jam Records. In 1988 came his debut, *The Great Adventures of Slick Rick*. The flagrantly foul but really, really funky "Treat Her Like a Prostitute" had the streets in a vise grip, but radio didn't show Ricky or the song much love because of the nasty anti-female sentiment. Better received was a duet with the then red-hot Al B. Sure! entitled "If I'm Not Your Lover," which hit number two in 1989. That same year came Ricky's masterpiece, the gritty, fractured fairy tale "Children's Story," which went top five and would years later make its way to Montell Jordan's "This Is How We Do It." His career was on fire, but Ricky's life was a mess. In

1990 he was arrested after shooting at his cousin and leading the cops on a chase. He was put in jail, and while out on bail (thanks to Def Jam's Russell Simmons) laid down *The Ruler's Back* in three weeks. The album would drop in 1991. While in prison (he was released in 1997), Ricky returned with *Behind Bars* (1994). The album made some noise, as did 1999's *The Art of Storytelling*, but by then Ricky's legal problems were overshadowing his recording efforts. Even though he had lived the majority of his life in the United States, owned property here, paid taxes here, was married to an American, and was the father of American-born kids, he wasn't technically himself a citizen. The drama unfolded in 2002 when Ricky, after performing on a Caribbean cruise ship, was arrested by the INS as the rapper reentered the United States. Rick was going to be deported because of that pesky little detail—you know, the one about not being a U.S. citizen. Adding to his problems was a 1996 law that called for foreigners who'd been convicted of violent felonies—which Ricky had—to be kicked out. Caught in a quagmire, Ricky kept being denied bail, but after seventeen months behind bars, he was released in 2003. Three years later it was back on when the INS began another attempt to deport him. A trial is set for a future date.

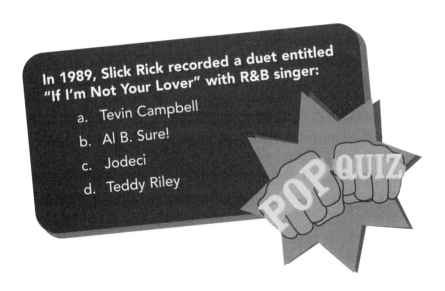

In 1989, Slick Rick recorded a duet entitled "If I'm Not Your Lover" with R&B singer:

a. Tevin Campbell

b. Al B. Sure!

c. Jodeci

d. Teddy Riley

POP QUIZ

Queen Latifah

Queen Latifah held it down as one of the finest flow stresses in hip-hop. She was the first female solo rapper to go gold (1993's *Black Reign*). In addition, throughout the years, Latifah has proven to be a savvy businesswoman, skilled actress, solid singer, and all-around media presence. All hail the Queen indeed.

Latifah was born Dana Owens in Newark, New Jersey. At the age of eight, her cousin dubbed her Latifah, meaning "delicate" or "sensitive." Nothing personal, but delicate La ain't. Latifah began rapping and a little beatboxing while she was still in high school. After graduating and attending college, she adopted the nickname she'd been given so long ago, adding the royal honorific for extra impact. Soon after, she got down with the Native Tongues crew, whose members were hugely instrumental in injecting a conscious Afrocentric vibe in hip-hop. Latifah recorded a demo that got her a deal with NYC's Tommy Boy Records, who released her single "Wrath of My Madness" in 1988. Hot. Fire hot. Girlfriend was like seventeen, eighteen and she had the poise and skills of someone twice her age. "Wrath" was followed up with the funky hip-hop house-flavored "Dance for Me." In 1989, Latifah's album *All Hail the Queen* was met with great press and support from the fans. The album also contained the girl-power jam "Ladies First" featuring Monie Love and made its way into the R&B top ten. Not one to rest on her laurels, Latifah used her newfound creative profile to co-found (with old friend Shakim Compere) Flavor Unit Entertainment. Based in Jersey, Flavor Unit was responsible for discovering a handful of acts, none bigger than Naughty by Nature. With business on lock, Latifah got back to making music, but 1991's *Nature of a Sister* lacked both the cultural, artistic impact and commercial appeal of its predecessor. Along with a slump in sales, La's contract with Tommy Boy was up and the label chose not to re-up with their star. As if the indignity of being dropped wasn't bad enough, Latifah suffered an even greater and more personal loss when in a short span of time she was the victim of a carjacking and her beloved brother Lance died in a motorcycle accident.

Down but far from out, Latifah took time off to mourn and then came back stronger and more focused than ever. Now with Motown, she blessed fans with 1993's *Black Reign*. Dedicated to her late brother, the album was Latifah's biggest seller to date. It made its way to gold and contained Latifah's biggest single, the funky and feminist "U.N.I.T.Y." The hard-hitting anthem earned a Grammy in 1994 for Best Rap Solo Performance. Along with dropping hot rhymes, Latifah continued making strides with her acting career. With well-received roles in *Jungle Fever*, *House Party 2*, and *Juice* already on her résumé, she moved from big to small screen in 1993 when she joined the cast of the sitcom *Living Single*. The popular series ran until January 1998, and during that run the public's attention was shifted from Latifah the rap artist to Latifah the actress/comedienne. To her credit, Latifah excelled on both fronts. She returned to film in 1996 with *Set It Off*, playing a tough-as-nails lesbian bank robber with fierce conviction. Latifah was breaking the law offscreen as well. The same year *Set It Off* set it off, the Queen got popped when the cops found a loaded gun and weed in the car she was driving—too fast. Latifah pleaded guilty to a misdemeanor weapons charge. Public service announcement: rappers, if you've got a piece and some smoke in the whip, try to obey speed limits. Thank you.

Following the cancellation of *Living Single*, Latifah headed back to the base to begin work on her fourth album, *Order in the Court*, which hit stores in 1998. The album had a more R&B sound, with Latifah splitting it up between rapping and singing. Thanks to singles "Bananas (Who You Gonna Call?)" and "Paper," *Order in the Court* did respectable numbers, and that same year Latifah showed her versatility again with buzzed-about roles in *Sphere* and *Living Out Loud*. In 1999, she returned to television but this time as the host of her own daytime talk show, *The Queen Latifah Show*. The chat fest ran in syndication for two years and brought the rap star even deeper in the mainstream, making her a household name. The year 2002 saw La messing up again when, after being stopped by the police, she failed a sobriety test. Latifah! The star got three years' probation following pleading guilty to reckless driving. Luckily for the Queen, the legal skirmish was muted when she hit the cinema again, this time with a supporting role in the critically acclaimed musical adaptation of the Broadway show *Chicago*. Starring alongside Richard Gere and Renée Zellweger, Latifah's sparkling, sexy performance came damn near close to stealing the film and she was awarded Best Supporting Actress nominations from the Screen Actors Guild, Golden Globes, and even the Oscars. Two years later Latifah flexed her vocal chops with the unexpectedly solid covers collections *The Dana Owens Album* and 2007's *Trav'lin Light*. She continues to enjoy a flourishing acting career both in film and TV, as a spokeswoman for Cover Girl, and by hosting award shows. But the coolest thing? Latifah continues her reign as an all-around fly girl—er, woman—who no matter what she did, always kept it hip-hop.

"LATIFAH CONTINUES HER REIGN AS AN ALL-AROUND FLY GIRL—ER, WOMAN—WHO NO MATTER WHAT SHE DID, ALWAYS KEPT IT HIP-HOP."

MC Lyte

MC Lyte wasn't the first girl to go for hers—hip-hop's earliest days saw undersung female forces like Pebbly Poo, Sha-Rock, and Sequence. But MC Lyte's profile was higher than her foresisters, and because of that, along with unquestionable, revered talent, Lyte helped to tear down barriers and raised the bar not just for female rappers, but rappers in general. Lana Moorer was born in Queens and raised in Brooklyn. She began rhyming at the age of twelve, after falling under rap's spell when some older cousins who lived uptown turned her on to the genre's greats. Raised in a family that stressed education, poetry, and music (her stepfather, Nat Robinson, ran indie label First Priority), Lyte began making little homemade tapes with her stepbrothers Milk and Gizmo, a.k.a. Audio Two. Audio Two had already earned their rep with their 12-inch "Top Billin'" (1987), a track the guys had originally cooked up for their kin. Audio Two signed to their pop's label, and in 1988 lil' sis recorded the landmark single "I Cram to Understand U." With her husky vocals (many thought that Lyte was a young boy rather than a teenage girl) and remarkably mature and wise content (the song dealt with a girl in love with a crack addict), "I Cram to Understand U" became an instant sensation and led to Lyte securing a deal—okay, it was with her dad's label. But the indie did enjoy major-label distribution, so to be fair, a suit had to sign off. Lyte's full-length debut was the terrific *Lyte As a Rock*, and a year later in '89 came the follow-up, *Eyes On This*. Both albums showcased a lyricist wise beyond her years, with a flow honed in NYC's rough-and-ready rap club circuit and lyrics that spoke to Lyte's childhood love of language. The two albums are also widely considered Lyte's best work and *Eyes On This* produced the hit "Cha Cha Cha" (number one rap) and "Cappuccino," which spoke out against the violence that was tearing the cities of America apart. For her three-peat, Lyte turned to writer/producers Wolf & Epic, who had previously worked with Bell Biv DeVoe. Not surprisingly, 1991's *Act Like You Know* contained a little more R&B/soul flavor. Still selling moderately well, Lyte then came back two years down the road with *Ain't No Other*. The single "Ruffneck," which laid out what Lyte looked for in a dude, was big (in fact, the first gold single by a woman rapper) and earned Ms. Lyte a Grammy nomination for Best Rap Single.

After watching "Ruffneck" wreck shop, Lyte took a little breather as she settled into the mid-'90s (not her age, the decade!) and up and switched labels. Her first LP on Elektra was 1996's *Bad As I Wanna B*. That CD featured the club banger "Cold Rock a Party," a duet with a then up-and-coming Missy Elliott. The duet was big in the streets and clubs and set up the equally popular *Seven & Seven* (1998). That CD also featured Missy along with LL, who produced "Play Girls Play." Lyte's second gold single was a collabo with Xscape, "Keep On Keepin' On." The song also appeared on the *Sunset Park* soundtrack.

Along with music, Lyte tried her hand at acting, appearing in long-canceled shows *Moesha*, *In the House*, and *New York Undercover*. Always astute and politically conscious, Lyte became very active in a number of social causes including Rock the Vote and AIDS awareness. In 2003, she attempted to call it a comeback with *Da Undaground Heat, Vol. 1*. It didn't do much, but even with weak sales on this, you couldn't front. Lyte was and remains one of the flyest females in the game and she's earned her place in hip-hop's hall of fame.

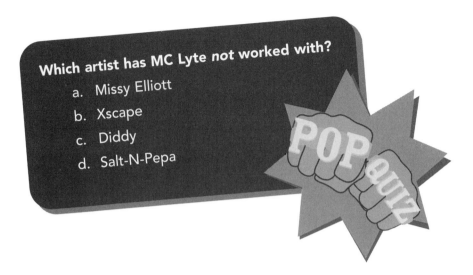

DJ Jazzy Jeff & the Fresh Prince

Run-D.M.C. might have made rap palatable to a mainstream audience, but it took DJ Jazzy Jeff & the Fresh Prince to make it kid-friendly. Where gangsta provocateurs like Ice Cube posited themselves as *AmeriKKKa's Most Wanted* (the glowering manifestation of white America's worst fears about young black men), the rapper formerly known as the Fresh Prince cultivated a friendly, eminently accessible persona as the popular class clown entertaining classmates with goofy stories about shopping with his mom and fighting Mike Tyson. Along with Run-D.M.C.'s first albums and the timeless display of lyrical virtuosity that is "The Super Bowl Shuffle," DJ Jazzy Jeff & the Fresh Prince's *He's the DJ, I'm the Rapper* served as a gateway drug for white suburbanites who'd later experiment with stronger stuff from Public Enemy, Snoop Dogg, and N.W.A.

Will Smith is rap's Mr. Clean. He's probably the least controversial rapper of all time, but his wholesome image has nevertheless attracted criticism. "Will Smith don't gotta cuss in his raps to sell records / Well I do, so fuck him and fuck you too," Eminem quipped on "The Real Slim Shady." Even Bow Wow has derided Smith's music as "bubblegum." Smith's popularity with white America has reaped huge rewards critically and commercially, but it's come at the expense of his hip-hop credibility. He could probably get elected president, but the guardians of hip-hop authenticity revoked his ghetto pass long ago.

A bright student at Overbrook High, a legendary high school in Philadelphia where legendary figures such as Solomon Burke and Wilt Chamberlain once matriculated, Smith had the grades and SAT scores to get into a top college like MIT, but chose to pursue a career in hip-hop instead. At a house party, he met Jeff Townes, a widely respected DJ who spun under the name DJ Jazzy Jeff.

The two began performing together and in 1987 released their debut album on Jive Records, *Rock the House*. The album scored a minor hit in "Girls Ain't Nothing but Trouble," but it was the duo's next album that would catapult the pair to superstardom.

From its *Dummy's Guide to Hip-Hop* title onward, 1988's *He's the DJ, I'm the Rapper* aimed unapologetically at scoring with a huge mainstream audience. "Parents Just Don't Understand" was a goofy story song about shopping at the mall and the mischief that ensues when the Fresh Prince "borrows" his parents' car without permission. Anybody with a parent could relate to the song's lighthearted subject matter, and Jeff's pop-friendly production made the song irresistible to radio programmers. More hits followed, most notably "A Nightmare on My Street," a tongue-in-cheek homage to Wes Craven's classic horror movie *A Nightmare on Elm Street*.

In 1989 DJ Jazzy Jeff & the Fresh Prince won the first ever rap Grammy for "Parents Just Don't Understand" and released *And In This Corner . . .* The album scored a minor hit with another wacky story song, "I Think I Can Beat Mike Tyson," but failed to replicate its predecessor's success.

Will Smith's animated performances in music videos and lyrical tomfoolery made him a natural for television. Accounts differ as to how Smith ended up starring in *The Fresh Prince of Bel-Air*, but one credible account posits that he got in one little fight and his mom got scared and told him he was moving in with his auntie and uncle in Bel-Air. Whatever the case, the fish-out-of-water sitcom about a brash West Philadelphia kid cavorting with the upper classes was a sizable hit that lasted six seasons.

Boosted by his television success, Smith and Jeff—who made guest appearances on *The Fresh Prince of Bel-Air*—headed back into the studio and recorded 1991's *Homebase*, a comeback album that went double platinum and spawned one of the duo's biggest hits, the breezy, Grammy-winning anthem "Summertime."

By the time "Summertime" reignited Smith's music career, his film career was already up and running. He made an inauspicious film debut in the little-loved Ted Danson/Whoopi Goldberg vehicle *Made in America* (yes, there was once a time when Ted Danson and Whoopi Goldberg were billed above Will Smith), but turned a lot of heads with his risky, adventurous performance as a charismatic gay con artist in Fred Schepisi's adaptation of John Guare's play *Six Degrees of Separation*.

But it was as a wisecracking action hero that Will Smith became one of Hollywood's biggest, most bankable names. He led a sprawling ensemble cast in the 1996 sci-fi blockbuster *Independence Day*, one of the top-grossing smashes of all time. Smith returned to sci-fi the next year with another ubiquitous smash, *Men in Black*. The brash kid from West Philly was officially an international movie star whose fame transcended hip-hop and national borders.

As Smith's acting career rocketed to the stratosphere, his recording career began to take a backseat to cranking out big-budget popcorn fare. Nineteen ninety-three's under-performing *Code Red* was the last album credited to DJ Jazzy Jeff & the Fresh Prince before Smith went solo with 1997's *Big Willie Style*, a pop-rap opus that spawned the monster hits "Men in Black"—the theme song to Smith's cinematic blockbuster—"Miami," "Just the Two of Us," and "Gettin' Jiggy Wit It."

"BUT IT WAS AS A WISECRACKING ACTION HERO THAT WILL SMITH BECAME ONE OF HOLLYWOOD'S BIGGEST, MOST BANKABLE NAMES."

Hip-hop critics increasingly wrote off Smith as a pop-rap lightweight, but he surprised a lot of film critics with his powerfully internal lead performance in the underrated Muhammad Ali biopic *Ali*. The 2001 Michael Mann film was a commercial disappointment but netted Smith an Academy Award nomination for Best Actor, a milestone for Smith personally and for hip-hop as a whole. Smith received a second Oscar nomination for *The Pursuit of Happyness* in 2007. With another actor in the lead the story of a homeless single father would have been a hard sell, but Smith's relaxed charisma made the film an unexpected blockbuster.

DJ Jazzy Jeff, meanwhile, returned to his hip-hop roots as an in-demand producer and DJ. Jeff's solo album, *The Magnificent*, and his *Hip-Hop Forever* mix series both traffic in organic underground hip-hop far removed from the glossy pop-rap of Will Smith, though he's continued to collaborate with Smith on some of the rapper's solo albums.

In the past twenty years Will Smith has conquered the worlds of film, television, and music and become one of the most famous people in the world. God only knows what he'll do next, but you can bet it'll be popular, mainstream, and free of cussing, drug references, or anything else that might offend. Smith lost hardcore hip-hop heads a long time ago, but gained the world in return. Not a bad bargain for an insanely wealthy and popular rapper who's not just a businessman: he's a business, man.

Will Smith received an Oscar nomination for Best Actor for which film?

   a. Six Degrees of Separation

   b. Ali

   c. Made in America

   d. Independence Day

POP QUIZ

BACK IN THE DAY:
'80s SOLO RAP

LL COOL J STARRED WITH QUEEN LATIFAH IN THE ROMANTIC COMEDY *LAST HOLIDAY*.

RUSSELL SIMMONS SIGNED LL COOL J TO DEF JAM IN 1984.

QUEEN LATIFAH GUEST STARRED AS DEE DEE ON *THE FRESH PRINCE OF BEL-AIR* WITH DJ JAZZY JEFF & THE FRESH PRINCE.

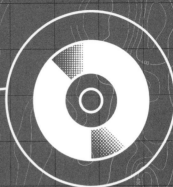

BIG DADDY KANE WAS
FEATURED ALONG WITH
MC LYTE ON THE *MO' MONEY*
SOUNDTRACK.

DOUG E. FRESH STARRED
IN *BROWN SUGAR* WITH
BIG DADDY KANE.

DJ JAZZY JEFF & THE FRESH
PRINCE RELEASED "SO FRESH"
FEATURING BIZ MARKIE AND
SLICK RICK.

SLICK RICK MET DOUG E. FRESH
AND JOINED THE GET FRESH
CREW IN 1984.

CHAPTER 2

IT'S A
G(ROUP) THANG:

'80s RAP GROUPS

Before hip-hop groups became a bunch of guys onstage hollering things like "I need a mic!" and "Put your hands up!" hip-hop groups stemmed from neighborhood crews, groups that felt there was either strength in numbers or all parties involved were necessary for success. Take N.W.A., for example. You had Dre as the producer, Eazy-E as the street genius/one guy with legitimate street credibility, Yella on the decks, Ren and Ice Cube as the MCs. Not good enough? Where would Run-D.M.C. be without Jam Master Jay? Heavy D without his Boyz? Salt-N-Pepa definitely wouldn't have been able to push it without DJ Spinderella. Though solo projects were eventually launched from a number of groups, those albums (some of them classic in their own right) would never have happened if it weren't for their original groups taking them to the next level.

EPMD

EPMD may not have been a household name (well, actually that sort of depended on your household), but the Strong Island duo was instrumental in bringing funky back. Their tough-as-nails flow combined with righteously rubbery grooves helped set the standard for gangster lean hip-hop.

Underground and proud of it, EPMD was Erick Sermon (a.k.a. the Green Eyed Bandit) and Parrish Smith (a.k.a. Pee MD). Both were raised in Brentwood, New York, and made separate moves into rap, coming together in 1987. Calling themselves EPMD—"Erick and Parrish Making Dollars"— the twosome dropped their first single, "It's My Thing," and signed to NYC indie Sleeping Bag/Fresh Records. Their debut album *Strictly Business* (1988) had the classics "You Gots to Chill" and the title track, and went gold like their next LP, 1989's *Unfinished Business*. Def Jam snatched them up and EPMD came through in 1990 with *Business as Usual* and, in keeping with the theme, *Business Never Personal* in 1992. Along with their own careers, EPMD created the Hit Squad, whose membership included the then rookie Redman, K-Solo, and the Virginia-based duo Das EFX. EPMD ceased to be in '93 and went the solo route, with Sermon dropping *No Pressure*, and Smith's *Shade Business* (1994). In 1997, EPMD reunited with the comeback *Back in Business*, followed up by *Out of Business* in 1999, which may have exhausted the amount of times they could use "business" in a title.

Salt-N-Pepa

Salt-N-Pepa were the embodiment of LL Cool J's "Around the Way Girl." In a genre that didn't give females much to choose from (skank ho or bull dyke), SNP blazed their own path.

Natives of Queens, New York, Cheryl "Salt" James and Sandy "Pepa" Denton were working at the local Sears when their co-worker and Salt's then best friend Hurby "Luv Bug" Azor offered the girls the opportunity to rap on a song he was producing for a college project. They cooked up "The Show Stopper" in 1985, and it was released under the name "Super

Nature." The track ended up being big on the streets and R&B charts. That unexpected success landed the girls, who were now renamed Salt-N-Pepa, a deal with Next Plateau. Their debut was 1986's *Hot, Cool & Vicious*, which featured DJ Pamela Green. The album yielded "My Mic Sounds Nice," "Tramp," and "Chick on the Side," which performed moderately, but everything changed when a San Francisco radio jock remixed the B-side of "Tramp," "Push It."

In 1987 "Push It" blew up in the Bay Area and then nationwide, going to number nineteen on the Billboard Hot 100. It also became one of the first rap records to earn a Grammy nomination. Soon afterward Salt-N-Pepa replaced their DJ with rapper/DJ Spinderella (Deidra Roper) and began work on their second album, *A Salt with a Deadly Pepa*. The album fared moderately well, and then in 1990 the group released their third LP, *Blacks' Magic*. That album got good reviews and equally strong sales, with the single "Expression" spending eight weeks atop the rap charts and eventually crossing to pop. The next single, "Let's Talk About Sex," would become the trio's biggest single to date, landing at the number thirteen spot on the Billboard Hot 100 chart.

As they got ready to record their fourth album, Salt-N-Pepa severed ties with Azor and signed a new deal with PolyGram. In 1993 the ladies delivered *Very Necessary* and it was a watershed moment. The CD marked the first time SNP publicly took creative control and was the biggest hit of their career. Like the first single, "Shoop," *Very Necessary* went to number four on the charts. "Shoop" was eclipsed by their top three duet with En Vogue, "Whatta Man," and another single, "None of Your Business," copped the Grammy for Best Rap Performance by a Duo or Group in 1995.

The ladies followed up *Very Necessary* with 1997's *Brand New* featuring the single "R U Ready." Soon after *Brand New*, SNP faded from view, choosing to concentrate on raising their kids, branching out into acting, and other endeavors. But they were back on the scene ten years later with a VH1 reality show, *The Salt-N-Pepa Show*, which followed the seasoned duo (minus Spinderella) as they attempted to reunite on and off the stage. The ladies may be reality stars these days, but they remain rap's greatest female group.

Salt-N-Pepa's highest-charting single on the Billboard Hot 100 was:

a. "Push It"

b. "Whatta Man"

c. "Shoop"

d. "My Mic Sounds Nice"

POP QUIZ

Eric B. & Rakim

There are few things hip-hop heads can agree on. Here's one: that Rakim is one of the best MCs ever. And that his DJ, Eric B., was pretty nice as well. Eric B. & Rakim might not have gone platinum, but they did something more important. They changed hip-hop. With Eric B. laying down make-it-funky, James Brown beats and Rakim dropping verses rich with metaphor, the team played off each other with a studied yet improvisational technique. Studious and soulful, Eric B. & Rakim are hip-hop's greatest duo.

At sixteen, Long Island's William Griffin Jr. converted to Islam and changed his name to Rakim Allah. Eric Barrier was born in Queens and started DJing in high school, eventually landing a gig at NYC's influential radio station WBLS. There he met Rakim and the two decided to join forces and create a hip-hop team. A year later, in 1986, the work paid off—for real. The guys came through with a little gem they called "Eric B. Is President/My Melody." The two-sided single (yeah, they had those back then) exploded and ruled as a bona fide street hip-hop anthem and rallying cry. The labels pricked up their ears and soon the cool duo were picked up by respected downtown indie 4th & Broadway. Their next two singles, "I Ain't No Joke" and "I Know You Got Soul," established their blueprint by fusing funky samples (Eric B. did more to help introduce the late James Brown to the new generation than anyone) and thoughtful, lean, and sturdy lyrics. Hip-hop fans gobbled it up like Skittles. Eric B. & Rakim were so revered that Ra's line "pump up the volume" was sampled on M/A/R/R/S's hit of the same name.

"THERE ARE FEW THINGS HIP-HOP HEADS CAN AGREE ON. HERE'S ONE: THAT RAKIM IS ONE OF THE BEST MCS EVER. AND THAT HIS DJ, ERIC B., WAS PRETTY NICE AS WELL."

In 1987 came the duo's first full-length album. Pushed and propelled by a huge underground buzz, *Paid in Full* climbed into the R&B top ten. Adding to the already booming hype, the hot British DJ team Coldcut did an innovative remix of "Paid in Full." This newer version and homage just caught fire overseas and helped bring the NYC duo to an even more far-ranging and international audience. The drum track that formed the essence of "Paid in Full" became one of those gotta-hear-it and everyone-knew-it jams. It was instantly so recognizable and fly that it even found new life as the foundation for Milli Vanilli's hit song "Girl You Know It's True." A backhanded compliment if ever there was one. Hmm, wonder if anyone got a check for that.

Boosted by their new status and commercial firepower, Eric B. & Rakim moved to MCA Records and firmed up their legend status with 1988's *Follow the Leader*, featuring the classic eponymous single. A year later Rakim enjoyed top ten pop shine for the first and last time when he guested on Jody Watley's "Friends."

Let the Rhythm Hit 'Em came in 1990, followed by *Don't Sweat the Technique* two years after that. It was Eric B. & Rakim's last, but the inevitable solo careers were stalled by years of legal hassles. The drought ended in '95 when Eric B. released a self-titled album on his own label, while Rakim dropped 1997's *The 18th Letter* and 1999's *The Master*. A real comeback became a possibility when Ra signed to Dr. Dre's Aftermath Entertainment label, yet after numerous delays the much-anticipated CD never saw the light of day and Rakim and Dre eventually parted ways.

Run-D.M.C.

These days folks take for granted that white kids in the suburbs will buy a rap record. But in the '80s, that was a fantasy—until Run-D.M.C. Hip-hop groups have come and gone, but none, absolutely none, had the impact of the three guys from Hollis, Queens. They crossed over in a way that no rappers had before. They broke down barriers, were the first rap act on MTV, forged a coalition between rap and rock, and delivered the 'hood to the 'burbs and beyond.

Run (Joseph Simmons) was the kid brother of Russell Simmons, who in the early '80s formed Rush Productions and co-founded the landmark hip-hop label Def Jam. Russell encouraged Joe and his friend Darryl McDaniels (D.M.C.) to join together as a rap duo. They took Russell's advice, and in 1982, after graduating from high school, recruited another friend, Jason Mizell (Jam Master Jay), to work the turntables.

A year later, Run-D.M.C. released the 12-inch "It's Like That"/"Sucker MCs." Breaking new ground, the song shockingly became a top twenty R&B hit. So did their next joint, "Hard Times"/"Jam Master Jay." In 1984 came more hits, "Rock Box"—one of the first rap songs to incorporate heavy metal guitars—and "30 Days." Later that year, the group's self-titled LP was released. It wasn't just rap's sound that was shook up. It was its style. Unlike their flashy peers, Run-D.M.C. looked like B-boys. They wore tight jeans, leather jackets, and Adidas shell toes. In fact, the group was so linked to Adidas that in time they'd earn an endorsement deal—the first rappers to do so. Run-D.M.C. looked like the kids buying their records.

By 1985's *King of Rock*, Run-D.M.C. were rap's biggest stars. Cuts like the title track embraced rock and roll and rap—laying the foundation for groups like the Red Hot Chili Peppers and Korn. That fusion of genres finally made its way to the white kids on 1986's *Raising Hell*. The album was introduced by the top ten R&B single "My Adidas." Soon after followed the group's biggest hit, a cover of Aerosmith's "Walk This Way." Featuring Steven Tyler and Joe Perry, "Walk This Way" exploded, going all the way to the number four spot on the pop charts, and *Raising Hell* became the first rap album to go number one R&B and top ten pop. Additionally, Run-D.M.C. paved the way for all hip-hop music, becoming the first rappers to get airplay on MTV.

The next year Run-D.M.C. dropped *Tougher Than Leather*, paired with a feature film of the same name—which tanked. Run-D.M.C.'s shine was starting to fade as fans were now checking for tougher, politically savvy groups like Public Enemy.

Two years later, in 1990, Run-D.M.C. came back with the appropriately titled *Back from Hell*—their first album not to reach platinum status. Run and D were both battling demons and their turmoil led to them becoming born-again Christians. Their faith inspired 1993's *Down with the King*. It was just what the Lord ordered and the title track became a top ten R&B hit as the album went gold.

After a lengthy break they came back, again, with the totally whack *Crown Royal*, which bombed. Despite that, Run-D.M.C. continued to rule, thanks to sold-out tours with old pals Aerosmith. In 2002 they were touring with Aerosmith full-time, but then tragedy struck. Hard. A few weeks after ending their tour, thirty-seven-year-old Jam Master Jay was murdered at his Queens recording studio. The still unsolved death of rap's best-known DJ shook the hip-hop community to its core and ended an era.

Following Jay's murder, Run and D vowed to never perform as Run-D.M.C. again. D focused on charity efforts and a solo career. Run dropped an utterly awful album in 2005 on his big brother's label; the CD went nowhere and thankfully disappeared. On a more positive note, Run and family became unlikely but fantastic reality TV show stars with MTV's *Run's House*.

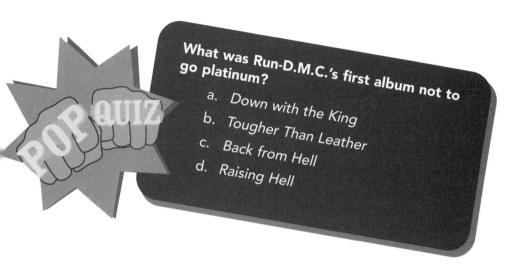

Public Enemy

With politically charged lyrics and incendiary beats, Public Enemy made rap dangerous and controversial. They were the most radical commercial hip-hop act of their time. They were dynamite.

Carlton Douglas Ridenhour a.k.a. Chuck D was a graphic design student who DJed at his college radio station. It was there that he met Hank Shocklee, who had been crafting mixtapes. He convinced Chuck to rap over a song called "Public Enemy No. 1," which started getting played on the college station and made its way to Rick Rubin. The Def Jam co-founder/producer reached out to Chuck in the hopes of signing him. Initially Chuck said no, but then began to formulate a rap group driven as much by exploring radical sound as espousing radical Afrocentric politics. To accomplish this impressive goal, Chuck brought on Shocklee, college friend Bill Stephney, DJ Terminator X (Norman Lee Rogers), and Nation of Islam adherent Professor Griff (Richard Griffin). Griff's role was to act as the choreographer (working on a variation of step dancing mixed with some paramilitary flourishes) of the proposed group's backup dancers, the Security of the First World. Chuck then recruited another old pal, William Drayton. The ever-clever Drayton created Flavor Flav, the comical yin to Chuck's deadly serious yang. Yes, years before *Flavor of Love*, Flav was a viable artist.

PE's debut, *Yo! Bum Rush the Show*, came in 1987. The critics dug it, but it failed to really make much impact. Not so with 1988's *It Takes a Nation of Millions to Hold Us Back.* With Shocklee's Bomb Squad production providing dense, eclectic tracks, Chuck's searing rhymes, and Flav's jokes, *Nation of Millions* got a massive thumbs-up from the rock and rap press who were impressed and invigorated both by the searing sonics and the agitprop. While PE wasn't the first group to attempt to bring a social agenda or consciousness to an audience, the way they pulled it off and the groundbreaking production took rap into a whole new era. If the Black Panthers had a band, they would have been PE.

"IF THE BLACK PANTHERS HAD A BAND, THEY WOULD HAVE BEEN PE."

All the acclaim was briefly overshadowed by some questionable and vile remarks made by Griff in an interview with the *Washington Times*, stating that Jews were responsible for "the majority of the wickedness that goes on across the globe." He later denied making these comments, claiming they were taken out of context and not his words. The mainstream media, and in fact most of PE's white fans and critics who had sincerely championed the group, were angry and Chuck was faced with a tough dilemma. Should Griff stay or should he go? As it turned out, Griff did both—he was fired, brought back, and then left for good after dissing PE in another interview.

With the drama still circling, PE headed back to the studio. But all hell broke loose, again with 1990's single "Welcome to the Terrordome," which contained lyrics that some considered inflammatory. Even so, *Fear of a Black Planet* was a pop and R&B top ten hit, fortified by "911 Is a Joke" and "Can't Do Nuttin' for Ya Man." The following year's *Apocalypse '91 . . . The Enemy Strikes Black* (featuring a new version of "Bring tha Noize" recorded with thrashers Anthrax) debuted at number four pop, but PE was starting to lose steam.

Worn down by external forces such as Flav's run-ins with the law, PE took a breather but returned in '94 with *Muse Sick-N-Hour Mess Age*. It got mixed reviews and had lackluster sales. In 1995, Chuck took Public Enemy off the road, cut ties with Def Jam, developed his own label, and made a stab at reenvisioning PE. He dropped a solo CD, 1996's *The Autobiography of Mistachuck*, and started planning a new PE joint with the Bomb Squad on board. The comeback began with the soundtrack to Spike Lee's *He Got Game* (1998), which earned PE their best reviews in years. In 1999 arrived *There's a Poison Goin' On . . .* but it didn't do much and again Chuck chilled. He returned a few years later and during the 2000s came through with a series of remix/B-side/live projects, all of which made little impact. In 2007, Public Enemy introduced their pioneering music to a younger generation of hip-hop fans with their tenth full-length album, *How You Sell Soul to a Soulless People Who Sold Their Soul?*

KRS-One/Boogie Down Productions

Fronted by MC KRS-One, Boogie Down Productions helped usher in gangsta rap and the backpack clique.

Laurence "Kris" Parker was born in Brooklyn, and after dropping out of high school he headed to the South Bronx where he floated in and out of homeless shelters and social services. Spending much of his time at public libraries (it's there that he studied for his GED), Kris began to write rhymes and tag under the name KRS-One (Knowledge Reigns Supreme Over Nearly Everyone). In 1985, nineteen-year-old Kris met social worker Scott Sterling at a Bronx shelter. Sterling was a DJ who performed as Scott La Rock. Together Kris and Scott decided to form Boogie Down (as in the Bronx) Productions.

BDP's first single was 1986's "Crack Attack," and a year later came their album *Criminal Minded*. The indie release got love from the hardcore and is today considered a classic, typified by the sizzling "9mm Goes Bang," which was one of the first rap songs to find a commonality musically with reggae. The buzz attracted Jive Records, who signed BDP. Sadly, shortly after the triumph, Scott was shot and killed while breaking up a fight.

Seeing BDP as a living tribute to and an emotional extension of the late La Rock's work and creativity, Kris recruited kid brother Kenny as DJ, D-Nice, and Ms. Melodie, who was Mrs. One for a bit. The new BDP dropped *By All Means Necessary* in 1988, and it too was championed and hailed for being not just good but one of the first rap albums to seriously address social issues. Kris's MO and his activist soul was clear from tracks like "My Philosophy" and "Stop the Violence." He also took that spirit to higher levels by founding the (woefully short-lived) Stop the Violence Movement and orchestrating the fund-raising track "Self-Destruction."

That next year BDP came back with the brainy, stripped-down *Ghetto Music: The Blueprint of Hip-Hop*. Again tackling the issues of urban America, KRS-One was gaining a wider audience. Yet the faithful turned on BDP after 1990's *Edutainment* because they thought Kris was getting a bit too preachy and just this side of flat-out pedantic. Two years later, Kris's antiviolence stance was called into question when pop-rappers PM Dawn questioned Kris's self-proclaimed teacher status. In response, KRS physically attacked PM Dawn during their NYC gig. Feeling the heat, KRS-One later apologized and backed away from view for a second.

Nineteen ninety-one saw *Live Hardcore Worldwide*, and then KRS-One made a cameo on R.E.M.'s "Radio Song," which at the time was a big mainstream move and a bit risky for both acts. The next year's *Sex and Violence* found BDP making some moves back to their earlier sound, which made critics happy, but the fans didn't pay much mind. Soon Kris scrapped BDP and recorded under KRS-One. His debut was 1993's *Return of the Boom Bap*, which did fairly well. He continued to be a major live draw as well as an in-demand lecturer, and while his recent solo CDs haven't connected, KRS-One remains the guardian of true school hip-hop.

Boogie Down Productions first signed to:

a. Def Jam

b. Uptown Records

c. Columbia Records

d. Jive Records

POP QUIZ

Beastie Boys

In 1989, New Yorkers 3rd Bass (Pete Nice; MC Serch, host of VH1's *The White Rapper Show*; and DJ Richie Rich) grabbed some shine with their release *The Cactus Album* and hits "The Gas Face" and "Pop Goes the Weasel" (a verbal beatdown to the bane of all honky homies, V-Ice). Yet when you're Googling white-boy rap acts, only one group really matters or managed to truly transcend the obvious. The Beastie Boys broke down doors, set new milestones, and proved that hip-hop was for everyone, by anyone who felt it.

"THE **BEASTIE BOYS** BROKE DOWN DOORS, SET **NEW MILESTONES**, AND PROVED THAT **HIP-HOP** WAS FOR EVERYONE, BY ANYONE WHO FELT IT."

Mike D (Mike Diamond), MCA (Adam Yauch), and Ad-Rock (Adam Horovitz) were products of NYC, where in the early '80s the downtown club scene incorporated rap and punk. It was in one of those underground punk clubs that the Beasties first made their rep. Diamond and Yauch formed the group in 1981 with drummer Kate Schellenbach and guitarist John Berry. In '82, the Beastie Boys dropped the EP *Pollywog Stew*, which no one outside of the punk scene cared about. That same year, the then teenage band met Horovitz, who fronted hardcore combo the Young and the Useless. In 1983, Schellenbach and Berry stepped out and Horovitz stepped in. The new lineup dropped the rap 12-inch "Cooky Puss." Based on a prank call to the local ice-cream chain Carvel, the track was huge in NYC's cool clubs, the ones where rappers and rockers mingled and future stars like Madonna held court.

By the time '84 came around, the Beasties had moved away from punk and more toward rap. That same year they hooked up with Rick Rubin. Def Jam signed the Beasties in 1985, and then came their first hit, "She's On It." Later that year, the trio was picked as the opening act on Madonna's The Virgin Tour, but their drunken stage show didn't go over well with Madge's mostly young female fans. In 1986 the Beasties toured with Run-D.M.C., which set up *Licensed to Ill*. Dissed by many critics, the album's mix of frat-boy yuks, metal, and hip-hop struck a chord with likeminded white kids, who helped make it the fastest-selling debut in Columbia Records history. Crediting the massive crossover single "(You Gotta) Fight for Your Right (to Party!)" (which remains not only their best-known hit, but possibly the bane of the Beasties' existence), *Licensed to Ill* was the biggest-selling rap album of the '80s. While some questioned the Beasties' right to dip so liberally into the culture, by 1987 they were the biggest hip-hop act on the planet, as well as one of the most vilified. After a bitter lawsuit against Rubin and Def Jam, the Beasties left the label, moved to Cali, decided to clean up their image, and signed to Capitol Records, where they have remained ever since. In Los Angeles they linked up with the Dust Brothers (Beck's *Odelay*), who produced the sample-heavy *Paul's Boutique*. Because it was so to the left of *Licensed to Ill*, fans and critics were caught off guard, and even with a minor hit, "Hey Ladies," it fell way short of previous sales. Years later *Paul's Boutique* would be hailed as ahead of its time and help introduce a more free-flowing way of working sampling into the mix.

In 1992 the Beastie Boys came back with *Check Your Head*, featuring the college/alt-rock radio hit "So What'cha Want." Then 1994's *Ill Communication* (with single "Sabotage") debuted at number one.

The band remained very much on the DL for two years, but individually released side projects. In '96 MCA put together the first of the Tibetan Freedom Concerts, which raised awareness and money for Tibet's oppressed citizens. The band's long-awaited fifth album, *Hello Nasty*, arrived in 1998—their third to hit number one. Fans had to wait until 2004 for *To the 5 Boroughs*, which received great reviews and strong sales. The Beasties hit the road, resulting in 2006's live documentary *Awesome; I Fuckin' Shot That!* In 2007, the group showed love to their fans in a new way by releasing an all-instrumental album called *The Mix-Up*.

N.W.A.

For years rap music was an East Coast thing because, well, that's where it came from. So it wasn't all that strange that even though there were rappers going for theirs on the other coast, it took a while before hip-hop fans started paying close attention to the West Coast and showing those artists love. Straight outta Compton, N.W.A. gave Los Angeles an image and intensity that many never thought possible. Call it hardcore, gangsta, or West Coast, N.W.A. put the pedal to the metal and brought L.A. front and center.

"CALL IT HARDCORE, GANGSTA, OR WEST COAST, N.W.A. PUT THE PEDAL TO THE METAL AND BROUGHT L.A. FRONT AND CENTER."

The group's leader, Eazy-E (Eric Wright), was a former dealer who used his profits to start up Ruthless Records and build a roster of artists. Things weren't going all that well until Eazy met Andre Young a.k.a. Dr. Dre, who was part of the World Class Wreckin' Cru, and Ice Cube (O'Shea Jackson). The two started writing songs for Ruthless and Eazy decided to give one of those songs, "Boyz-N-the-Hood," to a Ruthless act. When that group refused the track (hello poor career choices), Eazy figured he'd just create his own damn rap group. N.W.A., which stood for Niggaz With Attitude, consisted of Dre, Cube, Eazy, DJ Yella, the Arabian Prince, and the D.O.C.

N.W.A.'s first album, *N.W.A. and the Posse* (1987), was a party record that was ignored, but in '88 and with the addition of MC Ren (Lorenzo Patterson) the group started to retool their sound. The new N.W.A. embraced an aggressive, angry, often violent style. The first taste of this fresh N.W.A. was *Straight Outta Compton*, originally released in 1988 and then rereleased in February of 1989. Unrelenting and brutal, the album got barely any support from radio or the press, but nonetheless caught on fire among fans and the underground. The former party/good-time act suddenly was issuing songs like the hardcore "Fuck tha Police." That song was so inflammatory and controversial that the FBI warned N.W.A. and Ruthless to watch it. Ahh, remember when rap actually scared people?

A good portion of the political passion and fire dissipated when Ice Cube, who was embroiled in numerous financial disagreements with Eazy and Ruthless, left to go solo in 1989. Not wanting to show weakness or indicate that they needed Cube to make their brand of rap, N.W.A. put out the EP *100 Miles* (1990) and then a year later *Efil4zaggin* ("Niggaz 4 Life" backward). The album was as funky as it was filled with way-over-the-top misogyny and insanely violent rhymes. N.W.A. was selling crazy albums, but things weren't all good, as Dre started mapping out his exit strategy, motivated in great part by what he saw as a shady record deal and long-standing conflicts with management and the label.

While Dr. Dre was making his plans to leave, his soon-to-be-former group was clearly falling apart and on hard times. Ren and Yella also went the solo route, but no one paid much mind, while Eazy's own solo CDs only indicated that the savvy artist was sinking deeper and deeper into unintentionally comical self-parody. Then tragedy struck in 1995 when Eazy publicly announced that he'd contracted HIV. Even though basketball legend Magic Johnson had revealed his own positive status a few years earlier, acknowledgment of HIV/AIDS, especially within the hip-hop community, was unheard of. Soon after his admission, Eazy-E died from AIDS-related complications, becoming one of the first black celebrities and certainly the first rapper to pass from that disease. Thankfully the formerly feuding group members Cube and Dre had made amends with their former partner before Eazy's demise. Yet in many ways the end of N.W.A. was only the beginning.

Heavy D & the Boyz

Heavy D & the Boyz were crazy fun and cranked out a host of catchy hip-hop hits that helped make its leader, "the overweight lover," an unlikely sex symbol. Born in Jamaica, Dwight Myers moved to Mount Vernon, New York, as a kid. By junior high he was making his own homemade rap demos and in high school formed the Boyz (DJ Eddie F a.k.a. Eddie Ferrell, "Trouble" T. Roy a.k.a. Troy Dixon, and G-Wiz a.k.a. Glen Parrish). Their demo landed in Andre Harrell's hands, and he made the quartet the first signing on his soon-to-be-launched label Uptown. In 1987 Heavy D & the Boyz released *Living Large* and hit right away with "Mr. Big Stuff" and "The Overweight Lover's in the House," which played, uh, heavily on D's size. The album went gold in 1987. The group really broke through with 1989's *Big Tyme*. Working once again with Teddy Riley, this album showed a little more depth and sides to Heavy's lovable fat-guy identity. "We Got Our Own Thang," and "Gyrlz, They Love Me" became top ten R&B hits and the platinum album was the number one R&B album and went top twenty on pop. The good times were undercut by sadness when, while on a 1990 tour, "Trouble" T. Roy was killed in an accident. His shocking and unexpected death would become the subject of Pete Rock & C.L. Smooth's classic "They Reminisce Over You (T.R.O.Y.)" and a tribute song on Heavy D's *Peaceful Journey*.

Released in '91, *Peaceful Journey* also sold a million, and a good portion of that well-deserved success was because of the joyous single "Now That We Found Love," which made the big pop crossover. The Heavster was now big in more ways than one. His larger-than-large position was solidified by the sexy "Is It Good to You." *Blue Funk* was the next album, and though the 1992 gem was a tad tougher, it still went gold. While still working with his group, Heavy also began what would become a lucrative acting career. In 1993, he became VP of A&R at Uptown.

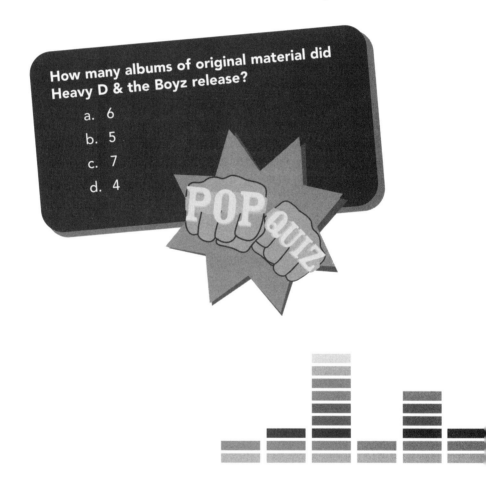

How many albums of original material did Heavy D & the Boyz release?

a. 6

b. 5

c. 7

d. 4

POP QUIZ

In '94 Heavy D & the Boyz came back platinum with *Nuttin' But Love*, which topped the R&B album charts. In '96 Heavy served briefly as the president of Uptown (following Harrell's splashy and short-lived move to Motown) and made his off-Broadway debut in a play written and directed by Laurence Fishburne. The next year a Boyz-free Heavy returned to music with *Waterbed Hev*, which went top ten pop and R&B. His seventh album, *Heavy* (1999), also went top ten. That same year he appeared in the films *Life* and the Oscar-nominated *The Cider House Rules*. By the new millennium, Heavy was acting full-time under his given name.

IT'S A G(ROUP) THANG: '80s RAP GROUPS

N.W.A. AND PUBLIC ENEMY BOTH RELEASED THEIR DEBUT ALBUMS IN 1987.

BOTH KRS-ONE AND RAP GROUP N.W.A. HAVE SONG DEALING WITH THE ISSUE POLICE BRUTALITY.

PUBLIC ENEMY AND THE BEASTIE BOYS WERE BOTH SIGNED TO DEF JAM RECORDS BY ITS CO-CREATOR RICK RUBIN.

THE BEASTIE BOYS AND SALT-N-PEPA BOTH APPEARED ON VH1'S *HIP-HOP HONORS*.

BOTH EPMD AND HEAVY D & THE BOYZ
SAMPLED POPULAR '70S SONGS FOR
TRACKS THAT BECAME CHART-TOPPING
SINGLES, ERIC CLAPTON'S "I SHOT THE
SHERIFF" FOR EPMD AND THIRD
WORLD'S "NOW THAT WE FOUND LOVE"
FOR HEAVY D & THE BOYZ.

RAKIM OF ERIC B. & RAKIM AND
ERIC SERMON OF EPMD BOTH
APPEARED ON THE FINAL EPISODE
OF MTV'S *YO! MTV RAPS*.

RUN-D.M.C. AND ERIC B. &
RAKIM ARE ALL FROM NEW
YORK CITY.

SALT-N-PEPA AND RUN-D.M.C.
ARE BOTH GROUPS COMPOSED OF
TWO MCS AND ONE DJ.

CHAPTER 3

BIG TIMERS:
'90s SOLO RAP

After hip-hop proved itself as a viable profession and lifestyle, the '90s saw a boom in the genre, creatively and sales-wise. Artists like the Beastie Boys and the Run-D.M.C./Aerosmith collaboration helped hip-hop branch out into white America (as did fat guys in suits who saw urban radio as a way to make some cash), solidifying the fact that hip-hop wasn't just for street corners in the city. *Yo! MTV Raps* brought hip-hop into homes via television, inspiring a new generation to pick up mics and drum machines all over the world. Eminem brought insane controversy to national media just from being a white guy who said all of the same things black artists had been saying for years. Women like Lil' Kim and Foxy Brown upped the sexuality ante tenfold. Backpackers like Mos Def and Common kept intellect within rhymes alive. Biggie and Tupac took beefing to the next level. Things happened at an accelerated rate in the '90s, and the artists represented here all played a major part in this hip-hop explosion.

The Notorious B.I.G.

On the basis of looks alone, the Notorious B.I.G. never should have made it past open mic night. As he indelibly conceded on the "One More Chance (Remix)," B.I.G. P.O.P.P.A. (no info for the D.E.A.) was a "heart-throb, never/black and ugly as ever." Sammy Davis Jr. and Janis Joplin long ago proved that movie-star looks weren't a prerequisite for pop stardom, but people who look like Notorious B.I.G. generally have to be twice as talented and work twice as hard just to get the same props and popularity as their more slender, conventionally attractive peers. Nobody ever accused the Notorious B.I.G. of coasting on his looks.

In life and in death, B.I.G.'s legacy is hopelessly wrapped up in friend turned rival Tupac Shakur. There are many reasons why Tupac's star has posthumously dwarfed B.I.G.'s, but much of it comes down to looks. Tupac Shakur wasn't just handsome: he was damn near pretty, with an almost feminine beauty, soulful brown eyes, and a gym-sculpted physique. The hip-hop nation was tantalized by the "Thug Life" tatted on Tupac's six-pack, but if B.I.G. ever tried to show off his belly in public, onlookers would flee in horror like extras in a *Godzilla* movie.

B.I.G. wasn't just what Jim Morrison calls a "large mammal." We all know fat people who are as graceful as ballerinas. B.I.G. was most assuredly not that kind of guy. In videos and interviews, he seemed to move with the greatest of difficulty. His humongous size seemed to make everything hard for him, from walking to rapping to talking to breathing. Seemingly nothing came easy to the man born Christopher Wallace other than writing. B.I.G. was the Raymond Chandler of rap, a natural-born storyteller with a flair for novelistic detail and pitch-black humor.

The pop music world is largely the domain of skinny, beautiful people, but Biggie kicked in the door and made himself comfortable through sheer talent and force of will. Like good friend and sometime collaborator Jay-Z, he made the leap from selling cocaine to selling millions of albums without ever shifting his hustler's mind-set. It was B.I.G. who first informed the world that the rap game was just like the crack game, an assertion that has become the ghetto gospel for all the hustlers, dealers, and aspiring rappers who followed in his path.

"B.I.G. WAS THE RAYMOND CHANDLER OF RAP, A NATURAL-BORN STORYTELLER WITH A FLAIR FOR NOVELISTIC DETAIL AND PITCH-BLACK HUMOR."

Born May 21, 1972, in Bedford-Stuyvesant, Brooklyn, Christopher Wallace was the son of a welder and a preschool teacher named Voletta Wallace. After Christopher's father left, Voletta strove to provide a stable and loving home life for her son, but even though Christopher was a bright student, the lure of the streets proved too hard to resist.

Christopher dropped out of school while still a teenager and began selling crack, much to his mother's horror. Voletta's warm, maternal presence would later form the soulful core of Nick Broomfield's empathetic documentary *Biggie & Tupac*. When Broomfield asked Voletta about the seeming incongruity between the middle-class existence she tried to provide for her talented son and the hard-luck tales he shared on his CDs, B.I.G.'s mother graciously conceded that her son was a storyteller first and foremost and one of a storyteller's central jobs involves making shit up. Voletta could certainly delineate between the facts of her son's life and the wild stories he spat on his records, even if censors, moralistic busybodies, and the uptight citizens' brigade couldn't.

Movies made an indelible impression on B.I.G. He took the rap name Biggie Smalls from a supporting character played by Calvin Lockhart in the 1975 blaxploitation epic *Let's Do It Again*, while his "Frank White" persona was an homage to Christopher Walken's melancholy kingpin from *King of New York*. But B.I.G. wasn't just vicariously experiencing the illicit thrill of criminality from the safe confines of a movie theater seat. No, he was out in the streets selling crack and racking up a formidable arrest record. In 1989 he was arrested on weapons charges and sentenced to probation. The next year he was busted for violating his probation, and in 1991 he was arrested in North Carolina for drug dealing and spent close to a year in prison, which in the early '90s doubled as a strange sort of finishing school for aspiring gangsta rappers.

B.I.G.'s lengthy stint in prison only strengthened his resolve to make it in hip-hop. After being released, he recorded a demo under the name Biggie Smalls that eventually found its way into the hands of *The Source* editors. *The Source* selected Wallace for its prestigious "Unsigned Hype" column, a star-making platform for everyone from Eminem to DMX to Common to Mobb Deep.

B.I.G.'s "Unsigned Hype" buzz led to another demo tape, which in turn attracted the attention of a hungry young hip-hop mogul-in-training named Sean "Puff Daddy" Combs. Combs had dropped out of Howard University to pursue an internship at Uptown Records, where, being a terribly ambitious overachiever, he quickly climbed the corporate ladder by bringing hip-hop closer to R&B and R&B closer to hip-hop. He struck gold commercially by injecting a hip-hop edge into the music of a tough-as-nails soul singer with a beautifully bruised voice named Mary J. Blige. Not coincidentally, B.I.G. made some of his first big appearances on remixes for Blige hits like "Real Love" and "What's the 411?" Uptown superstars Jodeci were another fine example of Combs's uncanny ability to reconcile the worlds of hip-hop and R&B. In the early '90s, his fusion of the two genres made him a hero to record execs. It also made him a villain to hip-hop purists.

Alas, Combs was seen as a little too ambitious. Top Uptown execs like Andre Harrell worried that the cocky young upstart was gunning for their jobs, so the brash young businessman was fired not long after Combs signed Notorious B.I.G. to Uptown. When Combs left the label, he simply took his star pupil with him when he founded Bad Boy Records.

Half of B.I.G.'s legendary debut, *Ready to Die*, was consequently recorded while the rapper was still signed to Uptown, and half was recorded after he'd joined the fledgling Bad Boy roster. But even before *Die*'s release, B.I.G. generated deafening buzz thanks to his bravura turn on the "Flava in Ya Ear (Remix)," a seminal posse cut that helped cement the growing stardom of both the Notorious B.I.G. and a combustible fount of energy named Busta Rhymes.

While working on *Ready to Die*, B.I.G. continued to sell crack to support himself and newborn daughter T'Yanna, a sideline Combs helped bring to a merciful halt. During this time B.I.G. befriended Tupac Shakur, a rapper whose name would become nearly as synonymous with B.I.G.'s as Puffy's.

When *Ready to Die* was released in 1994, it rivaled Nas's *Illmatic* as the instant classic that would officially bring grimy East Coast lyricism back to the forefront in the midst of Dr. Dre's G-funk invasion.

The Notorious B.I.G. hailed from the NYC borough of:

a. Brooklyn
b. Staten Island
c. Queens
d. The Bronx

POP QUIZ

Ready to Die began, literally, at the very beginning, with B.I.G.'s birth set against the soundtrack of his life: first Curtis Mayfield's "Pusherman," a sly in-joke considering the rapper's own drug-dealing past, and Sugarhill Gang's "Rapper's Delight," the landmark track that introduced the United States and the world at large to hip-hop. For the rest of the intro, vivid, impressionistic scenes ostensibly from B.I.G.'s childhood and tortured adolescence are juxtaposed with the music of the moment, namely Audio Two's "Top Billin'" followed by the unmistakable drawl of Snoop Doggy Dogg, a rather blatant sign of respect to a West Coast rival that somehow failed to kill the Bad Boy/Death Row beef in its infancy. The intro ended pretty much where B.I.G.'s music career began: with the black Frank White leaving prison with dreams of trading in the crack game for the rap game.

Ready to Die's rather extraordinary intro went a long way toward providing a sense of context for the rapper's life and music. It threw down the gauntlet by declaring that the album that followed wouldn't just reflect the scattered thoughts of the man behind it. No, *Ready to Die* set out to capture the totality of B.I.G.'s existence, from his days running the streets and ducking from cops to the outsized rewards that accompany the upper tier of hip-hop stardom. *Ready to Die* was a debut, but it also felt like a magnum opus. If B.I.G. was in fact as ready to die as his almost comically grim album title indicated, he'd nevertheless be leaving behind an impressive legacy.

The next track, "Things Done Changed," paid further homage to Death Row with a gloomy chorus borrowed from Dr. Dre's "Lil' Ghetto Boy." Then came "Gimme the Loot," which served as a showcase for B.I.G.'s most stunning display of technique, as the rapper rapped opposite a speeded-up version of himself so he could play both himself and a no-good accomplice trying to lure him further into the criminal underworld.

The songs that followed ran the gamut emotionally from suicidal despair to ecstatic joy and everywhere in between. "Everyday Struggle" split the difference between the two extremes by somehow managing to be both unbearably, almost suicidally grim (the chorus is, "I don't wanna live no mo'/Sometimes I feel death knockin' at my front do'/I'm livin' everyday like a hustle, another drug to juggle/Another day, another struggle," after all) and strangely uplifting. Notorious B.I.G. had obviously been through hell, but made it through to the other side.

The subject matter of *Ready to Die* wasn't exactly novel. In every 'hood there were hundreds of aspiring rappers bragging about selling crack, nailing groupies, and stacking paper, but few rappers could match the depth, richness, and visceral wallop of B.I.G.'s music.

"IN EVERY 'HOOD THERE WERE HUNDREDS OF ASPIRING RAPPERS BRAGGING ABOUT SELLING CRACK, NAILING GROUPIES, AND STACKING PAPER, BUT FEW RAPPERS COULD MATCH THE DEPTH, RICHNESS, AND VISCERAL WALLOP OF B.I.G.'S MUSIC."

Ready to Die began with B.I.G.'s troubled birth and ended with "Suicidal Thoughts," a grim bit of gangsta fatalism where B.I.G. contemplates suicide and an afterlife in hell before pulling the trigger and putting himself out of his misery. From its title onward, *Ready to Die* is one seriously bleak fucking album, so it's all the more remarkable that Combs managed to transform his weed-smoking, depressive, barely mobile, morbidly obese friend into one of pop music's unlikeliest superstars.

"Suicidal Thoughts" and "Everyday Struggle" might have been two of Biggie's deepest, most personal tracks, but the songs that introduced Biggie to the mainstream were slick, radio-friendly singles like "Juicy," "Big Poppa," and "One More Chance." Combs didn't just executive-produce and spearhead *Ready to Die*. Nope, he was impossible to miss in the album's Hype Williams–directed videos. They were a perfect team, the mountain of a man who was nobody's idea of eye candy and the manic, dancing goofball who couldn't resist the siren song of a video or news camera. Combs could also be heard ad-libbing throughout the disc, chipping in excitable cries of "Yeah, yeah" and "I like dat."

Ready to Die was released to ecstatic reviews and phenomenal sales. After a prolonged period of hibernation it now appeared that East Coast hip-hop was back thanks to Biggie, Nas, and the Wu-Tang Clan. Biggie's life suddenly shifted into overdrive. He wasted little time exploiting *Ready to Die*'s success by forming the rap group Junior M.A.F.I.A. as a vehicle for friend/lover Lil' Kim and buddies like Lil' Cease and appearing throughout its debut.

Biggie also made headlines by marrying fellow Bad Boy artist Faith Evans less than two weeks after meeting her at a Bad Boy photo shoot. Alas, with mo' money came mo' problems. After being shot and robbed at a New York studio, Tupac Shakur accused B.I.G. and Puff Daddy of being complicit in the attack, an unsubstantiated charge that led to a huge feud between Death Row Records and Bad Boy.

B.I.G. suddenly found himself on the receiving end of vitriolic diss songs like "Hit 'Em Up." Tupac was waging war on Bad Boy and Biggie at a time when both were at their commercial and critical zenith. Tupac's war with Biggie ended with the Death Row icon's murder in 1996. Further run-ins with the law and dark talk that Biggie might somehow have been involved in his rival's murder continued to haunt him throughout the recording of his second album, the eerily titled *Life After Death*.

Like a lot of follow-ups to classic albums, *Life After Death* was much bigger than its predecessor but not necessarily better. The runaway success of Tupac's *All Eyez on Me* led to a boom in double-disc sets, including *Life After Death*, which spread twenty-four tracks over two discs. Where *Ready to Die* was produced largely by Easy Mo Bee and featured only a few guests like Method Man on "The What," *Life After Death* was a star-studded affair featuring R. Kelly, The Lox, Jay-Z, Ma$e, Bone Thugs-

N-Harmony, Lil' Kim, Too $hort, and Faith Evans in addition to a battery of producers from Puff Daddy's Hitmen Squad and outside hitmakers like Kay Gee, RZA, DJ Premier, and Clark Kent.

Life After Death offered an embarrassment of riches but it lacked the tightness, cohesion, and focus of *Ready to Die*. Nevertheless, the album was a big hit with critics and fans and spawned a huge leadoff single in "Hypnotize"—yet another Bad Boy single sold largely on the basis of an insanely expensive, elaborate Hype Williams–produced music video.

In March of 1997, Biggie traveled to Southern California to promote the single and attended a party at the Petersen Automotive Museum alongside Puff Daddy, estranged wife Evans, and a number of known gangbangers repping the Crips and Bloods. After leaving the party in an SUV along with Bad Boy's security detail, B.I.G. was shot by an unknown assailant four times in the chest. He died shortly afterward.

The man who'd named his first album *Ready to Die* and his follow-up *Life After Death* fell victim to the early, violent death he'd prophesied in so many of his songs. *Life After Death* was released fifteen days after the rapper's murder and shocked no one by going directly to the top of the charts. The video for "Mo' Money Mo' Problems," the disc's second single, used previously shot footage of B.I.G. combined with new footage of Puff Daddy and Ma$e goofing around in shiny suits against an array of fantastical backgrounds. The rapper who bared his soul in track after track and wrote empathetically about the darkest, most crippling forms of depression was now associated, rightly or wrongly, with the gaudiest form of pop escapism. A subsequent video for "Sky's the Limit" directed by Spike Jonze went even further into fantasy by using prepubescent look alikes to play B.I.G., Lil' Kim, and Puff Daddy.

Puff Daddy, meanwhile, jump-started his solo career by releasing "I'll Be Missing You," a maudlin tribute track to B.I.G. featuring Faith Evans on the chorus and built around a clunky sample of the Police's "Every Breath You Take." Bad Boy went on to release three more discs featuring B.I.G.: 1999's *Born Again*, 2005's *Duets: The Final Chapter*, and 2007's *Greatest*

Hits, and while B.I.G. continues to be one of rap's most revered icons, his cult pales in comparison to the secular religion of Tupac worship that has built up around his fiercest rival.

The Notorious B.I.G. will never be as popular with teenage girls as Tupac, but for hardcore hip-hop heads who value lyricism and complexity over flash and washboard abs, his status as the greatest rapper of all time remains secure. Considering the incredible lengths Biggie had to travel just to get to the top and the formidable obstacles facing him along the way, it's a great feat that he's considered one of rap's most revered icons.

Which track was not on Biggie's *Ready to Die?*

a. "One More Chance"
b. "Big Poppa"
c. "Mo' Money Mo' Problems"
d. "Juicy"

POP QUIZ

Eminem

Since his 1999 breakthrough, Marshall Mathers has been hip-hop's most beloved honky. More importantly, he's kind of made that whole white rapper qualifier passé. Oh sure, being white gave Em a leg up—he's the first to cop to that. But trust. A novelty only takes you so far—just ask the supremely-talented-but-who-really-cares whitey Bubba Sparxxx. When it comes to this white boy, Eminem may be a cat you either love or hate, but on this you can't front. He made it hot to be trailer trash and more often than not brought his very own thing to the game.

Em grew up outside of Kansas City, but spent much of his youth traveling between there and Detroit. It was in Detroit, actually nearby Warren, that

Em began to rap when he was fourteen. He formed a group with a friend and they called it Manix and M&M, derived from Em's initials. Knowing that hip-hop didn't have a lot of use for most white guys who rap, Eminem figured that the way to win over Detroit's underground was to battle rap against other MCs. Over time he became quite a popular draw, in good part because of the novelty, but also because he had talent.

Em's growing profile resulted in other rappers trying to form groups with him. One such early act was Soul Intent, who put out Eminem's first single in 1995. Performing on the B-side was a local kid named Proof who dug Em so much that he asked his fair-haired friend to start another group. Bringing in a few other guys, they became known as D12—even though they were a six-man crew. Things were going well, but soon the demands of fatherhood and supporting his girlfriend/soon-to-be wife and lyrical nemesis, Kim, slowed Em's career down. This new reality began to filter into his raps, which were increasingly bitter as well as drawn not from the streets but his life.

In 1996, Em dropped the indie *Infinite*, which was met by mostly silence. Shaking it off, he decided to create a no-holds-barred alter ego: Slim Shady. He didn't have to go far for inspiration. He and his mother had a poisonous relationship, a beloved uncle had committed suicide, and Kim had moved away with their daughter, Hailie. Adding to his rage, Eminem was drinking and taking drugs. That darkness along with caustic humor was heard in *The Slim Shady EP*. The buzz was starting to get loud.

Myth has it that Dr. Dre stumbled on Em's demo at Jimmy Iovine's (president of Interscope Records) crib. Reality is that Em came in second, freestyle division, at 1997's Rap Olympics MC Battle in L.A. and Iovine asked for a tape, which he then played for Dre. After getting past his initial shock over Eminem's melanin count, Dre began recording his new protégé. "Just Don't Give a Fuck" was the first single, and along with his marrying Kim, it made Em's 1998 memorable. That year Interscope signed the MC and the hype campaign kicked off.

The Slim Shady LP appeared in 1999, complete with the massively massive "My Name Is," and the just merely massive "Guilty Conscience." Both helped the debut sell over three million units. Fans loved it, both white and black, and having one of the most respected names in rap, Dr. Dre, did a lot for Eminem's visibility and cred. Not to mention it was kind of hot that, for once, a black guy was pimping whitey. But with the love came some hate thanks to Em's graphic and often over-the-top violent lyrics. Yet even critics had to acknowledge that this white boy had skills and a unique perspective.

> **"FANS LOVED IT, BOTH WHITE AND BLACK, AND HAVING ONE OF THE MOST RESPECTED NAMES IN RAP, DR. DRE, DID A LOT FOR EMINEM'S VISIBILITY AND CRED. NOT TO MENTION IT WAS KIND OF HOT THAT, FOR ONCE, A BLACK GUY WAS PIMPING WHITEY."**

After guesting on Dre's 2001, Em came roaring back in 2000 with The Marshall Mathers LP, which sold close to two million units in its first week out, making it the fastest-selling rap record—ever. With the success came more controversy and drama. Em got into public beefs with everyone from guys down with Insane Clown Posse (Motor City's other "white meat") to Christina Aguilera. On top of that, Em's mom sued him for defamation of character, and he got into it with a Detroit club patron over a perceived come-on to Kim. Plus he was accused of having violent and anti-female lyrics (e.g., "Kill You" and "Kim"). Understandably, this infuriated gay and women's groups. As always, the controversy didn't hurt sales or prevent Em from getting nominated for several key Grammys, but to many activist groups those nominations were an approval of Em's use of hate speech. To silence those critics (and make good TV), Eminem enlisted a fan, Elton John, to perform the haunting "Stan" with him at the telecast. Boom. Critics shut down. TV ratings up. Grammy committee looks edgy and Em grabs some statues.

In 2001, Eminem reformed D12, who released the popular *Devil's Night*. After finishing up a tour, Em made the by now expected foray into films—with a difference. He starred in *8 Mile*, which was directed by the well-known Curtis Hanson. The critically acclaimed film was loosely based on Em's life and worked both as a biopic and a really good flick. Its theme song, "Lose Yourself," won an Oscar for Best Original Song, as well. After what seemed like nonstop touring and promotion, Em stepped out of the spotlight for a minute.

His reentry in 2002 was "Without Me," the first single from *The Eminem Show*, which, as by now the pattern, debuted at number one and sold millions. The next single, "Cleanin' Out My Closet," brought the f-you vibe down a notch and was sort of reflective—sensitive thugs and all that. Still in the public eye and still picking fights with easy targets (e.g., techno star Moby), Em came through again with '04's *Encore*, another chart-topping multiplatinum hit. What was different were songs like the anti-war "Mosh" that showed Em had more thematic range than previously indicated. By now running his own Shady Records, whose roster included D12 and fellow Motor City rapper Obie Trice, Em was going nonstop. Until he stopped. He canceled the European leg of his tour due to exhaustion. Soon after, he checked into rehab to deal with "dependency on sleep medication," later addressing the issue on "When I'm Gone." The year 2005 ended with *Curtain Call: The Hits*, which went to number one. Shocking.

Em kicked off 2006 by remarrying Kim, and then in April, around the time when he and the wifey split again, tragedy of the real kind struck. Proof, fellow D12 member and Em's best friend, was killed in Detroit. The loss of his family and friend kept Eminem away from the spotlight and studio, although he did produce Obie Trice's *Second Round's On Me* and popped up on Akon's hit "Smack That." Em ended 2006 with *Eminem Presents the Re-Up*, a compilation featuring Shady artists, none of whom have been able to sustain a career without the white boy's guidance.

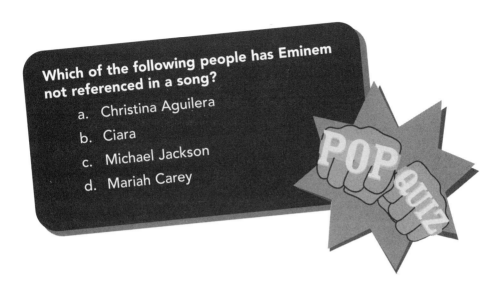

DMX

By the late '90s, hip-hop had reached a crossroads. What began as impromptu street jams in the park had grown into a huge business whose reach and influence stretched far beyond national borders. The super-stars of rap's golden age were pawning their fat gold chains just to pay the rent. Public Enemy, once the conscience of hip-hop, was now record-ing for a crazy, doomed Internet label called Atomic Pop, while fellow conscious rap icon KRS-One worked a white-collar job at Warner Bros. The unsolved murders of Tupac and Notorious B.I.G. inspired heated debate as to whether hip-hop was causing violence or merely reflecting it. The music had lost two of its strongest, most charismatic voices and was increasingly dominated by questionable instant stars whose greatest gift involved being in the right place at the right time. In B.I.G.'s absence, producer turned mogul turned rapper Sean "Puff Daddy" Combs went from being the cheesy camera hog dancing around in glitzy videos to starring in videos himself.

In this vast sea of glamour and glitz, the guttural cry of a grimy rapper, Yonkers-born Earl Simmons, stood out as a lone voice in the wilderness. Actually it was more of a feral bark, an agitated cry of rage from some-where deep within the soul of America's suffering underclass. Just as 50 Cent cannily exploited widespread resentment toward Ja Rule as a springboard to megastardom, DMX, consciously or unconsciously, rode the anger and resentment toward the jiggy new hip-hop order of Puff Daddy to megaplatinum sales and household name status. Simply put, DMX was the anti-Puffy.

The story of DMX is a narrative that ripples through the long, glorious, sad, and triumphant story of black music in America. It's the story of a man perpetually torn between heaven and hell, salvation and sin, the church and the streets. It's the history of a man torn between the antithetical imperatives of gospel and blues, an American genre that looks upward to heaven for guidance and inspiration and an equally indigenous homegrown art form that sings of sorrows straight out the bowels of hell.

"IN THIS VAST SEA OF GLAMOUR AND GLITZ, THE GUTTURAL CRY OF A GRIMY RAPPER, YONKERS-BORN EARL SIMMONS, STOOD OUT AS A LONE VOICE IN THE WILDERNESS."

Earl Simmons was born December 18, 1970, in Baltimore, though his family moved to the New York suburb of Yonkers soon after. His childhood was characterized by frequent bouts of trouble. An early predilection toward violence resulted in numerous stints in group homes and prisons, but Simmons eventually discovered a gift for music that would become his personal and professional salvation.

Though he initially toiled as a DJ, Simmons quickly segued into rapping. He decided to name himself DMX after a digital drum machine and set about pursuing a career as an MC. In 1991, he became the subject of *The Source*'s much-vaunted "Unsigned Hype" column, a vastly influential showcase for unsigned rappers that had provided crucial early breaks for everyone from Notorious B.I.G. to Eminem to Mobb Deep to Common.

Rappers featured in "Unsigned Hype" seldom remain unsigned for long. DMX was no exception. In 1992 he signed to Columbia Records and cut the single "Born Loser." Alas, the song's title proved apt: "Born Loser" was a flop and DMX was subsequently dropped. In the words of 50 Cent, DMX spent the next few years "patiently waiting to blow."

Bad Boy and Death Row were reportedly both interested in signing DMX, but the rapper instead chose to follow friend Irv Gotti to Def Jam, which was then experiencing a prolonged commercial slump. Gotti signees Ja Rule, Jay-Z, and X quickly and dramatically ended that drought. In 1997 DMX appeared on "4, 3, 2, 1," an LL Cool J single that would become infamous for igniting a feud between Cool J and guest rapper Canibus after the veteran rapper interpreted a Canibus rhyme as disrespectful.

While Canibus and LL Cool J battled it out on wax and in the press, DMX went on to score a string of high-profile guest turns on hits like Ma$e's "24 Hours to Live" and The Lox's "Money, Power & Respect." Ironically, both songs were for Puff Daddy's Bad Boy label, a strange pairing that proved that even the flashiest pop-rap big shots jonesed for an unadulterated shot of DMX's gritty street swagger. More importantly, both singles found DMX collaborating with The Lox, a respected Yonkers trio who'd join forces with DMX's Ruff Ryders clique after parting ways with Bad Boy.

DMX's guest appearances served to fuel anticipation for his 1998 solo debut, *It's Dark and Hell Is Hot*. DMX glared sullenly from the disc's blood-red cover, his scowl betraying a hard life filled with bone-deep emotional scars. His agitated, staccato flow aimed for maximum visceral impact. He didn't rap so much as he shouted, screamed, and barked lyrics full of threats, hatred, and self-pity.

Just as DMX's style and flow can be read as a gritty antidote to mainstream hip-hop's blinding shininess, the production on his early albums seemed like a direct rebuke to the lazily sample-based beat-biting of Puff Daddy. The beats DMX generally spit over were hard, gloomy, and synthetic, the product of synthesizers pumping out angry assaults of noise. Gangsta rap's long reign at the top of the pop charts deadened a lot of listeners to the genre's violence and aggression, but the over-the-top über-violence of DMX's lyrics, like "If you got a daughter older than fifteen, I'ma rape her/Take her on the living room floor, right there in front of you" (from "X Is Coming"), broke through even the most jaded listener's defenses.

In 1998 DMX followed in Tupac Shakur's footsteps by making the leap onto the big screen in *Belly*, the eagerly anticipated feature film directorial debut of Hype Williams, arguably the most influential music video director in hip-hop history. *Belly* had all the makings of an instant hip-hop classic. It was helmed by the hottest video director alive, was shot by the brilliant cinematographer Malik Sayeed, and starred three of rap's biggest and most charismatic performers: DMX, Nas (who also contributed to the film's script), and Method Man.

Belly confirmed Williams's singular genius for creating effortlessly iconic, eye-popping imagery, but the film's plot was a convoluted mess and its improvised dialogue often felt amateurish and stilted. Though it was released to mixed reviews and unimpressive box-office numbers, it has subsequently become a favorite in hip-hop circles. A sequel is reportedly in development.

"EVEN AUDIENCES WHO FOUND DMX'S RECORDED OUTPUT UGLY AND REPELLENT COULDN'T DENY THE FORCE OF HIS STAGE PRESENCE."

Hot off the success of *It's Dark and Hell Is Hot*, DMX embarked on the Hard Knock Life tour alongside labelmates Ja Rule, Method Man, Redman, DJ Clue, and Jay-Z. Though Jay-Z was the ostensible headliner (it was the Hard Knock Life tour after all, not the Hell Is Hot tour), DMX was nearly as big a draw as Jay-Z himself. Even audiences who found DMX's recorded output ugly and repellent couldn't deny the force of his stage presence.

Over a half decade had elapsed between the ill-fated release of "Born Loser" and the quadruple-platinum success of *It's Dark and Hell Is Hot*. With his recording career firing on all cylinders, DMX was intent on making up for lost time. When his sophomore set, the cheerfully titled *Flesh of My Flesh, Blood of My Blood*, was released in December of '98, it gave him the unique distinction of scoring two consecutive number one smashes in the same year.

Flesh of My Flesh, Blood of My Blood boasted an even darker cover than its predecessor. It showed a shirtless, scowling DMX covered in pig's blood, an appropriate image for an album as dark and uncompromising as his debut. From *Flesh of My Flesh, Blood of My Blood* onward DMX worked extensively with Swizz Beatz, a producer whose unique style sharply divided critics and audiences. To fans, Beatz was a fresh new maverick whose synthesizer-based production marked a much-needed evolutionary step up from the sample-based beats of rap's past. To critics, however, the much sought-after beatsmith was a shameless hack charging huge fees for beats that sounded like the product of a bored adolescent fucking around with a cheap Casio.

When Marilyn Manson appeared on *Flesh's* "The Omen" it marked a collaboration between two of white America's preeminent bogeymen, larger-than-life representations of every parent's worst fears. DMX had reached the pinnacle of pop stardom, but his name soon began popping up in stories that had nothing whatsoever to do with hit tours, movie roles, or back-to-back number one albums.

In 1999 DMX was arrested in Teaneck, New Jersey, on a variety of charges. In 2000, meanwhile, the enterprising rapper/actor was arrested for aggravated unlicensed operation of a vehicle (try saying that three times in a row fast), speeding, failure to signal, driving without a license, failure to notify the DMV of an address change (undoubtedly the most gangsta of all the charges brought against Dark Man X), and possession of marijuana. In other words, DMX was a veritable one-man vehicular crime wave.

This decade DMX has seemingly popped up more in the police blotter than in the pop charts. He became a real-life version of *Mr. Show*'s Ronnie Dobbs, a recurring character famous for getting arrested under the most ridiculous of circumstances. The hits kept coming, but so did the arrests. The cops spent so much time arresting the popular rapper, actor, and ex-con, it's a wonder they didn't just set up a special DMX Task Force to monitor the superstar's moves twenty-four hours a day.

DMX's constant run-ins with the law only served to increase his street credibility. He didn't have to pretend cops were after him: he had the arrest record and glowering mug shots to prove it. As his personal life spiraled out of control, his career became a massive tug-of-war between his better angels and his formidable demons.

In 2000 and 2001, DMX leveraged his pop stardom into prominent roles in *Romeo Must Die* and *Exit Wounds*, big, dumb Joel Silver–produced action blockbusters that cast the rapper opposite international movie star Jet Li and over-the-hill ponytail enthusiast Steven Seagal, respectively. The films were substantial commercial hits but were derided by critics as formulaic junk that squandered DMX's smoldering presence and tormented, intense persona. In 2003, *Cradle 2 the Grave* reteamed DMX with Jet Li but failed to equal *Romeo Must Die*'s impressive box-office tally.

It seems sadly telling that DMX delivered his most memorable performance in one of his least-seen vehicles, 2004's *Never Die Alone*. Director Ernest Dickerson's adaptation of cult paperback hero Donald Goines's novel is like one of X's songs: a grim, ugly, utterly unsentimental wallow in the depths of human misery and degradation. DMX's charismatic drug dealer is utterly without redeeming qualities yet strangely fascinating all the same.

On the recording front, 1999's . . . And Then There Was X, 2001's aptly named The Great Depression, and 2003's Grand Champ continued X's string of consecutive platinum-selling number one albums. After Grand Champ's release, DMX announced plans to retire from rap (perhaps to concentrate more on getting arrested in new and novel ways), but like most hip-hop retirements, it didn't last.

The year 2006 brought X's puzzlingly underpromoted and thoroughly anti-climactic comeback album Year of the Dog . . . Again, his first album since leaving Def Jam (where he would have worked under old collaborator Jay-Z) and signing with Sony. Where Def Jam president Jay-Z managed to turn his return to hip-hop into a cultural event roughly on par with Jesus's return, Again slipped into stores with little in the way of press or promotion. The public's appetite for X's contradictory persona had once seemed insatiable. Now it appeared hip-hop heads had grown tired of the almost comically self-destructive rapper.

Before returning to rap, DMX talked about following Ma$e in abandoning rap to pursue a preacher's life, but his arrest record spoke louder than his godly words. This decade DMX has been arrested for everything from impersonating an FBI officer (not a smart move if you're one of the most famous and recognizable people on the planet) to an endless string of driving violations. Someone seriously needs to stage an intervention to take away X's car keys before he gets himself into even more trouble.

Though still in his thirties, DMX has accomplished enough for ten lifetimes. He's sold over twenty million albums, five of which debuted at number one. He's starred in hit movies. He's toured huge venues. He's written an autobiography and starred in his own BET reality show (DMX: Soul of a Man). Yet X seems to have devolved from the main attraction to a one-man freak show. Yes, he has attained more than he could have ever imagined back when "Born Loser" tanked fifteen years ago. But it'd be nice, if not overly realistic, to imagine that his best years might still somehow be ahead of him, that someday he'll find that perfect role or killer track that'll catapult him back into the spotlight so he can once again be known primarily for his remarkable talent instead of his equally remarkable genius for self-destruction.

How many albums has DMX released that debuted at number one on the Billboard 200?

    a. 5

    b. 6

    c. 4

    d. 7

POP QUIZ

Busta Rhymes

Hip-hop fans could be mistaken for imagining that the great gods of hip-hop issued a pronouncement from on high that Busta Rhymes must appear on every rap or R&B album made between 1995 and 2000. Since erupting onto the hip-hop scene with his starmaking verse on A Tribe Called Quest's classic posse cut "Scenario," Rhymes has redefined hip-hop ubiquity by appearing constantly in singles, videos, movies, commercials, advertising, video games, DVDs, posse cuts, hooks, and everywhere else an injection of high-energy star power was needed. To get away from Rhymes's charismatic growl in the mid- to late '90s, a hip-hop fan would need to move to Afghanistan, join the Taliban, move into a cave, and denounce all forms of music as evil and decadent. Even then you'd probably still hear Rhymes's rasp booming out of passing jeeps.

As he documents in "Been Through the Storm" on *The Big Bang*, Rhymes's father was a rough-hewn Jamaican immigrant who moved to New York and fell in love with Rhymes's hardworking mother. Rhymes enjoyed a loving and supportive home life growing up, but the lure of the streets was too strong to resist. Not even a thriving high school basketball career could keep him from pursuing the perilous existence of a street-corner hustler.

Busta Rhymes (Trevor Smith) discovered an early gift for hip-hop and embraced a sect called the Nation of Gods and Earth, a controversial off-shoot of the Nation of Islam, a group that ironically enough is itself a controversial offshoot of traditional Islam. The Nation of Gods and Earth was founded by a Korean War veteran who called himself Clarence 13X and was mysteriously murdered in 1969. Followers of the sect are known as Five Percenters due to their belief that five percent of mankind consists of enlightened divine beings who understand the true nature of existence and must educate and liberate the minds of the eighty-five percent of humanity that is mentally deaf, dumb, and blind. According to the Five Percenters, the remaining ten percent understand the true nature of existence but sneakily keep it to themselves rather than uplifting the masses. The Nation of Gods and Earth preaches the divinity of the Black Man, and its traditions and teachings are spread orally so it's no surprise that the sect has found a huge following in hip-hop, where rappers tend to think they're God no matter what the Bible, Torah, or Koran might say. Rakim, the Wu-Tang Clan, and Brand Nubian are some of the big-name rap acts who've become Five Percenters. References to Five Percent terminology and its concept of Supreme Mathematics frequently pop up throughout Rhymes's lyrics.

Like many of his peers, Busta first experienced professional success as a teenager: he wasn't even old enough to drink legally when his group Leaders of the New School released its major-label debut, *A Future Without a Past*, in 1991. The disc exploded with youthful high spirits and infectious energy. Tracks with names like "Homeroom," the delightful single "Case of the P.T.A.," "Lunchroom," and "Afterschool" betrayed the fact that the group members were essentially still kids themselves. Leaders of the New School were pretty much the same age as their teenage fan base.

Leaders of the New School would go on to record another album, 1993's *T.I.M.E.*, but it was clear even then that Rhymes was destined for bigger and better things. Accordingly, his contribution to "Scenario," the final track on A Tribe Called Quest's timeless 1991 masterpiece *The Low End Theory*, was the verse heard round the world. "Scenario" was originally conceived as a Native Tongues posse cut where A Tribe Called Quest's Q-Tip and Phife Dawg would share mic time with De La Soul and Leaders of the New School. Alas, De La Soul's verses were removed from the final version, allowing Rhymes's star to shine even brighter.

Rhymes's "Scenario" lyrics bordered on nonsensical with their agitated talk of going "Rowr, rowr like a dungeon dragon," but as is generally the case in the style-obsessed realm of hip-hop, it wasn't what Busta Rhymes was saying that made him a huge instant star. No, it was the way he said it. He is a master of hip-hop style. On a technical level, he's one of the dopest rappers in the game, with a liquid flow that runs the gamut from machine-gun staccato aggression to silky, laid-back smoothness and everywhere in between.

"ON A TECHNICAL LEVEL, [BUSTA'S] ONE OF THE DOPEST RAPPERS IN THE GAME, WITH A LIQUID FLOW THAT RUNS THE GAMUT FROM MACHINE-GUN STACCATO AGGRESSION TO SILKY, LAID-BACK SMOOTHNESS AND EVERYWHERE IN BETWEEN."

After "Scenario," Leaders of the New School became more popularly known as Busta Rhymes and some other dudes. Rhymes was clearly the group's breakout star, and his fame created tension within the group—most notably between Rhymes and Charlie Brown, who began to resent the attention Rhymes was receiving in the press. Charlie Brown also probably seethed with rage over his inability to kick a football, pitch effectively, or convince a delusional, blanket-addicted peer that the Great

Pumpkin does not, in fact, exist, but it is possible that we're getting our Charlie Browns confused. In any case, the long-simmering tension between Rhymes and the non–comic strip Charlie Brown reached a public apex during an infamous episode of *Yo! MTV Raps* where the painful awkwardness between Rhymes and Brown became embarrassingly apparent to even the dimmest home viewer.

When Leaders of the New School's *T.I.M.E.* failed to replicate *A Future Without a Past's* modest success, the group broke up and Rhymes surprised absolutely no one by pursuing a solo career. In 1993, he joined a large army of hip-hop fixtures in the cast for the Doctor Dre and Ed Lover vehicle *Who's the Man?* Yes, Doctor Dre (no, not that Dr. Dre) and Ed Lover were once popular enough to score their own feature-film vehicle. In 1994, A Tribe Called Quest's "Oh My God" became one of the first rap songs to feature a Busta Rhymes hook.

Rhymes had been ready for his close-up since "Scenario," so when his debut album, *The Coming*, hit shelves in 1996 the response was less "Why now?" than "What the hell took so long?" Then again, Rhymes didn't exactly maintain a low profile between the release of his last disc with Leaders of the New School and his first solo release: his unmistakable rasp could be found on songs by Craig Mack, Buju Banton, KRS-One, and Brand Nubian. Like Ludacris and Redman, he became known more for attention-grabbing, high-energy guest appearances than his generally uneven albums.

Busta Rhymes was even better known for videos than his songs. With his trademark dreads, incredibly expressive face, and boundless energy, he was a natural for music videos and quickly became one of the few acknowledged masters of the form. *The Coming* boasted a monster first single and video in "WOO-HAH!! Got You All in Check," an outrageous blast of comic-book bravado that director Hype Williams used as a springboard for some of his zaniest and most flamboyant imagery. Rhymes and Williams enjoyed a mutually beneficial relationship: Rhymes was Williams's muse, and Williams in turn helped develop Rhymes's persona as a larger-than-life total entertainer.

Given Rhymes's runaway popularity in music videos, it's no surprise that Hollywood eventually came calling. He enjoyed a substantial supporting role in John Singleton's *Higher Learning*, a well-intentioned but hopelessly muddled kitchen-sink college melodrama undone by bizarre miscalculations like casting Jewish actor Michael Rapaport as a confused college kid who becomes a neo-Nazi. Apparently Woody Allen and Jackie Mason weren't available. *Higher Learning* similarly enraged the entire male gender, and plenty of lesbians as well, by featuring a lesbian kiss between original Buffy Kristy Swanson and Jennifer Connelly that wasn't even remotely hot. Damn you, John Singleton! Damn you to hell for that inexcusable missed opportunity. The ninth circle of hell is too damn good for you.

Rhymes's sophomore release, *When Disaster Strikes*, scored another memorable hit and video in "Put Your Hands Where My Eyes Could See." In their many groundbreaking videos together, Hype Williams essentially transformed Rhymes into a human cartoon, a hip-hop Jerry Lewis spitting out jets of anarchic excitement in every direction. Late 1998 saw the release of *Extinction Level Event*, an album that boldly, and it turns out incorrectly, predicted that the world would end in the year 2000. Busta Rhymes must have been sorely disappointed when his New Year's Eve party at the end of 1999 failed to climax in the end of life as we know it. The album featured the hugely successful collabo with Janet Jackson, "What's It Gonna Be?!" Rhymes's final album for Elektra, 2000's *Anarchy*, was a gaudy, star-studded affair featuring guest appearances or production from J Dilla, Jay-Z, M.O.P., Lenny Kravitz, Raekwon, Just Blaze, Scott Storch, Swizz Beatz, Rockwilder, and Ghostface Killah.

By the release of *Anarchy*, Busta Rhymes had leveraged his hip-hop fame into a thriving multimedia empire. He was now a one-man brand, but as his fame and profile rose in other media, the rapper's albums began to seem less and less essential. In 2000 he scored another big movie role as Samuel L. Jackson's sidekick in John Singleton's thoroughly disappointing *Shaft* remake. A voice-over gig as "Reptar Wagon" in *The Rugrats Movie* did little to boost Rhymes's street credibility, nor did his perform-

"BY THE RELEASE OF *ANARCHY*, BUSTA RHYMES HAD LEVERAGED HIS HIP-HOP FAME INTO A THRIVING MULTIMEDIA EMPIRE. HE WAS NOW A ONE-MAN BRAND."

ance in the now forgotten Sean Connery film *Finding Forrester*, a movie that failed to find an audience.

Though he remained ubiquitous, Rhymes's increasingly irrelevant Elektra albums suggested he desperately needed a change of pace musically. In the early part of this decade, he hooked up with J Records, the label run by music industry legend Clive Davis. J Records spared no expense on *Genesis*, his much buzzed-about debut for the label, hooking Rhymes up with production by Dr. Dre, Just Blaze, The Neptunes, and Pete Rock. The result was Rhymes's strongest album in years and spawned hits in The Neptunes' remix of "Pass the Courvoisier" and "What It Is." Rhymes's chemistry was particularly strong with Dr. Dre, who produced many of the album's best tracks and tapped Rhymes for "Holla," a track from the soundtrack to *The Wash*.

Busta Rhymes's next album, *It Ain't Safe No More*, didn't fare nearly as well with fans or critics, and the pop-minded rapper didn't exactly endear himself to the grimy hardcore demographic by singing his way through "I Know What You Want," a collaboration with Mariah Carey. Where all of his previous albums went platinum, *It Ain't Safe No More* limped its way to gold status.

Yet again it seemed like Rhymes had run out of steam creatively and needed a new beginning. That's when Dr. Dre pulled a power move and signed the veteran rapper to his Aftermath Entertainment label. King Tee, Rakim, and Truth Hurts could all vouch that signing to Aftermath wasn't exactly a guarantee of huge commercial success, but the pairing of hip-hop legends Dre and Rhymes had tongues wagging throughout the hip-hop nation.

To commemorate leaving J Records and signing with "Dre Records: Aftermath, bitch!" (as the rapper so eloquently put it), Rhymes had his signature dreadlocks cut off, a seminal landmark in hip-hop that was reported far and wide. Sure enough, Busta's Aftermath debut, humbly titled *The Big Bang*, was easily the rapper's best album since *Genesis*, as well as the culmination of everything he had achieved over the course of his impressive career.

Though Dinco D, Charlie Brown, and Cut Monitor Milo were nowhere to be found, the disc found Rhymes collaborating with many crucial figures from his venerable career. "New York Shit" was a classic New York City anthem produced by DJ Scratch of EPMD fame, while "You Can't Hold the Torch" brought back the vibe of vintage Native Tongues with a lush beat by J Dilla and a stellar contribution from Q-Tip, who also guested on the monster opening track "Get You Some." "Been Through the Storm," meanwhile, is an epic autobiographical opus with a hook by Stevie Wonder.

The Big Bang debuted at number one and went platinum, but expectations for the album were so high that it was nevertheless viewed by some as an underperformer. With arguably the most respected producer in rap behind him, the future seemingly couldn't look brighter for Rhymes, but regular run-ins with Johnny Law have cast a dark shadow over the rapper's life. He's been in and out of court on assault charges and generated an avalanche of negative press when he refused to talk to cops in connection with the murder of one of his bodyguards.

Given the rapper's decade and a half of ubiquity and notoriety, overexposure should have killed Rhymes's career a long time ago. But fans and haters alike can be certain that he won't be exiting the public eye anytime soon.

For which animated film did Busta Rhymes lend his voice?

a. Toy Story

b. Happy Feet

c. Racing Stripes

d. The Rugrats Movie

POP QUIZ

Ja Rule

When Tupac Shakur's brief, eventful life ended in a flurry of gunshots in Las Vegas in the fall of 1996, it left a huge void at the center of hip-hop. Just as Bruce Lee's equally mysterious death gave way to an army of sketchy imitators with names like "Bruce Le" and "Bruce Li," Tupac's untimely passing created a tidal wave of derivative gangsta rappers angling unashamedly for the icon's vacated throne. In New Orleans, an enterprising entrepreneur, shameless self-promoter, and mediocre rapper named Master P created an impressive if short-lived empire out of Tupac worship, his signature cry of "Uhhhh," nepotism-P and his brothers C-Murder and Silkk the Shocker were three of the label's biggest stars—and bloated, filler-filled CDs with crudely Photoshopped covers selling a comically gaudy version of hip-hop excess taken to its extreme. In New York, an agonized loner named DMX fruitfully channeled Tupac's bottom-less rage and tormented persona for fun and profit. Since the famously unsolved murder of Suge Knight's meal ticket, the Church of Tupac has threatened worship of the almighty dollar as rap's unofficial religion.

From Run-D.M.C.'s old stomping ground of Hollis, Queens, a diminutive rapper named Jeffrey Atkins with the unusual distinction of being both a bicentennial and leap year baby (his birthday is February 29, 1976) threw his bandanna into the Tupac sweepstakes with invaluable assistance from Irv Gotti. As an A&R man, Gotti brought both Jay-Z and DMX into the Def Jam fold and was looking to catapult Rule, who was raised a Jehovah's Witness by his single mother, onto the hip-hop A-list. Not content to merely A&R for another man's label, Gotti was intent on becoming the next Suge Knight, a larger-than-life figure who engendered both loyalty and fear. He saw Ja Rule (an acronyn for Jeffrey Atkins Represents Unconditional Love's Existence) as his Tupac, a superstar who could turn his dreams into reality.

Gotti introduced Rule to hip-hop via "Can I Get A. . . ," a 1999 smash hit single from the *Rush Hour* soundtrack that helped solidify Jay-Z's superstardom and proved to be a starmaking vehicle for both Gotti—who produced the track—and Rule. The song briefly promised to do the same for a female rapper named Amil, but after Jay-Z parted ways with Amil her career sank as quickly as it had risen.

Ja Rule's voice on "Can I Get A . . ." was fresh, yet reassuringly familiar, a raspy, gritty growl with echoes of both Tupac's authoritative bass and DMX's agitated bark. The song's video only cemented Rule's growing stardom. With his finely honed abs, muscles, tattoos, and lucrative aversion to wearing shirts, he clearly modeled himself after Tupac visually as well as vocally.

> **"WITH HIS FINELY HONED ABS, MUSCLES, TATTOOS, AND LUCRATIVE AVERSION TO WEARING SHIRTS, [JA RULE] CLEARLY MODELED HIMSELF AFTER TUPAC VISUALLY AS WELL AS VOCALLY."**

In the aftermath of the track's crossover success, rumors circulated about a Murder Inc. supergroup pairing Rule with two other Gotti-associated superstars: DMX and Jay-Z. Like most hip-hop rumors, talk of an album-length collaboration between the trio didn't lead anywhere, but it was nevertheless apparent that Ja Rule's star was on the rise. In 1999 Rule joined Def Jam labelmates and fellow rap superstars Jay-Z, DMX, Redman, Method Man, and DJ Clue on the well-received Hard Knock Life tour.

That year also saw the release of Ja Rule's Def Jam/Murder Inc. debut, *Venni Vetti Vecci*, which took its title from Julius Caesar's "Veni, Vidi, Vici," or "I came, I saw, I conquered," a typically humble assertion from a rapper whose heady existence was starting to outstrip his wildest dreams. Yet even as *Venni Vetti Vecci* reached platinum status, a dark cloud loomed on the horizon in the form of a drug dealer turned rapper who called himself 50 Cent after a legendary '80s street hustler.

The success of *Venni Vetti Vecci* ignited Gotti's crossover dreams. Angling for a big chunk of the pop market, he steered Rule's sophomore album into a much more commercial, radio-friendly direction. Just as Death Row undercut the street swagger of its gangsta icons with R&B hooks, Gotti started pairing Rule with R&B singers, most notably Ashanti, a pretty young singer Gotti was grooming to be Murder Inc.'s next big pop star.

Rule 3:36 (2000) was an even bigger smash than Rule's debut, going triple platinum in the States and spawning the hit singles "Put It On Me," "Between Me and You," and "I Cry." Then in 2001, *Pain Is Love* was released, to become Ja's biggest-selling album of his career. It spawned the hit singles "Livin' It Up" and "Always on Time," featuring Ashanti. But Rule's popularity with mainstream audiences came at a steep price. With every sugary single, glossy video, and collaboration with an R&B princess, his street credibility took a steep hit, until the rapper had become a laughingstock among hardcore hip-hop heads.

The streets increasingly saw Rule as an opportunistic pop star playing at being a gangsta. He was seen as an Irv Gotti creation who would flounder without powerful connections. Rap fans began wondering which Ja Rule was authentic: was it the grimy-voiced thug hollering "Murda!" at every opportunity or the grinning superstar cavorting and crooning his way through slick videos alongside Jennifer Lopez and Ashanti? Wasn't Murder Inc. an awfully grim name for a label that churned out sticky cotton candy like the "I'm Real (Murder Remix)"?

In 2000 Ja Rule made his feature film debut in *Turn It Up*. On paper at least, the project looked promising. It was produced by Madonna and Guy Oseary's production company, Maverick Films, and co-starred Pras of seminal hip-hop trio The Fugees. But by the time the film was released Pras was already a sinking star and the film tanked at the box office. A brash new crop of superstars was bubbling just under the surface with names like Lil Jon, T.I., and The Game, but Rule was increasingly aligning himself with the stars of yesterday. Besides co-starring with Pras, Rule (and Murder Inc.) befriended controversial, much-demonized Death Row head honcho Suge Knight as well as equally reviled *Source* owners Ray "Benzino" Scott and Dave Mays.

Rule was making friends with all the wrong people and alienating and antagonizing an impressive bevy of hip-hop power brokers. DMX, after collaborating with Rule in the late '90s, accused his onetime friend of shamelessly copying him and recorded withering diss tracks like "Do You" and "Ruled Out." In an ironic twist, Gotti produced a diss track for DMX called "We Don't Give a Fuck," apparently without realizing it was directed at Rule.

But DMX was hardly the only rapper taking shots at Rule, whose massive crossover success and popularity among teenage girls made him a huge target. Rule couldn't have known it at the time, but the seeds of his professional downfall were planted the moment 50 Cent got into a booth and recorded "How to Rob," a satirical tour de force that fired potshots at just about every major rapper as it outlined an epic robbing spree targeting rap's richest players.

Fiddy's deal with Columbia Records never led to an album, but tracks like "How to Rob" attracted the attention of Eminem. In an unprecedented move, 50 Cent was signed to both Eminem's Shady Records and Dr. Dre's Aftermath Entertainment, a unique position that gave him a very prominent platform from which to launch repeat attacks on Rule and Murder Inc.

As a former crack dealer who'd famously been shot and stabbed multiple times, 50 Cent enjoyed the street credibility that Rule sorely lacked. Furthermore, 50 Cent had made his name via the underground mixtape scene so he was immune to charges of being an ersatz major-label creation like Rule. In 2002, his "Wanksta," which many people perceived as a diss track about Ja Rule, was everywhere. You couldn't turn on the television without seeing the video on BET or MTV. It blared out of passing cars and dominated Top 40 and hip-hop radio. It was prominently featured on not one but two multiplatinum albums. It was the second single off the *8 Mile* soundtrack, the huge-selling companion to Eminem's smash-hit autobiographical film, and it was a bonus track on 50 Cent's *Get Rich or Die Tryin'*. Just in case anyone lingered under the assumption that 50 didn't despise Rule with every fiber of his being, the rising superstar included two more blistering diss tracks in Rule's direction in the form of "Back Down" and the mixtape favorite "Life's on the Line," both of which could be found on 50's legendary major-label debut.

It was an old show business story: one star rose as another fell. 50 was seen as gangsta rap's future and Ja Rule came to symbolize its past. The irony of course is that 50 Cent and Ja Rule, two Queens street kids who conquered the pop world but couldn't seem to get along, have far more in common than either would like to admit. Both rappers owe a debt to Tupac they can't repay. Neither seems partial to wearing shirts, which would only cover up their well-defined abdominal muscles and elaborate tattoos. Both rappers appeal to teenage girls despite the bloodthirsty nature of their lyrics, and neither is averse to crooning a few bars or aiming unapologetically for mainstream radio play.

A lot of rappers are empowered by high-profile beef, but 50 Cent's constant attacks on Ja Rule irrevocably harmed Rule's career. Ja Rule followed up to his little-seen, little-loved debut with more film appearances, but his roles were limited to tiny cameos. In 2004's *Shall We Dance* he is listed only as "Hip-Hop Bar Performer." As his career skidded he lurched into self-parody. The *Adult Swim* show *The Boondocks* featured a Ja Rule–like character named Gangstalicious who is revealed to be gay. Albums from underground acts like Lifesavas and Party Action Fun Committee included withering parodies of Rule's increasingly ridiculous thugged-out persona.

Irv Gotti and Murder Inc.'s fortunes sank with Rule. Gotti had always been fascinated by crime. He took his name from the notorious Gotti crime family, and as his career as a producer and label head stalled, he grew closer to a seminal '80s street legend named Kenneth "Supreme" McGriff. Gotti's ties to McGriff attracted the unwanted attention of the federal government, which became convinced Gotti was laundering money for McGriff through Murder Inc. Around this time Murder Inc. changed its name to The Inc., but minor cosmetic changes did nothing to reverse the label's losing streak. In December of 2005, Gotti and his brother were acquited of all criminal charges.

Gotti and his brother were innocent, but Rule's career never recovered from 50's withering attacks. *Blood in My Eye* (2003) and 2004's *R.U.L.E.* moved away from the R&B hooks and sugary melodies that characterized Rule's hits with Ashanti, Jennifer Lopez, and Lil' Mo for a harder street sound more in line with his debut. *R.U.L.E.* featured one of his strongest singles in "New York," a hard-hitting anthem that matched Rule's grimy flow with stellar assists from Fat Joe and Jadakiss and an icy synth-drenched sound straight out of a '70s B movie. Not content to merely destroy Rule's career, 50 announced his intention to go after any rapper who collaborated with his archnemesis and promptly attacked widely respected veterans Fat Joe and Jadakiss for the unforgivable crime of sharing a track with Murder Inc.'s fading golden boy.

Ja returned in 2008 with *The Mirror*, but only time will tell if Rule will ever be able to recapture the popularity of his early days. For now his once formidable, now fading career stands as a cautionary tale about the dangers of selling out and the impossibility of regaining lost credibility.

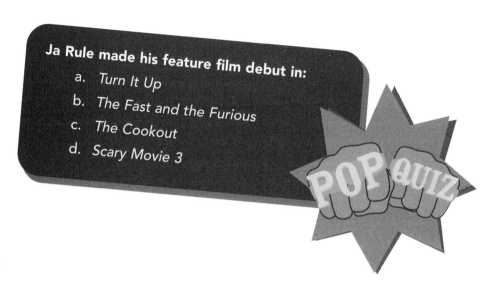

Master P

What makes Percy Miller a.k.a. Master P's saga so dope is that unlike many of his contemporaries, he made his money (and music) working totally outside of the confines of the "industry" and way underneath any mainstream radar. That most of his No Limit roster lacked basic skills wasn't the point. Miller gave the people what they wanted, and judging by the sales, clearly what the people, especially outside of NYC or L.A., wanted was No Limit. Even if it sorta sucked.

P was raised in the violent projects of New Orleans, seeing firsthand the drug/hustler's life. He also was a skilled baller and won a scholarship at the University of Houston, but eventually decided to study business in the Bay Area. He inherited a sizable stack of chips in the late '80s and invested it in No Limit, a record store in the Bay. While working at the store, P figured out that even though the major labels were all over hip-hop, there was an audience not being serviced, so in 1990 he turned No Limit, the store, into a label—one that would feature hardcore hip-hop. In 1991 he dropped a single and then in '94 he had a regional hit with *The Ghettos Tryin to Kill Me!* Soon enough P moved back to NOLA and threw all his energy and business savvy into cranking out hardcore rap. By the mid-'90s, No Limit had an in-house production team (Beats by the Pound) and was releasing upwards of ten albums a year, all overseen by P and his in-house crew. If other better-known labels were going for quality, P was after quantity and keeping the overhead crazy low. That meant that soon he was living very large.

"IF OTHER BETTER-KNOWN LABELS WERE GOING FOR QUALITY, P WAS AFTER QUANTITY AND KEEPING THE OVERHEAD CRAZY LOW. THAT MEANT THAT SOON HE WAS LIVING VERY LARGE."

Soon P became an artist, too, with '95's *99 Ways to Die* and '96's *Ice Cream Man*. With the release of '97's *Ghetto Dope*, P had an empire—all without radio or TV shine. He kept making moves and formed the group Tru with younger brothers Silkk the Shocker and C-Murder. From rap, P then shifted to movies, releasing straight-to-video ghetto drama and then the theatrical release *I Got the Hook Up* in '98. By now, P had distribution deals with a small indie label, yet he maintained almost total creative control. In 1997, he was back in the studio, and in quick succession came the hugely popular *Only God Can Judge Me*, *Ghetto Postage*, and *Game Face*. By the 2000 mark, P's clout had begun to wane a bit and he shifted some of his attention to grooming his son, Lil Romeo, who had a decent career of his own along with a Nickelodeon sitcom. Yet even though he was no longer *the* man, P still kept making records, and in 2005 he came back with *Ghetto Bill* and *Living Legend: Certified D-Boy*. The next year he also made an appearance on the TV show *Dancing with the Stars* (he sucked), released his thirteenth album, *America's Most Luved Bad Guy*, and joined forces with old New Orleans nemesis Cash Money to raise money and support for Katrina victims.

Juvenile

Like Master P, Terius Gray a.k.a. Juvenile grew up in NOLA's projects. And Like P, Juve helped put his hometown in contention. He fell under rap's spell and began performing while a teen, and in 1995 released an indie record, *Being Myself*. Juvenile then met NOLA's Cash Money Millionaires—Ronald "Suga Slim" and Brian "Baby" Williams—the crosstown rivals of Master P's No Limit Soldiers. With them in his corner and the label's wizard Mannie Fresh behind the boards, Juve delivered 1996's *Solja Rags*. It did great on the underground circuit, and then came Juvi's 1998 breakthrough, *400 Degreez*. That CD contained the top ten hits "Back That Azz Up" and the ridiculously innovative "Ha." Like that, Juve went from NOLA hero to MTV star. In 1999, CMM rereleased *Solja Rags* in order to cash in, and then Juve laced his fans with a new album, *Tha G-Code*. Two years later came *Project English*. All of the albums went platinum-plus and Juvi was easily Cash Money's money guy and biggest star. In keeping with the "mo' money mo' problems" dictum, it was only a matter of time before drama ensued between the label and its star. In 2002, Juvenile flew the coop to form his own crew, the UTP Playas, with whom he recorded *The Compilation*. The album tanked and a year later Juve went back to Cash Money, dropping *Juve the Great* and the hit "Slow Motion." In 2005, Juve re-upped with UTP and shot off "Nolia Clap" and then went label hunting again. As he linked up with Atlantic Records, Mother Nature in the form of the catastrophic Hurricane Katrina slammed into Louisiana and destroyed Juve's Slidell home. Katrina's wrath and political fallout became the main lyrical inspiration for his chart-topping 2006 album, *Reality Check*.

Common

Gap spokesman and cool-ass conscious rapper, Chi-Town's Common was born Lonnie Rashid Lynn. He first started making hip-hop under the name Common Sense and appeared in *The Source* magazine's "Unsigned Hype" column. In 1992 Common dropped his indie debut album, *Can I Borrow a Dollar?*, which gave him some sway in the underground community. Amazingly, the man who would eventually become almost the poster child for crunchy had critics on his ass for misogynistic lyrics. In '94 Common stepped his game up with *Resurrection*, and the single "I Used to Love H.E.R." got love for its clever metaphors and analogies about the current state of hip-hop. The song even provoked a short and meaningless tiff with Ice Cube. After finding out that there was a ska band with the same tag, Common Sense became Common, leaving Chicago for Brooklyn. His first album under the new name dropped in 1997 on a different label, Relativity. *One Day It'll All Make Sense* was intelligent and street-smart and boasted a hot lineup of guests including Lauryn Hill and Erykah Badu. The latter would become Common's boo, while the former cameoed on "Retrospect for Life." Over the next couple of years, Common would up his profile with a slew of guest spots with like-minded artists such as Pete Rock, Mos Def, Talib Kweli, and The Roots.

With a buzz growing and alliances with the cool clique, Common inked a major-label deal and enlisted The Roots' ?uestlove to produce 2000's *Like Water for Chocolate*. The CD was a must-own among the alternative hip-hop crowd, while the silky single "The Light" (featuring soul singer Bilal) became a radio hit, earning a Grammy nod for Best Rap Solo Performance. *Like Water* was Common's biggest commercial achievement to date and he rode the wave, appearing in 2002 on Mary J.'s *No More Drama*, which was repackaged with the track "Dance for Me (Remix)." That same year Common created the experimental *Electric Circus*. Perhaps due to its less commercial sound, the CD failed to reap many rewards. By now a familiar face and voice on the music scene, Common joined up with fellow Chicagoan Kanye West to create 2005's *Be*. Bristling with energy, *Be* included the Grammy-nominated "The Corner" and ended up on numerous critics' top ten lists. Two years later, Common was back in the lab with Kanye working on what would eventually be the first number one album of his career, 2007's *Finding Forever*, and also making big-screen moves as part of the ensemble casts of the action flick *Smokin' Aces*, crime drama *American Gangster*, and comic book adaptation *Wanted*.

Mos Def

Many rappers get into acting as another avenue of expression. Mos Def did the reverse. Born Dante Smith in Brooklyn, Mos began acting while a teen, with his highest-profile gig being the short-lived Bill Cosby series *The Cosby Mysteries*. Despite his success, Mos wanted more, and he literally flipped the script and started rhyming. He made inroads quickly, performing in NYC underground showcases, and in 1996 popped up on CDs from De La Soul and Da Bush Babees. By 1997, Mos had released an indie single, "Universal Magnetic," which brought him to the attention of a then upstart rap label, Rawkus Records. Over time Rawkus would become a mecca for the second wave of so-called alternative/conscious hip-hop. One of the label's "biggest" (truth be told, gauging by commercial rap standards, nobody was getting rich) was Black Star, consisting of Mos, high school friend Talib Kweli, and DJ Hi-Tek. A few years earlier, Ohio native Tek and Brooklynite Talib had formed Reflection Eternal. Their single "Fortified Live" was one of Rawkus's first releases in 1997.

A year later the two brought Mos into the crew, and the result was 1998's critically praised *Black Star*. The self-titled LP, also revered by hipsters and heads, became one of most talked-about and inventive rap albums of the year. With its conscious POV and nimble beats, it would set the stage for Mos and Talib to go for their solo selves.

Mos proved that Black Star was no fluke and that he was no joke when in 1999 he delivered his solo joint *Black on Both Sides*. Jazzy, smart, and influenced only by the late-'80s Native Tongues movement, the album yielded two singles—"Ms. Fat Booty" and the smooth "Umi Says."

In 2000, Talib and Hi-Tek resurrected Reflection Eternal, recording an album entitled *Train of Thought*. That CD generated a few minor hits, including "Move Somethin'" and "The Blast," but earned not much more than, once again, the devotion of the faithful and the press.

Now the newly crowned guardian of new-school "conscious" rap, Mos took his time reentering the studio following his solo debut, choosing to return to his first love. He kicked off the twenty-first century with key roles in several acclaimed films, including *Monster's Ball*, *Bamboozled*, *Brown Sugar*, and *The Woodsman*. Then he made the bold move from cinema to the Broadway stage, co-starring in the Pulitzer Prize–winning *Topdog/ Underdog*. While hitting the boards, Mos also hit the studio, constructing the much talked-about Black Jack Johnson with legendary black rock artists such as Parliament-Funkadelic's Bernie Worrell. Black Jack Johnson strove to grab rock music away from whack rap/rock hybrids like Limp Bizkit (whose frontman, Fred Durst, Mos openly dissed) and give it back to black musicians. Mos and the group played around NYC, and he would incorporate them on his second solo CD, 2004's *The New Danger*, which received mixed reviews. In '06, after more high-profile and noted acting gigs, as well as a performance in *Dave Chappelle's Block Party*, Mos Def released *True Magic*, sort of. The CD was a contract-fulfilling obligation to the major label, Geffen Records, that had taken over Rawkus years back, and neither the label nor Mos seemed all that into it. The album came and went without anyone really paying any attention.

Talib Kweli

While Mos was venturing out into differing disciplines, Talib stayed with hip-hop. In 2002 he delivered *Quality*, which found him collaborating with a slew of new partners, including Kanye West. Kanye handed Talib "Get By," and the combo of smart, thoughtful lyrics and West's soul-stoked grooves made it the biggest hit of Talib's career. His profile got an even bigger leg up when Jay-Z appeared on "Get By (Remix)." The pairing of the most mainstream rapper and the backpack king might have seemed strange, but it seems not only did the critics dig Talib, so did Jigga, which was driven home when on 2003's "Moment of Clarity" Jay shouted Talib out, saying, "If skills sold, truth be told/I'd probably be, lyrically, Talib Kweli." Sweet.

The one-two of "Get By"'s success and Hova's seal of approval paved the way for 2004's *The Beautiful Struggle*. While the CD was the most overtly commercial thus far, it failed to connect the way its predecessor had. The prevailing thought was that with all of the attention finally being focused on him (none other than 50 Cent also publicly showed Talib some love), Kweli had felt the stress of heightened expectations and maybe those pressures to live up to the justified hype got to him. Or maybe *The Beautiful Struggle* wasn't all that. Whatever the reasons, after his brief fling with the majors, Talib returned to his roots by signing with a NYC-based indie. In 2007, one of rap's most respected if underappreciated MCs came back with the less hyped *Eardrum*.

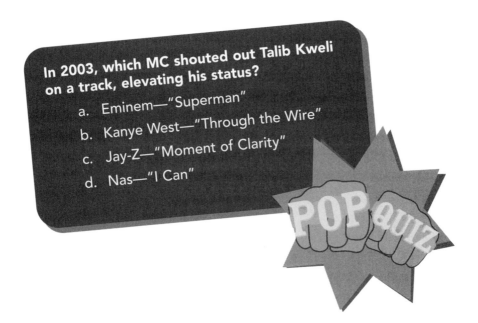

In 2003, which MC shouted out Talib Kweli on a track, elevating his status?

a. Eminem—"Superman"

b. Kanye West—"Through the Wire"

c. Jay-Z—"Moment of Clarity"

d. Nas—"I Can"

Even if you don't know from firsthand (or ear) experience, every damn person alive knows that hip-hop music and culture had its start in the East, specifically NYC. By the '90's—or, more to the point with the advent of N.W.A.—the other coast grabbed its share of the brass, or actually platinum, ring. So now it's East and West Coast. But shockingly, especially to people who live in L.A. and NYC, there is a whole 'nother country out there, and it's from these strange foreign regions that other rap artists began to make their own noise and do so without a lick of support from kids from the BK.

Too $hort

One of the Kings of the Bay (as in Area, as in that mass of land outside of San Francisco, which is far too fabulous and foggy to support a rap scene) has got to be E-40. The artist born Earl Stevens and owner of numerous wacky nicknames (because no doubt E, like Wu-Tang, knows that everyone needs a few good alibis and aliases), such as "Charlie Hustle," "40 Fonzarelli," "40-Water," grew up in the Bay. E's initial career goal was to be as large as Too $hort.

Too $hort, like E-40, was a Bay guy. Pretty much no one in NYC or L.A. gave a damn about or even acknowledged him, but nonetheless he sold truckloads of records. $hort, a.k.a. Todd Shaw, actually was born in L.A. but moved to Oaktown in the early '80s. Soon after the relocation, he started hustling his own mixtapes out of the trunk of his car—the non-NYC version of those African guys who sell mixtapes on Canal Street. He signed to a local indie, releasing his first album way back in 1983. Over the years, he dropped a prodigious amount of product, making him by all accounts one of the first Left Coast rap dudes. No dummy, $hort established his Dangerous Music label (which would eventually change names to Up All Nite Music) in 1986, and its first release, *Born to Mack*, clocked nice numbers. Soon enough, the big guns started paying attention and

$hort got Jive Records to help distribute his thuggish tales of sex, more sex, some shooting, and more sex. With no love from radio, *Born to Mack* went gold and *Life Is . . . Too $hort* went platinum in 1989.

$hort kept on dropping CDs damn near every year, including 1992's *Shorty the Pimp* and 1993's *Get In Where You Fit In*, both platinum. Yet by '95, with the release of his album *Cocktails*, he was losing some of his appeal and faced stiffer competition. Even though his tenth album, *Gettin' It*, was his fifth to sell a mil, he decided to retire. Confirming the generally held opinion that most rappers have too much ego to stay away (paging Jay-Z), he came back with the aptly titled *Can't Stay Away* in 1999. The CD debuted top ten and went gold. Throughout the '90s Too $hort would record now and then, and although he did nice numbers, most would say that his glory days were behind him, yet his DIY legacy and underground hustle set a standard for those to follow.

The year 2006, though, brought his sixteenth (!!!) studio album, *Blow the Whistle*. With production duties largely handled by the more-than-prolific Lil Jon and Jazze Pha, the album scored a few radio jams with the updated production style, but nothing as large as his guest spot on Kelis's 2006 single "Bossy." Featuring collaborations with Snoop, will.i.am, Bun B, Rick Ross, and more, *Blow the Whistle* proved $hort still had what it takes to succeed on the mic, and in years to come it should be looked back on as a reinvention of his style.

E-40

Like $hort, 40 built up his hype with mixtapes, and after years on that grind he started to go for self and start his label, Sick Wid' It, to make moves beyond Vallejo, California. Said first move was 1994's EP *The Mail Man*, then the single "Captain Save a Hoe," and then the album *Federal*.

Jive Records sniffed him out and in '95 decided to distribute E's label and rerelease the early stuff. There were also new joints—'96's *Tha Hall of Game* and a successful single, "Rappers' Ball," featuring Too $hort, K-Ci, and produced by Bay Area star Ant Banks.

Tha Hall of Game brought 40 this close to a breakthrough, and after a one-year hiatus he came back in '98 with the double album *The Element of Surprise*, and then '99's *Charlie Hustle*. Neither effort did much to branch E out to a wider fan base. Subsequent albums *Loyalty and Betrayal* (2000) and *Grit & Grind* (2002) had similar results. Yet with a decade in the game, E seemed cool with getting mad love from the Coast as well as the South, and in 2003 he delivered his last Jive CD, *Breakin News*.

E returned in 2006 on a new label (Warner Bros.) and with a new CD, *My Ghetto Report Card*. The album (executive-produced by Lil Jon) became his first trip into top ten land, while the singles "Tell Me When to Go" and "U and Dat" hit radio and MTV hard. The anthems gave the Bay's hot trend of the moment, hyphy, its first taste of mainstream exposure. More importantly, the success also revitalized interest and respect for a seasoned champion who, it seemed, had finally gotten his commercial due.

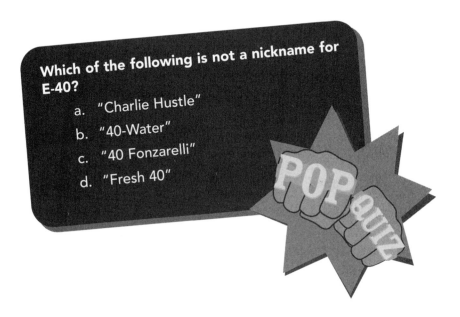

Which of the following is not a nickname for E-40?

a. "Charlie Hustle"

b. "40-Water"

c. "40 Fonzarelli"

d. "Fresh 40"

POP QUIZ

Lil Jon

Lil Jon is one multifaceted mother . . . The ATL-based rapper/producer has made hits not only for himself and his group, the Eastside Boyz, but he's put the platinum sparkle into smashes like Usher's massive "Yeah!" and counts among his satisfied clients Ciara, the Ying Yang Twins, T.I., Snoop Dogg, Ice Cube, and Pitbull, who Jon helped put on. The former club DJ and Animal from the Muppets lookalike helped kick off the Dirty South era and was one of the main forces behind bringing crunk to the masses. Gee, thanks. Jon started out as a club DJ and in 1993 got the call from Jermaine Dupri. The producer/label head tapped Jon to become the executive VP of A&R for Dupri's thriving So So Def label. While holding down that gig, Jon hosted an Atlanta radio show and started producing and remixing for ATL stars like Xscape, Total, and Usher. From there and with a nice little rep to his name, he became an artist in his own right. He formed the Eastside Boyz, introducing the group on 1996's *Get Crunk, Who U Wit: Da Album*, which produced the sizable club anthem "Who U Wit?" Over the next five years Jon kept cranking out the crunk, but remained an ATL thang until he broke through nationwide with 2001's "Bia', Bia'," featuring Ludacris, Too $hort, and Chyna Whyte off of *Put Yo Hood Up*. Jon & the Eastside Boyz fired back with *Kings of Crunk* (2002). The CD and the single "I Don't Give A . . ." caught fire, big time. By 2003 Jon was not only making hits for himself, he was a sure-shot go-to guy for other artists. A beat along with Jon's mumbling, over-the-top delivery and persona propelled the diminutive dude to the next level. Jon's cartoonish steez was so ubiquitous and so recognizable that comedian Dave Chappelle hilariously lampooned Jon's signature expressions "Yeaaahh!" and "Whaat!?" The hugely imitated parody ended up making Jon an even bigger star. In 2004, Lil Jon gathered up the Boyz and a mess of guests including Ice Cube and punk rock gods Bad Brains to add their own flavor to his *Crunk Juice*, released on his longtime label TVT. The CD was a platinum banger, but the always savvy Jon knew that trends come and go, especially in hip-hop. By '06, as crunk was fading and with the Eastside Boyz on hold, Jon, outrageousness in full effect, concentrated on making fly music and bringing his fans the next hot jam.

Lil' Kim

To call Lil' Kim outrageous would be an understatement. Since emerging from Notorious B.I.G.'s outsized shadow over a decade ago, the tiny little woman with the great big personality has lived her life in screaming tabloid headlines. She's the closest thing hip-hop has to Madonna: a brassy, sexually explicit provocateur prone to dramatic reinvention and obscene, attention-grabbing antics. Lil' Kim has the distinction of being one of the best-loved and most hated female rappers alive. But whether you love her or hate her—there are plenty of folks in both camps—there's no denying that Lil' Kim has left an indelible imprint on hip-hop. Her career is living proof that sex sells, but she proved long ago she's much more than just a pretty face and a pair of silicone tits. Depending on who you ask, Lil' Kim is either a hero or a harlot, a feminist pioneer or a shameless skank whose sexually explicit shenanigans have set the fairer gender back decades. Yes, everybody's got an opinion about Lil' Kim, and they're usually extreme: there seems to be no middle ground for this most divisive of cultural icons.

> **"SHE'S THE CLOSEST THING HIP-HOP HAS TO MADONNA: A BRASSY, SEXUALLY EXPLICIT PROVOCATEUR PRONE TO DRAMATIC REINVENTION AND OBSCENE, ATTENTION-GRABBING ANTICS."**

Kim was born on July 11, 1975, in Bedford-Stuyvesant, Brooklyn, a neighborhood immortalized by Spike Lee as the tension-filled setting for his 1989 masterpiece *Do the Right Thing*. Kim's childhood and adolescence were characterized by unrelenting misery and a total absence of security and stability. Her parents divorced when Kim was still a preteen. Her relationship with her father was volatile and charged with tension. When her father moved to another state, Kim was essentially left homeless. She began living with her mother again, but money was so scarce that Kim and her mother occasionally lived inside the family car.

Kim's luck began to change dramatically when she met the man who would become her lover, mentor, and friend, a fat, charismatic drug dealer and larger-than-life father figure named Christopher Wallace who rapped under the name Biggie Smalls. B.I.G. took an immediate liking to the diminutive MC and made her a core member of a group he was putting together called Junior M.A.F.I.A. (for Junior Masters At Finding Intelligent Attitudes).

Kim quickly emerged as the standout member of Junior M.A.F.I.A. In 1995 the group released *Conspiracy*, which spawned a pair of hits in "Player's Anthem" and "Get Money," both of which featured Notorious B.I.G. The chorus of "Get Money" was mockingly reprised by Tupac on "Hit 'Em Up," a legendary diss song directed at Notorious B.I.G. and everyone even vaguely connected to him.

From the very beginning of her career, Lil' Kim's life had all the makings of a hip-hop soap opera: beefs, betrayal, infidelity, and sexual competition gone awry. The melodrama began when former friends B.I.G. and Tupac Shakur had a falling-out after Tupac became convinced that B.I.G. and Sean "Puff Daddy" Combs were involved in a shooting/robbery that left Tupac wounded but hungry for revenge.

Combs and B.I.G. tried to deflate a conflict that somehow got blown up into a media-promulgated coastal rivalry, but Tupac continued his attacks not just on B.I.G. but also on Lil' Kim, Puff Daddy, Junior M.A.F.I.A., Mobb Deep, and just about every rapper residing east of Los Angeles. In "Hit 'Em Up" 's most notorious lines Shakur bragged about fucking Notorious B.I.G.'s wife, R&B singer Faith Evans, and mocked Prodigy's sickle-cell anemia. Tupac was clearly hitting below the belt, and the lines about fucking B.I.G.'s wife must have been especially painful for Kim, whose high-profile affair with her mentor made her arguably the most famous mistress in hip-hop history. B.I.G.'s conduct was pretty much par for the course, however, for superstars in a genre where rappers brag in verse after verse about how indiscriminately they lay the pipe, then get on TV and brag about how much they love their wife.

Kim's already stormy relationship with Notorious B.I.G. grew even more complicated and stressful when she became pregnant with B.I.G.'s seed. She has gone public about having the pregnancy terminated. Ironically, Kim's old archnemesis Tupac is one of the few other big-name rappers to publicly espouse pro-choice views.

But Kim and Tupac's similar views on reproductive rights did nothing to keep Tupac's beef with New York's top rap icons from spiraling out of control. On September 13, 1996, Tupac was gunned down in Las Vegas. On March 9, 1997, B.I.G. was killed in Los Angeles. He was twenty-four years old. B.I.G.'s death cast a long, dark shadow over Kim's otherwise thriving career.

In 1996 Kim released her first solo album, *Hard Core*. The album's title boasted a cheeky double meaning, referring both to the disc's over-whelming sexual explicitness and to Kim's rugged, violent lyrics. Kim was hardly the first female rapper to flaunt her sexuality, but *Hard Core* nevertheless took raunchiness to X-rated extremes. Men all over the world were fascinated by a rapper who could spit hardcore gangsta shit *and* star in their most perverted sexual fantasies. Kim was smartly and lucratively marketed as a down-to-earth round-the-way girl who'd do things in bed that would make porn stars blush.

Hard Core went double platinum and scored three hit singles: "No Time" (with Puff Daddy), "Crush on You" (with Junior M.A.F.I.A.'s Lil' Cease), and "Not Tonight (Remix)." Kim turned the "Not Tonight (Remix)" into a raucous celebration of female empowerment by inviting Left Eye of TLC, radio personality turned rapper Angie Martinez, Missy Elliott, and Da Brat to contribute verses.

The year 1997 was the best of times and the worst of times for Kim. She should have been ecstatic over the runaway success of *Hard Core*, but whispers began circulating that she wouldn't be able to make it without

B.I.G. Haters insisted that without her Svengali behind her she would recede into obscurity. Such hate speech exemplifies hip-hop's innate sexism: if a female MC is spitting hot verses, heads assume there must be a dude ghostwriting for her, but if an estrogen-fueled MC kicks nothing but garbage, heads assume she's writing her own lyrics.

The similarity between B.I.G.'s and Kim's flows and lyrics only fueled talk that B.I.G. was writing Kim's lyrics and that she would flounder in his absence. So the stakes were extremely high for her first disc since B.I.G.'s passing. Needless to say, she did nothing to quiet talk that she was crassly exploiting B.I.G.'s legacy when she named her second solo CD *Notorious K.I.M.* Then again, if anyone in rap had earned the right to call herself "Notorious" it was the 4'11" dynamo born Kimberly Jones.

Notorious K.I.M. proved that Kim's gift for provocation was as sharp as ever. On the single "How Many Licks," a female answer to Too $hort's classic sex rap "Freaky Tales," she invites convicts to masturbate to her image, rapping, "This verse goes out to my niggas in jail/Beatin' they dicks to the *XXL* magazine/You like how I look in the aqua green? Get your Vaseline." Kim was out to prove that female rappers can be just as nasty as male MCs, but she fell victim to hip-hop's vicious double standard. Male rappers can brag about fucking armies of groupies every day without catching flak, but female rappers as hardcore as Kim risked being called sluts, tramps, and worse.

Kim's in-your-face sexuality was augmented by breast enhancement surgery that the legendary exhibitionist showed off in microscopic outfits leaving little to the imagination. Ever the fashion-forward risk-taker, Kim regularly sported hair colors unseen in nature and made headlines for a fashion sense that can best be described as "hooker chic." Though Kim didn't put out an album between *Hard Core* and the millennium, she was seldom out of the news, even if people tended to talk more about what she wore than what she had to say.

Kim's acting career never quite got off the ground. Her prominently credited role in the smash hit teen comedy *She's All That* was little more than

"KIM'S IN-YOUR-FACE SEXUALITY WAS AUGMENTED BY BREAST ENHANCEMENT SURGERY THAT THE LEGENDARY EXHIBITIONIST SHOWED OFF IN MICROSCOPIC OUTFITS LEAVING LITTLE TO THE IMAGINATION."

a glorified cameo, and her performance in the cross-dressing basketball comedy *Juwanna Mann* inspired no one to speculate that the actress would soon join Will Smith and Queen Latifah in the rarefied company of popular rappers nominated for acting Oscars.

Notorious K.I.M. went platinum and silenced many, if not all, of the haters and paved the way for one of Kim's biggest successes: the single and video for "Lady Marmalade," the smash hit posse cut from the über-successful *Moulin Rouge!* soundtrack. Kim, the song, and *Moulin Rouge!* were a match made in heaven. Like Kim, the film was a big, gaudy, campy celebration of excess, tawdry glamour, and flashy sexuality, so it was fitting that Kim, similarly demonized pop star Christina Aguilera, white-trash superstar Pink, sultry R&B sexpot Mýa, and co-producers Missy Elliott and Rockwilder covered the classic disco anthem about a brazen New Orleans streetwalker. The ubiquitous video featured all five confidently sexy pop stars strutting through a brothel-like milieu in revealing lingerie and flamboyant hairstyles. Shockingly, the song and the video both became huge crossover hits. Like "Not Tonight (Remix)," "Lady Marmalade" was a brassy, fun celebration of female unity that appealed strongly to pop audiences. It became Kim's first number one hit and won a Grammy for Best Pop Collaboration with Vocals.

But it hasn't all been girl power, slumber parties, female solidarity, and "I Am Woman" sing-alongs for Lil' Kim. Hip-hop likes nothing better than red-hot girl-on-girl action, and Lil' Kim and rival Foxy Brown, the scourge of nail salon employees everywhere, have given them plenty of that via their long-standing beef. Kim and Brown were once friends but jealousy, rivalry, and accusations of creative theft led to an explosive hatred that gained momentum when Brown recorded a vitriolic diss of Kim on Capone–N–Noreaga's "Bang Bang." A lot of hip-hop beefs stay on wax, but Kim and Brown's battle led to an infamous 2001 gunfight outside radio station HOT 97 between entourage members in Kim and Capone–N–Noreaga's respective camps that in turn led to a perjury conviction for Kim along with a year in prison and, of course, a hit reality show, BET's *Countdown to Lockdown*.

Foxy Brown and Capone–N–Noreaga certainly weren't alone in beefing with Lil' Kim this decade. In 2003 she scored one of the biggest hits of her career with *La Bella Mafia*'s "Magic Stick," an irresistibly randy duet with 50 Cent that could have been even bigger if Kim and the eternally quarrelsome Curtis Jackson hadn't had a falling-out that led to no video hitting MTV or BET. *La Bella Mafia* scored another Grammy-nominated hit in the Kanye West–produced hyper-soul banger "Came Back for You." Ironically, West used the "Came Back for You" beat on a mixtape track called "Half Price" where he pays irreverent homage to Kim's, um, cosmetically enhanced gifts.

La Bella Mafia became Kim's third straight solo platinum album, but more trouble lurked on the horizon for her when in 2006 former Junior M.A.F.I.A. members Lil' Cease and Banger (formerly known as Larceny) testified against her in her perjury trial, then defended their actions in a series of street DVDs. In a hip-hop community where snitches are reviled as subhuman, Kim's unwillingness to reveal what she'd seen outside HOT 97 was viewed by many in hip-hop as honorable—even if it resulted in plenty of negative press as well.

The free-floating drama in Kim's life and career fueled her fourth solo album, 2005's *The Naked Truth*, a scathing, highly personal album that dealt extensively with her many beefs and public feuds. *The Source* famously gave the disc five mics, a designation reserved for instant hip-hop classics. Not surprisingly, the glowing review generated controversy and heated talk that Kim must have slept her way to five mics.

Countdown to Lockdown became one of the most popular shows in BET history, proving that the public's appetite for Lil' Kim's patented brand of sexed-up melodrama remains strong. God only knows what the next chapter in the Kimberly Jones saga will bring—more outfits of questionable tastes? more beef? more outrageousness?—but chances are good that we won't stop gawking anytime soon.

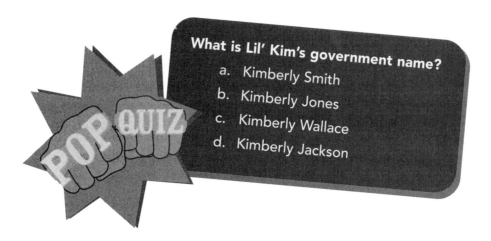

What is Lil' Kim's government name?
a. Kimberly Smith
b. Kimberly Jones
c. Kimberly Wallace
d. Kimberly Jackson

POP QUIZ

Foxy Brown

Let's say someone said the name "Foxy Brown" and asked if you knew who that person was. Even if you were a rap fan, it wouldn't be all that strange that you'd have no idea that the woman in question was (once) a platinum-selling star instead of a tabloid fixture and perpetual perp. Girlfriend has mad skills, but she also clearly is just mad and over the last few years has spiraled down from one of the best females in the game to an unpleasant mixture of Naomi Campbell and DMX.

Born and raised in the BK, Foxy Brown (Inga Marchand) got her start as a teen. In 1994 she nabbed first place at a local talent show and then went for hers on freestyle. Word got around and the production duo the Trackmasters, digging Foxy's style, brought her down to the studio to add some Brooknam flavor to LL's 1995 single "I Shot Ya." The song ended up becoming pretty damn hot and a hit, and in turn that led to Foxy getting calls (and more to the point, work) from performers that included R&B

trio Total ("No One Else"), love man Case ("Touch Me, Tease Me"), and Foxy's Brooklyn buddy Jay-Z. It was the on the come-up rapper who invited Foxy to spit something on *Reasonable Doubt*'s leadoff single, "Ain't No Nigga." As everyone knows, that single paid off nicely for all who were involved, including Miss Brown. Following the track's success, Foxy started getting courted by the major labels and she chose to sign with Def Jam in 1996.

Her debut came that same year and announced her arrival with flair. Hitting the number seven spot in its very first week out, *Ill Na Na* (a reference to Foxy's lady parts) featured production by the Trackmasters and guest spots from Method Man and Kid Capri. Foxy utilized her looks and sex appeal, but she also had the toughness that you get when you grow up in the BK. Fans ate up both her hardcore rhymes and her hot image, but the latter drew some heat since at the time of *Ill Na Na*'s release, Foxy was still technically a teenager.

Foxy's feminine flow helped land her a spot in 1997's short-lived rap supergroup The Firm, which also included Nas, AZ, and Nature. *Nas, Foxy Brown, AZ, and Nature Present The Firm: The Album* enjoyed pretty good sales, but probably owing to the number of egos and differing styles, the much-hyped group faded from view.

That brief move into high concept also helped set the stage for Foxy's sophomore joint. That CD, *Chyna Doll*, would enter into Billboard chart history books when it triumphed as the very first album by a female hip-hop performer to enter the Billboard Top 200 a.k.a. the album chart at number one. Eve has been the only other female MC to achieve that distinction, with 1999's *Ruff Ryders' First Lady*. *Chyna Doll* would go platinum, but even so, the single "Hot Spot" failed to make any real impact.

Even so, Foxy kept herself in the public eye. She used her good looks and hip-hop babe image to become a Calvin Klein jeans spokesmodel. On the personal front, she ended her engagement to then hot rapper Kurupt in 1999. That wasn't the only relationship she was having difficulty carrying on. Over the next year, Foxy found that longtime champions such as

Jay and Nas were no longer right by her side. That situation combined with an ongoing battle with Def Jam contributed to hard times for her.

In 2001, Foxy came back with perhaps the strongest, most artistically challenging CD of her career. *Broken Silence* was smart, introspective, and soulful, and more importantly it showed that Foxy had more to offer than her sexiness and more to talk about than material goods and getting laid. Yet despite getting mainly positive reviews, *Broken Silence* failed to sell the number of copies that the label had grown to expect, further setting into motion the schism between artist and executives. Foxy would bolt from Def Jam, and not under good terms, two years after her third CD's release.

A year later, in 2004, Foxy mended fences with Jigga, who was now Def Jam's prez. To show the love, Jay signed Foxy to Roc-A-Fella and enlisted her to join his "Jay-Z and Friends" tour. The Foxster began work on what was slated to be her fourth CD, then titled *Black Roses*. But her relationship with Roc-A-Fella fizzled before *Black Roses* saw the light of day. In 2007, Foxy left the label that Jay founded and signed with Koch Records to release projects through her own Black Rose Entertainment, including her first since 2001, *Brooklyn's Don Diva*.

Career took second stage to the drama unfolding outside of the studio. In 2004 it was alleged that Foxy, who had always been known for a temper, supposedly mixed it up with two nail technicians over a bill—totaling a paltry twenty bucks—that Foxy refused to pay. Somehow Foxy didn't get charged for the incident until the following year and continuously denied any wrongdoing, rejecting pleas, lesser charges, and the whole nine. Finally in 2006, she was sentenced to three years' probation and anger management classes.

That legal entanglement wasn't the only sign that Foxy's world was unraveling. In 2005, the lawyer representing her in the manicurist smackdown case let it be known that his client was almost completely deaf (there will be no jokes or puns about "Def" rappers) and because of that condition he couldn't communicate with her. Foxy fired her lawyer but later confirmed the sad announcement about the hearing loss, which she claimed had occurred without warning while she was in the midst of recording sessions.

Adding to the nonsense, in the winter of 2007 Foxy was busted again for pitching a fit (as well as beauty products) at a Florida beauty supply store. There was supposedly spitting (and not of sixteen bars), slapping, and struggling involved. Luckily no one was injured. A month later, Foxy who by now was doing more appearances in courtrooms than studios, pleaded guilty for violating probation by leaving NYC without the permission of the court. Judges involved in her various cases were not having any of her diva antics—deaf or not. The very real threat of incarceration hung over Foxy's pretty head, and on September 7, 2007, she was sentenced to one year in jail for violating her probation from her earlier altercation with two manicurists. For her part, she kept insisting that she was just misunderstood and being victimized. Can we all say hot mess? Damn, girl!

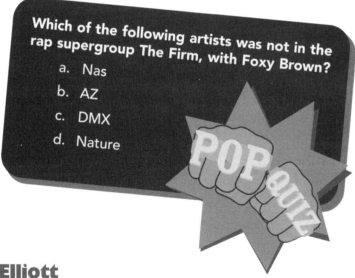

Which of the following artists was not in the rap supergroup The Firm, with Foxy Brown?

a. Nas

b. AZ

c. DMX

d. Nature

POP QUIZ

Missy Elliott

When Missy Elliott's "The Rain (Supa Dupa Fly)" hit airwaves in 1997, it was utterly unlike anything anyone had ever seen. The song itself was weird enough—a trippy, arty, surreal hip-hop nursery rhyme with giggly, borderline nonsensical lyrics, a wiggy drum pattern, and a rapper/singer who floated above the track with the playful innocence of a bored, caffeine-addled kid fucking around with a tape recorder. Then there was the imagery. Throughout the video Elliott seemed to be wearing an inflated garbage bag in a wind tunnel for a look that suggested a drugged-out Michelin Man in drag, while the use of distorted lenses gave the video a psychedelic quality. Like the song itself, the video moved to a languid, stoned, vaguely screwed-up rhythm. Even without the track's regular references to marijuana, it was evident that the people behind the song and video were smoking some seriously strong shit.

> **"THROUGHOUT THE VIDEO ELLIOTT SEEMED TO BE WEARING AN INFLATED GARBAGE BAG IN A WIND TUNNEL FOR A LOOK THAT SUGGESTED A DRUGGED-OUT MICHELIN MAN IN DRAG, WHILE THE USE OF DISTORTED LENSES GAVE THE VIDEO A PSYCHEDELIC QUALITY."**

It would be hard to imagine a more striking debut for any artist. Like few debut videos before or since, "The Rain (Supa Dupa Fly)" announced the arrival of a major new talent in hip-hop and R&B. Actually, make that two new talents, since Elliott's partnership with visionary producer/rapper Timbaland is central to her historic success. Elliott and Timbaland would go on to become one of hip-hop's all-time great duos, right up there in the pantheon alongside moneymaking Eric and Parrish of EPMD, DJ Premier and Guru, Snoop and Dre, and Pete Rock and C.L. Smooth.

For MTV viewers gobsmacked by "The Rain (Supa Dupa Fly)"'s audacity and originality, it sure seemed like Elliott emerged out of nowhere, but as is generally the case, the road to pop fame was long and littered with setbacks. Elliott began her musical career as part of an all-girl group called Sista in the late '80s. She hired a friend named Timothy Moseley to oversee Sista's demos, but it was a live, a capella performance for Jodeci's DeVante Swing that led to Sista scoring a record deal with Elektra Records.

Sista subsequently moved to New York, where they lived in the same building as Tweet and Ginuwine, both of whom would go on to have solo careers of their own. Elliott worked on Jodeci's final two albums and recorded an album with Sista that was shelved. She and Timbaland then began producing and writing for acts like 702, Total, and Destiny's Child, but perhaps their most important collaboration, commercially and creatively, was with a teenager named Aaliyah who achieved some measure of infamy when mentor R. Kelly tried to marry her at fifteen. Elliott and Timbaland helped refine Aaliyah's sound and style and a close musical and personal friendship was formed.

But as fruitful and profitable as Elliott's relationship with Aaliyah was, she still hungered for the spotlight. She appeared on tracks by Aaliyah, Gina Thompson, and MC Lyte and in 1997 released *Supa Dupa Fly*, perhaps the most critically acclaimed and influential debut hip-hop album ever released by a woman or man. Elliott continued to collaborate with other strong female artists. For example, she was part of the star-studded lineup of Lil' Kim's "Not Tonight (Remix)" and later collaborated with Kim again on the equally successful "Lady Marmalade" cover from the *Moulin Rouge!* soundtrack.

Supa Dupa Fly made Elliott and Timbaland pop stars who were also critics' darlings. Critics and fans alike hailed the duo's ability to craft perfect, radio-friendly pop songs while simultaneously experimenting with avant-garde sounds that blurred the lines between techno, glitch-hop, and straightforward hip-hop.

Where *Supa Dupa Fly* was released to near universal acclaim, its 1999 follow-up, *Da Real World*, received much more mixed reviews. The CD was a much darker, less commercial album, filled with paranoid rhymes and aggressively minimalist beats. The disc's angrier, more controversial edge was captured indelibly by the title of its first single: "She's a Bitch." *Da Real World* nevertheless went on to score sizable hits in the aforementioned "She's a Bitch," "Hot Boyz (Remix)," and "All N My Grill."

After going dark with *Da Real World*, Elliott embraced club music, club drugs, and her own raging libido with her third solo album, 2001's *Miss E . . . So Addictive*, a veritable concept album about the joys of sex. The single "One Minute Man" (with Ludacris and Trina) was a sly putdown of premature ejaculators, while "Get Ur Freak On" confirmed Missy Elliott and Timbaland's genius for making adventurous, arty singles that thoroughly charmed mainstream audiences.

Late in the fall of 2001, Elliott experienced a devastating personal setback when close friend and collaborator Aaliyah died in a plane crash. She was twenty-two. Rather than sink into depression, Elliott channeled her sadness and grief into making one of her most joyful and infectious albums, 2002's *Under Construction*. The CD marked a distinct return to the high spirits and innocent fun of rap's old school, so it's poetically fitting that the disc's monster single, "Work It," featured an attention-grabbing vocal part played backward.

Elliott's full-figured physique long stood in sharp contrast to the tiny little frames of the R&B sexpots she wrote hits for, but before the release of *Under Construction* she lost a great deal of weight and the album's cover showed off her drastically slimmed-down physique. *This Is Not a Test!* (2003) was a solid effort but lacked the clear-cut marketing hooks of many of Elliott's previous albums.

The Cookbook of 2005, meanwhile, marked the first Missy Elliott album not produced entirely by Timbaland. He produced half the disc, while Elliott and others handled the rest. If nothing else, the album confirmed that Elliott was capable of making compelling music without her longtime partner and friend.

In 2006 it was announced that Robert De Niro and his production company were looking to use Elliott's life story as the basis for an autobiographical film that may or may not star the rapper/singer/songwriter/icon herself. It seems like an apt culmination to the Horatio Alger saga that is Elliott's career. That career has had all the makings of a larger-than-life melodrama, so it's only fitting that Elliott's remarkable story will hopefully be making the trek all the way to the silver screen.

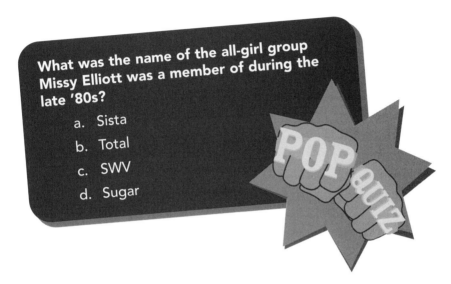

What was the name of the all-girl group Missy Elliott was a member of during the late '80s?

    a. Sista

    b. Total

    c. SWV

    d. Sugar

POP quiz

Eve

If she wasn't so damned lucky, Eve might just qualify as the single unluckiest person in hip-hop. Her life and career have been characterized by insane amounts of bad luck and good fortune. As a young MC she received the break of a lifetime when Dr. Dre, a god of hip-hop and legendary starmaker, signed her to his Aftermath Entertainment label. Eve then joined Last Emperor, Hittman, and Rakim in the impressive ranks of Aftermath artists who were released from their contracts without ever putting out an album. Eve scored another huge break when fellow Illadelph hip-hop act The Roots featured her on their classic single "You Got Me"— perhaps LL's "I Need Love"'s only real competition as the definitive hip-hop love song—but even that triumph was marred when Eve failed to appear in the music video, an oversight that led many to assume that her verse was actually delivered by former rapper Erykah Badu, who sang the haunting hook and appeared in the video. Eve scored another colossal potential break when Dr. Dre signed her to Aftermath a second time, but who knows if her second stint on the label will turn out any differently than her first.

Eve's presence on "You Got Me" begs the question: what if she had gone the underground route? What if she'd hooked up with Mos Def or Talib Kweli or Little Brother or 9th Wonder or J Dilla instead of Swizz Beatz and DMX? What if she'd channeled her inner Maya Angelou when composing her verses instead of spitting for the streets and for the radio? What if she'd sought out Roots drummer/producer ?uestlove as a mentor and sonic architect instead of a one-time collaborator? This alternate path is fascinating to contemplate, if inherently only theoretical in nature.

For someone who scored a number one album while barely out of her teens, the road to stardom has been surprisingly drawn-out and littered with roadblocks and obstacles, both personal and professional. Born Eve Jihan Jeffers in Philadelphia, Pennsylvania on November 10, 1979, her parents divorced while she was still a preteen. Between the ages of twelve and fourteen, Eve lived with her mother and grandmother before her mother remarried.

Eve discovered a love for language and wordplay early. In high school she dubbed herself "Gangsta" and formed an all-girl group called EDGP (pronounced "Egypt"). After high school, she exploited her good looks and roughhewn charm by working as a stripper and table dancer—a less than respectable gig that came back to haunt the rapper when footage of her apparently engaged in an act of sexual congress hit the Internet and Eve neither confirmed nor denied that she was in fact the woman in the video.

Despite calling herself "Gangsta" in high school and working that pole during her wild, misspent youth, Eve is remarkable for her unwillingness to conform to hip-hop's hoary stereotypes about women. Though she's certainly confident in her sexuality, she's never trafficked in the overt, almost cartoonish vampishness of sexpots like Lil' Kim, Trina, or Foxy Brown, preferring a more discreet, understated form of sex appeal. She has long been affiliated with gangsta rap icons Dr. Dre and DMX, but there's nothing particularly thuggish about her music, though she can certainly spit that rough shit with the best of them and sometimes does. Yes, Eve has found success on her own terms. She's paved her own lane in hip-hop while drawing on the groundbreaking work of female hip-hop pioneers like MC Lyte, Roxanne Shanté, and Queen Latifah.

After parting ways with EDGP and leaving the strip game behind (no doubt to the chagrin of her long-term customers), Eve began making inroads in the music business. Her initial Aftermath stint was a promising dead end that resulted only in "Eve of Destruction," a track off the huge-selling *Bulworth* soundtrack that spawned one of the decade's most ubiquitous hits in the Pras/Ol' Dirty Bastard/Mýa collaboration "Ghetto Supastar (That Is What You Are)."

While Dr. Dre failed to make Eve a star, the rapper hooked up with a tormented Yonkers loner named DMX who saw infinite potential in the self-professed "pit bull in a skirt"—a nickname that certainly appealed to DMX's animal instincts—with the sexy purr and appealing gruffness. Eve signed with the Ruff Ryders camp, an outfit that helped make DMX one of the biggest stars in rap. Her buzz increased with attention-grabbing collaborations like the remix for DMX's "Ruff Ryders Anthem."

> **"[EVE] HOOKED UP WITH A TORMENTED YONKERS LONER NAMED DMX WHO SAW INFINITE POTENTIAL IN THE SELF-PROFESSED 'PIT BULL IN A SKIRT' ... WITH THE SEXY PURR AND APPEALING GRUFFNESS."**

Eve's much-anticipated debut album, *Ruff Ryders' First Lady*, found her working extensively with synthesizer enthusiast Swizz Beatz, the nephew of Ruff Ryders founders Chivon, Joaquin, and Darrin Dean. Beatz's early production style was characterized by extremely simple keyboard melodies that the producer reportedly used to knock out in fifteen to twenty minutes. Beatz subsequently discovered the magic that is sampling—an innovation that reignited his fading career. His unique style divided fans and critics, with some praising him for eschewing sampling in the Puff Daddy era, while others accused him of abandoning solid songcraft in the bargain. When Beatz was sued for allegedly borrowing from built-in melodies from keyboard manufacturers for the beats for tracks like Eve's "What Ya Want," the producer's detractors—who long suspected that Beatz was jacking beats from his Casio—responded with "No shit." Beatz was nevertheless a sought-after hitmaker and his amped-up production helped make stars out of DMX and Eve.

When released in 1999, *Ruff Ryders' First Lady* became only the second album by a female rapper to debut at number one. Foxy Brown's *Chyna Doll* was the first. *Ruff Ryders' First Lady* went double platinum and garnered strong reviews for Eve's formidable lyrical presence and the novel subject matter of tracks like "Love Is Blind," which explores domestic abuse.

For 2001's *Scorpion*, Eve reconnected with Dr. Dre, who produced two of the album's strongest tracks: the hard-hitting "That's What It Is" with Styles P of The Lox on hook duty and the Grammy-winning smash hit "Let Me Blow Ya Mind." A seductive exercise in slow-rolling funk, "Let Me Blow Ya Mind" was auspicious for another reason: it marked the first collaboration between Eve and Gwen Stefani of No Doubt, who sang the hook and appeared in the popular music video.

In retrospect, "Let Me Blow Ya Mind" represented Stefani's first tentative foray out of the ska and pop realm of No Doubt and into the trendy, hip-hop-influenced sounds of solo albums like *The Sweet Escape*. The collaboration between Stefani and Eve proved mutually beneficial. Stefani introduced Eve to a big crossover pop audience while working with Dr. Dre, and Eve gave Stefani some measure of hip-hop credibility. Incidentally, in 1999 the two women both appeared on Prince's ill-fated would-be comeback album *Rave Un2 the Joy Fantastic*.

Stefani, Eve, and Dr. Dre would go on to collaborate again on "Rich Girl," a Grammy-nominated single from Stefani's *Love.Angel.Music.Baby.* disc. Eve has also worked repeatedly with another strong female artist, Missy Elliott, most notably by contributing a scorching verse to a remix of Elliott's "Hot Boyz."

Like seemingly every rapper alive, however, Eve wasn't content to strut her stuff solely on wax. No, she longed to create a multimedia empire and began making tentative steps into film and television. She made a less than auspicious debut in a supporting role in *XXX*, a high-concept Vin Diesel blockbuster that aspired to give the world a James Bond for a totally X-treme, in-your-face, Mountain Dewtastic age and somehow managed to be even more insultingly idiotic than its premise would suggest.

Eve made a much stronger impression in *BarberShop*, which was released just a month after *XXX* and smartly showcased the rapper's girl-next-door likability and laid-back magnetism. *BarberShop*'s sprawling ensemble cast was full of standouts, most notably Cedric the Entertainer's Jesse Jackson–baiting turn as an outrageous provocateur, but the film nevertheless served notice that Eve could potentially develop into a strong character actress and not just a popular rapper who sometimes appeared in films. Compared to frequent friend and collaborator DMX's godawful Joel Silver–produced vehicles with Jet Li and Steven Seagal, Eve's sturdy turn in *Barber-Shop*, a big critical and commercial hit, was downright Oscar-worthy.

Eve's work in *BarberShop* did not go unnoticed. She returned in the film's thoroughly underwhelming sequel and in 2003 joined the throng of rappers headed to the small screen by executive-producing and starring in her own eponymous sitcom. *Eve* cast the rapper/actress as a romantically challenged businesswoman who ran a fashion design firm with two friends. Though it opened to mixed reviews, the UPN show lasted three seasons and snagged Eve an NAACP Image Award nomination.

The Woodsman of 2004 proved a much better venue for Eve's acting chops. The film was produced by bashful, spotlight-averse recluse Damon Dash for his Dash Films and co-starred renowned underground hip-hop legend Mos Def, but it couldn't be further removed from violent, shoddy rapsploitation fare like, um, Dash's *State Property* movies. On the contrary, it was a sober, understated character study about ex-con child molester Kevin Bacon's unsteady attempts to make a life for himself outside prison walls. Eve contributed in a memorable supporting turn as an initially sympathetic but ultimately concerned and distrustful co-worker of Bacon's.

Eve released her third solo album, *Eve-Olution*, in 2002, but despite appearances and/or production from Dr. Dre, Swizz Beatz, Scott Storch, Snoop Dogg, Nate Dogg, Jadakiss, and Styles P the album was a commercial disappointment. Where Eve's previous two solo albums breezed their way past platinum sales, *Eve-Olution* barely made it past gold. The record did score a minor hit in "Gangsta Lovin'," a collaboration with yet another pop star, Alicia Keys.

Ever the enterprising entrepeneur, Eve started a clothing line called Fetish and made headlines of a different kind when it was revealed she was dating Teodorín Nguema Obiang, the playboy son and heir of hated African dictator Teodoro Obiang Nguema. Needless to say, this did not endear Eve to human rights groups like Amnesty International who have been critical of the dictator's use of torture, but hey, who among us hasn't gone on at least a few dates with the heir of a reviled third world strongman? In any case, the pair are no longer together.

Eve had a run-in with the cops when she crashed her Maserati while cruising on Hollywood Boulevard the morning of April 26, 2007. She was arrested on suspicion of driving while under the influence, to which she pleaded no contest. The rapstress didn't let that stop her from returning to the mic in 2008, this time a little more "yorkie in a prom dress" than "pit bull in a skirt," with her fourth album, *Here I Am*, off Dr. Dre's Aftermath label and Swizz Beatz's Full Surface Records.

In a sense, Eve's re-enrollment in Dre's sonic boot camp brings her career full circle. She's proven conclusively that a woman can enjoy a thriving hip-hop career without catering to male fans' basest instincts (no small feat for a former stripper) or playing the studio gangsta. Eve continues to prove an inspiration not only to strippers looking to leave the sex trade behind, but for strong, independent women everywhere.

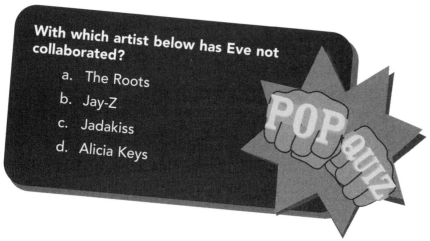

Da Brat

The tomboy-imaged Da Brat, born Shawntae Harris in Chicago in 1974, first broke on the scene after beginning to rap at the age of eleven and winning an amateur rap contest that featured the alluring grand prize of a meeting with Kris Kross (seriously). Her style was more along the lines of her male peers, and, post–Kris Kross meeting, So So Def label head Jermaine Dupri signed Brat and subsequently released her 1994 debut, *Funkdafied.*

Riding on the strength of the title track and succeeding singles "Fa All Y'all" and "Give It 2 You" (but mostly "Funkdafied," which went to number two on the charts), Brat became the first female MC to have an album go platinum and also enjoyed "Funkdafied" sitting atop the rap singles chart for nearly three months.

Nineteen ninety-six was a busy year for Brat, as it brought the difficult-to-spell *Anuthatantrum*, which, despite its confusing jumble of consonants and vowels, went on to break the Billboard top twenty as well as the R&B top five. Not one to let opportunities slip by her, Da Brat used this momentum to score some prestigious guest spots on tracks from the likes of peers Mariah Carey, the also platinum-selling Missy Elliott, and Lil' Kim. Brat also found herself on joints from not-often-discussed Dru Hill and Total, and her film debut came by way of the even-less-discussed "comedy" *Kazaam*, starring Shaquille O'Neal.

The year must have tired out Brat, as she didn't appear back on the radar until 2000's *Unrestricted*, which was released in conjunction with an arrest on the grounds of pistol-whipping a woman in a nightclub. Proving her longevity despite a four-year absence, Da Brat's third full-length album reached the top five on the pop charts.

The next year saw Da Brat back on the big screen in the collar-tugging Mariah Carey vehicle *Glitter*, and two years later, *Limelite, Luv & Nite-clubz* dropped with average content and a suspiciously Lil' Kim–looking cover. Also in 2003, Da Brat appeared on VH1's *The Surreal Life*. The year 2005 brought a guest spot on Dem Franchize Boyz' "I Think They Like Me (Remix)" alongside career-starter Dupri. Later that year, she was involved in an altercation at Dupri's Atlanta nightclub, Studio 72, where she was arrested on felony aggravated assault charges for allegedly hitting a waitress in the face with a rum bottle. Ouch!

Big Punisher

You know a guy has a weight problem when he's 150 to 200 pounds heavier than a buddy and mentor who calls himself Fat Joe. Sadly, that was the case for beloved rapper Big Punisher even before the tragic explosion in weight that led to his early death. Punisher's star burned out quickly and today his cult pales besides those of Tupac and Notorious B.I.G.—perhaps because getting cut down in a hail of gunfire is somehow deemed cooler than going down in a hail of White Castle sliders and frosty chocolate milkshakes—but for a brief period in the late '90s, Pun was one of pop music's unlikeliest superstars, a morbidly obese rhyme animal with a personality as big as his enormous frame.

Born Christopher Lee Rios on November 9, 1971, the man who would grow up to be Big Pun was a surprisingly athletic youth who excelled at

"[BIG] PUN WAS ONE OF POP MUSIC'S UNLIKELIEST SUPERSTARS, A MORBIDLY OBESE RHYME ANIMAL WITH A PERSONALITY AS BIG AS HIS ENORMOUS FRAME."

basketball and boxing. Like so many of his peers, Pun had a troubled childhood characterized by a stormy home life and periods of homelessness, but he found release in the form of hip-hop. He began collaborating with a group that dubbed themselves the Full A Clips crew, many of whom would later join Pun as part of his and Fat Joe's Terror Squad crew.

Big Punisher's career began to take off when he met mentor Joe and began collaborating with him on tracks like "Watch Out" and "Fire Water." In 1997 Punisher helped cement his growing stardom with an attention-grabbing verse on the Beatnuts' hit single "Off the Books." In 1998 Big Punisher released his solo debut, *Capital Punishment*. It was the first solo album by a Hispanic rapper to go platinum and spawned a massive crossover hit in the saucy party anthem "Still Not a Player." The adventurous, eclectic debut found Big Punisher collaborating with guests from across the hip-hop landscape, from Dead Prez and Wyclef Jean to Busta Rhymes and Black Thought. Critics hailed the deft lyricism of Punisher's rhymes and irreverent humor, and Joe would later pay homage to his late partner when he crowed on "New York" that he was spitting so hard that people were saying he must have found Pun's rhyme book. Joe and Pun collaborated on numerous projects together, including the Jennifer Lopez single "Feelin' So Good" and the 1999 self-titled Terror Squad posse album.

Throughout his brief career Pun wrestled with obesity. Concerned friends got him to enroll in a weight loss program at Duke University, where he lost over a hundred pounds that he later gained back during a life-ending orgy of food consumption that sent his weight rocketing upwards of seven hundred pounds. On February 7, 2000, Big Pun died of an obesity-induced heart attack. His follow-up album, *Yeeeah Baby*, was released two months later to mixed reviews but healthy sales.

Big Pun's early death cemented his iconic status. The year 2001 saw the release of the posthumous album *Endangered Species*, but allegations that Punisher abused his wife and squabbling between his widow and mentor Fat Joe over royalties for the record have cast a dark shadow over the rapper's legacy. Big Punisher was tragically killed by his gargantuan appetite without ever getting to witness the full fruits of the explosion of Latin musical talent he helped initiate.

Fat Joe

Fat Joe's not the flyest or most distinctive rapper. But there's just something about the dude that's hard to deny. He's paid his dues, logged his hours, and enjoyed a solid career—along with getting love from his fans and his peers.

Born in the South Bronx, Joe Cartagena got hip to rap through an older brother and soaked up the sound and rhymes of the music's pioneers. He started going for his own legacy as a teen and made a rep in NYC's underground community during the early '90s. Part of that respect came through his membership in the now semilegendary D.I.T.C. Crew ("Diggin' in the Crates"), whose ranks also included NYC sure shots Showbiz and A.G., Buckwild, Diamond D, O.C., the late Big L, and Lord Finesse—all street saviors. Joe worked both with the crew and popped up on various members' own joints.

Along the way, Joe met up with the late Big Pun. Because of Pun's status as one of the first Latino rappers to truly gain a national spotlight, the rotund rhymester would serve as a friend to many up-and-coming Latinos. Chief among them was Joe. Working hard, Joe finally got a chance to shine when he dropped his solo debut, 1993's *Represent*. The album yielded the number one rap single "Flow Joe." Having now made a mark, Joe came back in two years with *Jealous One's Envy*, featuring beats by

Premier and L.E.S. In this same time frame, Joe also joined LL's posse cut "I Shot Ya" (with Keith Murray and Foxy Brown).

Joe finally went back to focusing on his own thing when in the late '90s he jumped to Atlantic Records. With his own production deal, a perk most rappers get these days, Joey Crack delivered '98's *Don Cartagena*, featuring comrades such as Nas, Raekwon, Big Pun, and Puffy. In 1999, Joe formally introduced his longtime clique Terror Squad, who released an eponymous CD that same year. In late 2001, he returned to solo work with *Jealous Ones Still Envy (J.O.S.E.)*, which went gold and had contributions from Luda, R. Kelly, and soon-to-be TS member, female rapper Remy Ma. The album also had the Irv Gotti–produced hit "What's Luv?" featuring Ashanti and Ja Rule, which became one of 2002's biggest pop hits.

Everything Joe touched sold solidly and his rep among other rappers was impeccable, but despite the steadiness of his career he never had that breakout moment—until 2004. Joe brought Terror Squad back together with a new lineup. Pun, of course had passed away in early 2000 (morbidly overweight, the rapper died of a heart attack). Longtime boys Cuban Link and Triple Seis split with some degree of bad blood under the surface. Remy was fully on board, and this new TS (which was basically Joe and Ma) dropped *True Story* and then the single "Lean Back." Produced by Scott Storch, the track's impossible-to-forget hook and banging beats exploded, became the jam, and went to the very tippy top of the charts for three weeks. It was Joe's biggest moment—but one he'd never

> **"EVERYTHING JOE TOUCHED SOLD SOLIDLY AND HIS REP AMONG OTHER RAPPERS WAS IMPECCABLE, BUT DESPITE THE STEADINESS OF HIS CAREER HE NEVER HAD THAT BREAKOUT MOMENT— UNTIL 2004."**

repeat. The anthem also brought Joe his first real taste of intracity beef. It seems 50 Cent—at that point NYC's kingpin—was pissed at Joe for his prior collabo with 50's archrival Ja Rule on Ja's single "New York." Fiddy hit back at Joe with "Piggy Bank" (off 50's *The Massacre*) and snarled, "That fat nigga thought 'Lean Back' was 'In Da Club'/My shit sold eleven mil, his shit was a dud." Yeah, that's mean, but there was a grain of truth, because even though "Lean Back" was undeniable, the TS album was a relative disappointment in the sales arena.

Fat Joe went on the offensive and hit the mixtapes with a return shot alternately called "Fake Gangsta" or "Fuck 50." Set to the *Flintstones* theme, the diss song mocked 50's street cred (a risky move). Titled "My FoFo," the song would become a cut on Joe's 2005 release *All or Nothing*, a much-hyped, much-anticipated CD that fell short of expectations. After taking some time off, as well as slimming down to a merely hefty Joe, he came back in fighting form in November of 2006 with *Me, Myself & I*, which was done independently in partnership with Virgin Records. More hardcore and more unrelenting, the CD got folks paying attention to this vet once again, especially after the single "Make It Rain," which featured the man of the moment, Lil Wayne, took off on radio and in the streets. The turnaround proved that you can't sleep on Fat Joe.

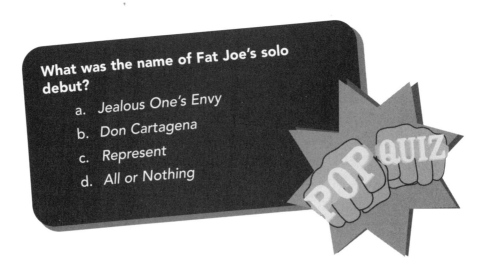

What was the name of Fat Joe's solo debut?

   a. Jealous One's Envy

   b. Don Cartagena

   c. Represent

   d. All or Nothing

POP QUIZ

Nas

When your debut is universally hailed as one of the greatest hip-hop albums of all time, what do you do for an encore? That's the dilemma that's plagued Nas ever since *Illmatic* was released in 1994 to deafening critical acclaim and bewilderingly modest sales. *Illmatic's* enduring legend has been a blessing as well as a curse for the legendary MC. It ensured Nas a prominent place in hip-hop history, but it also made it inevitable that each of his subsequent albums would be compared to *Illmatic* and found lacking. Of course Nas hasn't exactly made it easy for people to forget about *Illmatic* by naming one of his follow-ups *Stillmatic* or having Columbia release a tenth anniversary version of his classic debut.

Upon *Illmatic's* release, Nas was heralded as nothing less than hip-hop's boy messiah, a preternaturally gifted lyrical prodigy who'd save the genre. On his last album he generated headlines and inspired fevered debate on the state of rap music by provocatively proclaiming hip-hop dead. In between, he has been lionized as a hero and demonized as a sellout. He's experienced giddy highs and agonizing lows.

Nas is barely into his thirties, but he's managed to cram several lifetimes' worth of experience into his very eventful life and career. Born September 14, 1973, Nas is the son of jazz musician Olu Dara, a cornet player, singer, and guitarist whose nomadic, lusty lifestyle Nas made the subject of "Poppa Was a Playa," a standout track from his *Lost Tapes* CD. In addition to being a player, Nas's poppa was also apparently something of a rolling stone, so after Dara bolted in the mid-'80s, it was largely left to Nas's mother, Fannie Ann Jones, to raise him in the legendary Queensbridge projects, the stomping ground for Juice Crew legends like MC Shan and Marley Marl.

Between the Juice Crew blowing up and the soulful wail of his father's horn, Nas grew up immersed in music. Though extraordinarily smart, he, like many of his hip-hop peers, had little use for the white man's textbooks and tales of European glory, so he dropped out of school after eighth grade and embarked on a journey of intellectual self-discovery. He became particularly interested in African history and religion, themes he would go on to explore extensively in his music and in his starring role in *Belly*.

During his teen years, Nas lived the street life while simultaneously trying to break into hip-hop as Nasty Nas. His big break came when he met Large Professor, a rapper/producer best known as the front man for Main Source, a group loosely affiliated with the Native Tongues posse. Through Large Professor, Nas scored his first major national exposure via a guest appearance on "Live at the Barbeque," a track from Main Source's classic 1991 album *Breaking Atoms*. The appearance generated lots of positive buzz that Nas was unable to leverage into a record deal. Then again, in the early '90s hip-hop had fallen under the blunted spell of Dr. Dre's G-funk movement, so Nas's East Coast superlyricism wasn't considered commercially viable.

The Wu-Tang Clan would help create a market for grimy New York rhyme spitters, but their wildly influential debut—as classic in its own right as *Illmatic*—wouldn't drop until 1993. Thankfully, the long lag time between his "Live at the Barbeque" appearance and *Illmatic*'s 1994 release gave Nas plenty of time to build a classic solo debut, to craft the ten perfect tracks that would be his ticket to pop music immortality.

To help realize his dreams of stardom, Nas hired a white rapper and businessman named MC Serch to act as his manager. As a founding member of 3rd Bass, Serch recorded hits like "The Gas Face" and "Pop Goes the Weasel." More importantly, he helped provide crucial breaks for Nas, Non Phixion, MF DOOM (who guested on "The Gas Face" as part of KMD), and the melanin-deficient jokers on VH1's *The White Rapper Show*, which Serch hosted in 2007.

After featuring Nas on "Back to the Grill" from his *Return of the Product* solo album, Serch helped his young charge secure a record deal with Columbia, and sessions for *Illmatic* began in earnest. For his first album Nas snagged a dream team of respected East Coast producers.

Though Nas was largely an unknown commodity, he'd already developed a formidable reputation on the basis of his guest appearances and his solo turn on "Halftime" from Serch's soundtrack to *Zebrahead*, so it wasn't hard finding top-notch beatsmiths to work on the project. After parting ways with Main Source to concentrate on his ill-fated solo debut, Large Professor produced three *Illmatic* tracks. Pete Rock of the legendary duo Pete Rock and C.L. Smooth contributed "The World Is Yours," while DJ Premier of the equally legendary duo Gang Starr added his trademark beat wizardry to three tracks: "(Memory Lane) Sittin' in Da Park," "Represent," and "N.Y. State of Mind." A Tribe Called Quest frontman/producer Q-Tip and up-and-coming beatsmith L.E.S. completed the disc's remarkable lineup of revered sonic architects.

Lyrically Nas's dense, poetic lyrics and aggressive delivery were seen as a continuation of the super-scientific rhyme schemes of golden age heroes like Rakim. Creatively if not commercially, *Illmatic* was hip-hop's answer to *Thriller*. Its weakest cut was stronger than most rappers' best track. Every track on the album could be a more than respectable single. *Illmatic* boasted a number of virtues that would become increasingly rare in the decade to come, both in hip-hop and in Nas's own uneven subsequent albums. It was tight, it was focused, it was conscious, and it was wholly devoid of filler, gratuitous guest appearances (the only other rapper on the album is AZ), or blatant ploys for radio spins or club play. Nas worked with a bevy of strong-willed producers, yet the album maintained a strong sense of continuity musically as well as lyrically. It was clear that Nas had made exactly the album he had set out to make, one that would become the gold standard against which all other promising solo debuts would be compared.

> **"CREATIVELY IF NOT COMMERCIALLY, *ILLMATIC* WAS HIP-HOP'S ANSWER TO *THRILLER*. ITS WEAKEST CUT WAS STRONGER THAN MOST RAPPERS' BEST TRACK."**

Yes, *Illmatic* had everything except hit singles and strong initial sales. Its disappointing sales have long been one of rap's most pressing mysteries. How could an album so many people loved sell so poorly? How could a disc praised to the heavens by critics, fans, and tastemakers everywhere limp toward gold status, while inane walking punch lines like MC Hammer or Vanilla Ice breezed their way to diamond sales?

It's safe to say that nobody was as unnerved by *Illmatic*'s commercial failure than Nas himself. Respect is all well and good, but you can't buy a house or pay for your children's education with glowing reviews from the *New York Times* or accolades from respected DJs. Nas had critics and he had the streets. Now he was gunning for the mainstream and platinum sales.

Though fans who cherished *Illmatic* no doubt disagreed, Nas felt a commercial makeover was in order. So the rapper hooked up with savvy manager Steve Stoute, who encouraged Nas to abandon his prophet-of-the-projects persona and reinvent himself as Nas Escobar, larger-than-life hip-hop mobster à la Raekwon on *Only Built 4 Cuban Linx*.

Sure enough, 1996's *It Was Written* accomplished Nas's goal of scoring hit singles, mainstream success, and multiplatinum album sales, but at a steep price to his artistic credibility. Suddenly he was following commercial trends, doing radio-friendly songs with R&B choruses courtesy of Lauryn Hill ("If I Ruled the World") and R. Kelly ("Street Dreams [Remix]"), and making big, flashy videos with Hype Williams. If *Illmatic* made Nas the poster boy for authenticity and real hip-hop, *It Was Written* made him the poster boy for selling out and creative compromise.

It Was Written nevertheless found an audience and generated positive reviews, even if they paled in comparison to the raves that greeted *Illmatic*. Lupe Fiasco has publicly stated that he patterned his own iconoclastic debut album, *Food & Liquor*, after *It Was Written*. On his sophomore effort Nas worked with Premier, L.E.S., and Dr. Dre but most of the album was produced by the undistinguished, pop-friendly production team the Trackmasters. Nas was making big moves commercially but he also seemed to be moving away from what made his debut so special.

The song "Affirmative Action" from *It Was Written* provided fans with a sneak preview of sorts for Nas's next project, a much-ballyhooed hip-hop supergroup called The Firm. Originally The Firm's lineup was Nas, jailbait du jour Foxy Brown, Cormega, and AZ, but Cormega was replaced during the recording of the album by Nature.

Expectations for The Firm's debut were high. The 1997 disc was one of the first releases by Dr. Dre's Aftermath label, and the fact that the king of West Coast gangsta rap was now collaborating with some of New York's biggest names only raised the stakes. *Nas, Foxy Brown, AZ,* and *Nature Present The Firm: The Album* (a bulky, cumbersome name that at least left no doubt as to the supergroup's exact lineup) would either be a smash or a pronounced disappointment.

Needless to say, dear reader, the album was no smash and Nas fans were left wondering why exactly the former savior of hip-hop was now pretending to be John Gotti alongside a second-rate Lil' Kim wannabe better known for her cleavage-baring outfits than her lyrics. Despite production by Dr. Dre and a snazzy single in "Phone Tap," *The Firm* was released to mixed reviews and underwhelming sales. Nas had taken a big risk and it failed to pay off.

Nas did little to win back the hearts and minds of the hip-hop faithful with two albums in 1999, *I Am . . .* and *Nastradamus*, despite the occasional return to *Illmatic* form like "Nas Is Like" and "N.Y. State of Mind, Part 2," both collaborations with DJ Premier from *I Am . . .* The gloomy *I Am . . .* single "Hate Me Now," meanwhile, is best known as the song that sparked a vicious feud between Puff Daddy and Steve Stoute after a video featuring Nas and Puff Daddy being crucified made it onto MTV against Puff's wishes.

Nas's blatant plays for commercial success hit a nadir with a pair of singles that seemed to contradict everything the rapper stood for. "You Owe Me" was an inane, Timbaland-produced club track whose chorus found Ginuwine crooning, "Shorty, say what's your price?/Just to back it up, you can hold my ice." Nas was a long way from the visceral grit of

Illmatic. "Oochie Wally," a sexed-up nursery rhyme featuring Nas collaborating with protégés the Bravehearts, was arguably even more insipid and embarrassing.

Commercially Nas had developed into a major artist, but he was steadily losing respect within the hip-hop community. His creative resurrection came from an unlikely source. On September 11, 2001, a date that will live in infamy for reasons that have nothing to do with hip-hop, Jay-Z launched a surprise attack on his New York rival in the form of "Takeover," a blistering diss song directed squarely at Nas.

"Takeover" reiterated many of the complaints fans and critics had been directing at Nas since *It Was Written*, like its contention that he had never released a follow-up worthy of *Illmatic*. Another diss track, "Super Ugly," meanwhile, veered into queasily personal territory by bragging about Jay-Z's sexual relationship with Nas's baby mama.

"Takeover" had the streets abuzz and helped cement the growing fame of its producer, a young man from Chicago with a staggeringly high opinion of himself named Kanye West. Hip-hop breathlessly awaited Nas's response, which eventually came in the form of a diss track called "Ether." Despite grade-school-level lyrics smearing Jay-Z as "Gay-Z" and Roc-A-Fella Records as "Cock-A-Fella," "Ether" was nevertheless considered a classic diss song that reignited interest in the rapper's career.

"'ETHER' WAS NEVERTHELESS CONSIDERED A CLASSIC DISS SONG THAT REIGNITED INTEREST IN [NAS's] CAREER."

Battling Jay-Z also helped reignite Nas's competitive spirit. Accordingly, his next album, *Stillmatic*, was seen by critics and audiences alike as a return to form. The following album, *God's Son*, was a hit with audiences and critics as well and spawned hits in "Made You Look"—which sampled the Incredible Bongo Band's classic break from "Apache"—and "I Can"—which sampled Beethoven.

In 2004 Nas released the double-disc set *Street's Disciple*, which featured "Bridging the Gap," a collaboration with his father, and received similarly glowing reviews but never quite caught fire commercially. In the midst of Nas's creative renewal the rapper fell in love and married R&B iconoclast Kelis, a musician known for her overt sexuality, daring fashion sense, and Neptunes-produced hit singles. The pair would go on to collaborate on numerous songs and Nas turned in a cameo in Kelis's attention-grabbing video for "Milkshake."

In late 2005 and early 2006 Nas shocked hip-hop by publicly ending his feud with Jay-Z and signing with hip-hop powerhouse Def Jam, where Jay-Z served as a controversial president and artist. He made even more headlines by naming his Def Jam debut *Hip Hop Is Dead* and turning it into a scathing examination of contemporary hip-hop.

The result is Nas's tightest, most focused album since *Illmatic*, a cohesive concept album haunted by the past and filled with ghosts. Jay-Z has received a lot of flack, rightly and wrongly, for promoting his own albums over other artists on his label, but he very graciously allowed "Black Republican," a powerhouse duet with Nas, to appear on *Hip Hop Is Dead* when its inclusion on *Kingdom Come* would no doubt have strengthened the Def Jam president's dimly received comeback album.

Considering all Nas has been through, it's hard to believe he's barely into his mid-thirties. *Hip Hop Is Dead* brings the rapper's career and life full circle. He began his career as hip-hop's savior and with *Hip Hop Is Dead* helped resurrect the genre he'll always be intricately associated with. Nas is hip-hop's poet laureate of the streets. Not bad for a kid from the Queensbridge projects who never even went to high school.

Before he signed to Def Jam Records, what record label was home to Nas?

a. Interscope Records

b. Columbia Records

c. Jive Records

d. Universal Records

POP QUIZ

Jay-Z

It's safe to say that as of 2007, the biggest, best-known, most money-earning, Beyoncé-dating, all-around king of the whole damn rap and beyond that world is Shawn Carter a.k.a. S. Carter a.k.a. Jay-Z a.k.a. Jay Hova a.k.a. Jigga a.k.a. Hov a.k.a. Mr. Carter, sir.

Is he lyrically the best? Some say yes, yes y'all, some say he's fallen off—but no matter how you cut it, Jay-Z pretty much has defined hip-hop and done so since his 1996 classic, *Reasonable Doubt*.

Jay was raised in Brooklyn's Marcy projects, and throughout his career he has kept close spiritual and lyrical ties to the hardcore housing complex. His dad left when he was just a kid. Lacking both a father figure and a second income with which to help support his family, Jay did what a lot of BK's finest did—turned to the streets and got his hustle on. As fans of his music and readers of his interviews know, Jay alludes to having engaged in some illegal activities in order to make some spending money. How deep into the game Jay was is unclear, but if you believe his rhymes (and you can), young Shawn was up to something. But he had interests that were less criminal-minded. His mom had purchased him a boombox and as a kid and into his teens, Jay, who attended high school in downtown Brooklyn with Trevor Smith (Busta Rhymes) and Christopher Wallace (Biggie), also had some desire to rap. He began to work his magic at Marcy and local parties. Going by the name Jazzy, he started to earn a rep.

After shortening his name to Jay-Z, he put all his energy into hip-hop. Helping him in those early days was a Brooklyn legend named Jaz-O, and it was through the more seasoned rapper that Jay figured out how to work the business end of the hip-hop game. Along the way Jay briefly hooked up with a now who-cares-about-them group known as Original Flavor, but soon Jay's budding entrepreneurial spirit took hold and he decided to make not only moves, but unlikely ones at that. Rather than signing with an already existing label, the route most rappers went, he wanted to create his own label. With the assistance and participation of good friends Damon Dash and Kareem "Biggs" Burke, he introduced Roc-A-Fella Records: a way to not only get his music out there, but to cut out the labels and keep the cash for himself and his partners. The independent thinking was, on paper, a ballsy play, especially from a guy who was basically unknown. But Jay and his boys had faith and soon Roc-A-Fella scored a distribution deal, initially with Priority Records and then with Def Jam. He had a label, he had a distributor, and more important-ly he had a record—1996's *Reasonable Doubt*.

Cut from true life, stripped-down, and urgent, *Reasonable Doubt* didn't set the charts (it peaked at number twenty-three) or cash registers on fire, but it was seen almost from the jump as stunning. It would also become not only a classic, but also the CD that Jay considered his masterwork. With the first hit single, "Ain't No Nigga," featuring Jay protégée, a then teenage Foxy Brown, *Reasonable Doubt* became the hip-hop album for the heads—a position no doubt helped by Jay's gangster drama themes, producers like DJ Premier, and rhyme assistance from the other half of Brooklyn's finest, Biggie. *Reasonable Doubt* would produce three other singles: "Can't Knock the Hustle" (featuring Mary J. Blige), "Dead Presi-dents," and "Feelin' It." The kid from Marcy and his upstart Roc-A-Fella had hit the ground running fast and furious, and overnight, NYC rap—hell, hip-hop—had a new savior and star.

With success under his belt, Jay dropped 1997's *In My Lifetime, Vol. 1*. With fans really paying attention and a more commercial sound, the CD hit

"REASONABLE DOUBT BECAME THE HIP-HOP ALBUM FOR THE HEADS— A POSITION NO DOUBT HELPED BY JAY'S GANGSTER DRAMA THEMES, PRODUCERS LIKE DJ PREMIER, AND RHYME ASSISTANCE FROM THE OTHER HALF OF BROOKLYN'S FINEST, BIGGIE."

number three on the charts. But even though it sold better, some didn't think it sounded better, and Jay's move toward a more radio-friendly approach and more obvious, poppy hooks worried his base. Sure there were some *Reasonable* moments ("Streets Is Watching"), but when you're sampling the Eagles' Glenn Frey—"The City Is Mine"—Jigga, please.

Jay kept up a rigorous work schedule and returned in 1998 with *Vol. 2 . . . Hard Knock Life*. His newfound love for pop hooks and sing-along choruses was in full effect, most notably on the hits "Can I Get A . . ." and "Hard Knock Life (Ghetto Anthem)," which brilliantly sampled the Broadway show *Annie*. Both songs were significant hits, and if Jay wasn't going as deep or autobiographical lyrically anymore, he was becoming a master of making crossover-savvy hip-hop that still had enough bite and poetic dexterity to satisfy the true believers. His third CD topped the charts and produced six hit singles, including "Money Ain't a Thang" (produced by Jermaine Dupri), "Jigga What, Jigga Who" (produced by Timbaland), and "It's Alright." Selling out? Maybe, but Jay was also cashing in—big time. He also had formed his own little family. There was chick rapper Amil, whose subsequent attempt to go solo would fail. The brightest light was Philly's Beanie Sigel, whose solo output included 2000's excellent *The Truth*, 2001's *The Reason*, and 2005's *The B. Coming*. Beanie also had a hand in the State Property posse, film, and clothing line, projects mainly overseen by Dame Dash.

Beanie's career was curtailed by frequent legal and jail issues—release from prison in August of 2005 on weapons charges after serving almost a full year, a very brief stint back in jail in November of 2005 for missed child support payments, and a 2006 assault conviction that resulted in a two-year probation sentence. There was also fellow Philly dude Freeway and Memphis Bleek. Bleek, a few years younger than Jay, grew up with his boss and had been down with Jay since the get. So deep is the love between the two that Jay, in verse, has basically promised that as long as he draws breath, Memph will have a career. To help foster that, on Bleek's last minimally selling CD, 2005's 534, Jay dropped the delicious solo joint "Dear Summer." In typical fashion, this throwaway gesture outshone Bleek's entire recording career.

As was now his pattern, Jay closed out the year with Vol. 3 . . . Life and Times of S. Carter (1999). The CD sold a gazillion copies and contained the smash "Big Pimpin'," featuring Houston's UGK and produced by Timbaland. Yet even though the album moved big numbers, many felt that the overreliance on guest stars (i.e., Mariah Carey, Dr. Dre, Juvenile, and the Roc crew) watered it down.

It was also in 1999 that Jay found himself faced with legal drama, when he was accused in the stabbing of Untertainment's CEO, Lance "Un" Rivera. Word on the street was that the normally laconic Carter lashed out because he thought that Rivera had a hand in bootlegging his CD. The incident allegedly took place at a NYC record release party for Q-Tip's CD Amplified.

In the beginning, Jay denied any involvement, after a felony assault charge indictment was handed down. Yet even so, he would later plead guilty to a misdemeanor assault charge and receive three years' probation. Not only did Jay escape jail time, he referenced the incident most famously on The Blueprint's "Izzo (H.O.V.A.)."

Perhaps chastened by less than astounding reviews and his legal issues, Jay made album number five a bit more scaled down. The Dynasty: Roc La Familia (2000) put the spotlight on the crew, although the boss did get to shine on The Neptunes' "I Just Wanna Love U (Give It 2 Me)." The album, as had been the routine, sold in the millions and went to number one.

With *The Blueprint* slated to come out, as fate would have it, on September 11, 2001, Jay spent much of the summer rallying the troops and hyping the CD. One such mechanism was his live shows. A few years prior, Jay along with the Ruff Ryders and DMX had taken hip-hop concerts to a whole new arena level with their sold-out, groundbreaking, top-of-the-line Hard Knock Life tour. No rap act, or at least none since the glory days of the early Run-D.M.C. shows, had pumped that much money and care into presenting their music, and the fans gobbled it up. With that in mind, Jay's much-promoted starring spot at the yearly HOT 97 radio-station-sponsored concert, Summer Jam, promised to be big. Jay delivered, debuting a new song, "Takeover." The cut had a verse that clowned Mobb Deep's Prodigy ("You's a ballerina/I got your pictures, I seen ya") and then added insult to injury by projecting huge pictures of Prodigy, as a kid, in a dance ensemble. If that wasn't enough to set the talk lines and hip-hop message boards on fire, *The Blueprint*'s version of "Takeover" also had a few choice things to say about Nas, ranging from the usual you-have-no-skills diss to trash talk about a former girlfriend, and mother of Nas's daughter, whom the two superstars had in common. As you'd figure, Jay's verses set it off and a fired-up Nas shot back with the searing "Ether." Both songs were mixtape staples and ratings boosts for NYC rap radio. "Ether" prompted Jay to volley back with "Super Ugly," dropping nasty verses over Nas's hit "Got Ur Self A . . ." "Super Ugly" was so vile—some such crap about Jay doing it with Nas's baby mama and leaving a used condom on the car seat—that even Jay would later admit his own mother disapproved. As you'd figure, the battle between two of rap's best lyricists and former friends was huge and created even more interest in *The Blueprint* as well as Nas's *Stillmatic*. Yet even if Jay and Nas had played nice, *The Blueprint* would have been major. The album not only sold well, it earned Jay the best reviews since his jump-off and was widely considered, along with his debut, as a superior hip-hop moment. The CD also found Jay going back to personal stories for inspiration. It had soul-drenched production, mainly from Kanye West, and was deeply intense and mature.

Jay revisited *The Blueprint* that same year with an *Unplugged* CD, featuring Jaguar Wright, Mary J. Blige, and The Roots as his house band. They would also later serve that function at Jay's farewell concert. The live CD showed just how good *The Blueprint*'s songs were and was also a big success. Next, Jay linked up with sometime guest artist R. Kelly for 2002's *The Best of Both Worlds*. The CD and ensuing tour were huge. Also huge was Jay's recorded output. Throughout 2002, he went into the studio and came out with about forty tracks, twenty-five of them forming the double CD *The Blueprint 2: The Gift & the Curse*. Despite the similar names, this set of CDs was less personal and a bit flashier. There were, as usual, a slew of hits. Topping the list was a reconfiguration of Tupac's "Me and My Girlfriend" on "'03 Bonnie and Clyde" with Beyoncé by his side, the first public acknowledgment of their status. Then in 2003 Jay returned the love by guesting on B's "Crazy in Love."

He had the hottest chick in the game wearin' his chain, millions upon millions, and the title of the king. All Jay needed to do was top himself. Again. He did that by announcing his planned retirement, but naturally he opted to exit with months of hoopla and a farewell album for the ages. *The Black Album* (2003) went straight to number one, like he always did, and contained hits like the Timbaland-produced "Dirt Off Your Shoulder" and "99 Problems," masterminded by former Def Jam co-founder Rick Rubin. *The Black Album* was so dope and so inspirational that Danger Mouse, best known as one-half of Gnarls Barkley, fused Jay's beats to the Beatles' *White Album* to come up with the mash-up masterwork *The Grey Album*, the rage of the Internet.

In 2004, Jay hit the good-bye trail for real. After giving a mountain of interviews, he topped it all off with the career retrospective, self-love fest Fade to Black concert. Held at NYC's Madison Square Garden, the sold-out show featured appearances from nearly every performer who'd ever

> ## "HE HAD THE HOTTEST CHICK IN THE GAME WEARIN' HIS CHAIN, MILLIONS UPON MILLIONS, AND THE TITLE OF THE KING. ALL JAY NEEDED TO DO WAS TOP HIMSELF."

been associated with Jigga and was not just an artistic high point, but became a fly DVD to boot. Jay had taken it from Marcy to Madison Square, fulfilling the hip-hop American dream. His stock was so high that when a second tour with R. Kelly imploded, Jay finished up selected tour dates on his own. The move effectively shut Kelly down, and although a flurry of lawsuits followed, Jay came out on top because he looked professional and stayed above the fray as Kelly bugged.

Jay had left the arena, and done it Jordan style—on top. What next? Simple. Become president of Def Jam Records. To sweeten the deal, and cause some more drama, Def Jam's parent company bought Roc-A-Fella, which resulted in some very public nastiness between former friends and partners Jay and Dame Dash. For his part, Dame would run a series of ventures, including his own label, which didn't do much, a lifestyle magazine (which folded), and various fashion concerns. He is currently concentrating more on nonmusical activities. With his new corporate gig, Jay became one of the few black major-label executives and one of a select number of rappers to make the move from studio to boardroom in more than figurehead position.

With his music career on lock, Jay kept on branching out into other fields. Currently he is a minority owner of the NBA's New Jersey Nets, who are slated to move to the BK within the next few years. He also co-owns a high-end sports club/bar, the 40/40 Club, which launched in NYC and now has an outpost in Atlantic City and Las Vegas, with more to come. So great is his clout and power that in 2006, after reading what he thought were negative statements from a Cristal representative, Jay banished the bubbly from his club and even excised mentions of it in his lyrics. The first evidence of which was 2006's spectacular *Reasonable Doubt* anniversary show, held at NYC's Radio City Music Hall. With a full string orchestra and Beyoncé filling in for Mary J., Jay re-created his classic album to rave reviews.

Jay continued to have a hand in the massively successful Roc-A-Wear apparel line, which in early 2007 he sold to clothing licensor Iconix for $204 million in cash. He also enjoyed a shoe deal with Reebok, the first non-athlete to do such. Along with everything else, Jay kept it tight at Def Jam. Under his tutelage, the label signed Young Jeezy and Rihanna. Both had very big albums, and Rihanna became the subject of gossip regarding her alleged relationship with the boss—a rumor that has been denied over and over.

Business was all good, but Jay still had a rapper's heart and drive, and in 2005 he stepped out of his exile with NYC's I Declare War gig. To make the show even more extra special, Jay brought out one special guest, Nas. Not only was beef over and out, but Nas signed to Def Jam that year. His appetite whetted by the love—and maybe because Def Jam needed a surefire hit—Jay announced that the hiatus was over and that he was going to come outta retirement with a new CD, *Kingdom Come*. The single "Show Me What You Got," which in a classic example of cross-marketing was also a Budweiser Select commercial, preceded the CD.

All of this paled in comparison to the buzz surrounding *Kingdom Come*. Although first-week sales were strong, approximately 700,000, the CD got very mixed reviews. It was pretty clear that while it's always cool to have Hova, *Kingdom Come* wasn't grade-A Jay. He would make a second attempt to win over critics in 2007 with his first concept album, *American Gangster*, inspired by the film of the same name, starring Denzel Washington as '70s Harlem drug kingpin Frank Lucas. You had to hand it to him. From Marcy to Madison Square and Avenue, no matter what Jay did or what cause he lent his name to—from shoes to bringing freshwater to Africa—he always remained on top.

Which of these brands has Jay-Z not endorsed?

a. Budweiser
b. Reebok
c. Hewlett-Packard
d. T-Mobile

POP quiz

BIG TIMERS:
'90s SOLO RAP

COMMON WAS FEATURED ON THE ROOTS' *THINGS FALL APART* ALONG WITH EVE (COMMON ON "ACT TOO" AND EVE ON "YOU GOT ME").

BLACK STAR IS COMPRISE
MOS DEF AND TALIB KWE
WHO FEATURED COMMOI
THE TRACK "RESPIRATION

EVE WAS IN THE RUFF RYDERS WITH DMX.

JA RULE WAS FEATURED ON THE JAY-Z SINGLE "CAN I GET A . . ."

DMX HAD A LONG-STANDING BEEF WITH JA RULE.

JAY-Z FEATURED EMINEM ON HIS SONG "RENEGADE."

EMINEM PRODUCED "RUNNIN'" FEATURING THE LATE TUPAC AND BIGGIE.

BIGGIE WAS ON "VICTORY" WI
BUSTA RHYMES ON DIDDY'S
(THEN PUFF DADDY) *NO
WAY OUT.*

Y BROWN WAS IN THE FIRM WITH NAS.

NAS WAS ON FAT JOE'S "JON BLAZE" WITH THE LATE BIG PUN.

BIG PUN WAS FEATURED ON *RYDE OR DIE VOL. 1* WITH JUVENILE.

E$P

E-40 HAS COLLABORATED WITH BOTH TOO $HORT AND MASTER P.

LIL JON SIGNED E-40 TO HIS IMPRINT BME.

ASTER P WAS ON MIA X'S "THE RTY DON'T STOP" WITH FOXY BROWN.

DIDDY WAS FEATURED ON LIL' KIM'S SINGLE "NO TIME."

LIL' KIM FEATURED MISSY ELLIOTT AND DA BRAT ON HER SINGLE "LADIES NIGHT."

DA BRAT WAS FEATURED ON BROOKE VALENTINE'S "GIRLFIGHT (REMIX)" WITH LIL JON.

CHAPTER 4

ALL TOGETHER NOW:

'90S RAP GROUPS

For whatever reason, hip-hop groups during the '90s seemed able to keep a lower profile than their solo counterparts. Maybe the media was still recovering from N.W.A. in the '80s, or maybe the Fugees' critical acclaim for *The Score* diverted attention away from other acts, because some of the most creative and influential hip-hop came from group efforts during the '90s. *De La Soul Is Dead*, *The Low End Theory*, and, of course, *Enter the Wu-Tang (36 Chambers)* were all released during the '90s, causing what had to have been a record-breaking amount of non-car-accident-related whiplash from necks turning so quickly and then bobbing uncontrollably. These groups spawned now commonplace artists like Method Man, Lauryn Hill, the RZA, Guru, and at least eight more courtesy of the Wu-Tang Clan alone. The '80s may have been the groundwork, but the '90s took collaborative efforts to the next level.

Gang Starr

Gang Starr didn't have big hits, their albums didn't go platinum—in fact they barely went gold. But even so, they rank as one of rap's most revered and defiantly underground duos because they played by their own rules.

Gang Starr was Beantowner Guru (Keith Elam) and H-Town's DJ Premier (Chris Martin). From 1989's *No More Mr. Nice Guy* through their swan song, 1999's *Full Clip: A Decade of Gang Starr*, they brought literate lyrics and a fluid, funky, and jazzy sound. Their vibe could be felt on classic albums *Step in the Arena* (1991) and the following year's *Daily Operation*. If you don't own either, cop them—now.

On their own, GS also wrecked shop. The rough-voiced Guru headed up the innovative series of Jazzmatazz projects in the late '90s and worked with a host of performers including jazz legend Herbie Hancock. As for Premo? His client list includes the late B.I.G., Nas, Jay, and Xtina's 2006 Grammy-winning smash "Ain't No Other Man." The irony is that Premo crafted hits for everyone but his own group, but you know Gang Starr wouldn't have changed up their steez to cash in. Nuff respect.

Native Tongues

The tail end of the '80s was the jump-off for a loose-knit clique called Native Tongues. Creative and cutting edge, Native Tongues was a funky lab for hip-hop's finest moments. The New York–based crew included De La Soul, London transplant Monie Love (now a popular radio jock and then the gal behind the exuberant 1990 hit "Monie in the Middle"), Queen Latifah, the Jungle Brothers, and A Tribe Called Quest. They were all friends and frequently popped up on each other's tracks, e.g. De La's "Buddy."

A Tribe Called Quest

Q-Tip (Jonathan Davis) and Phife (Malik Taylor) grew up in Queens and Tip met Ali Shaheed Muhammad in high school. Phife and Tip were MCs, Ali was a DJ—and they thought about forming a group. Luckily the guys went to school with the Jungle Brothers. The JBs (Baby Bam, DJ Sammy B, and Mike Gee) were an influential act, formed in 1986, who released several albums including 1989's seminal *Done by the Forces of Nature*, and they took a shine to their classmates and dubbed the nascent trio A Tribe Called Quest. Soon Tribe began to gig around NYC, and in 1989 Tip made a cameo on De La Soul's *3 Feet High and Rising*. A year later, Tribe dropped "Description of a Fool." That same year Tribe signed to Jive and released *People's Instinctive Travels and the Paths of Rhythm*. Like their friends De La, Tribe often sampled jazz and rock, e.g., "Can I Kick It?," which flipped Lou Reed's "Walk on the Wild Side." Also like De La, Tribe paid a price, literally, for unauthorized sampling. As good as their first album was, they outdid themselves in 1991 with the classic *The Low End Theory*, whose vibey grooves were a major influence on rap and helped jump-start neo-soul.

The album was a revelation and yielded the thunderous posse cut "Scenario," featuring Busta Rhymes, then a member of Leaders of the New School, who had a minor hit with "Case of the P.T.A." Tribe followed up their triumph with another, '93's *Midnight Marauders*, it too one of rap's finest. The CD had a somewhat tougher sound and contained Tribe's infectious "Award Tour." As always, the combo of Tip and Phife's volley of wordplay and Ali's seamless beats were state of the art.

In '94 Tribe joined the Lollapalooza Festival, which resulted in even more support from college alt-rock fans, and then came back in 1996 with *Beats, Rhymes and Life*. The album marked the introduction of the late J Dilla to Tribe's production staff, and while a solid collection, it was no match for what the group had done before. Also disappointing was 1998's *The Love Movement*. While on tour, Tribe announced their breakup.

Post-Tribe, Q-Tip appeared in several films, including Spike Lee's *She Hate Me*, and DJed throughout NYC. He also popped up on other artists' tracks (most notably Janet Jackson's 1997 "Got 'Til It's Gone") and then had his own hit with the flamboyant "Vivrant Thing" (1999). Tip would record two other solo CDs, but neither saw the light of day.

Along with Raphael Saadiq and ex–En Voguer Dawn Robinson, Ali formed soul supergroup Lucy Pearl. After the group's quick rise and fall, he returned to production, working on D'Angelo's *Brown Sugar*. Phife put out an indie CD, which didn't get much attention, and in 2004 and 2006 Tribe reunited for a handful of gigs.

At which music festival did A Tribe Called Quest perform in 1994?

a. Coachella
b. Woodstock
c. Lollapalooza
d. Bonnaroo

POP QUIZ

De La Soul

Like Tribe, De La Soul colored outside the lines and brought a free-form, idiosyncratic attitude, which they called the "D.A.I.S.Y. age" (Da Inner Sound, Y'all).

The trio formed in the late '80s when Posdnuos (Kelvin Mercer), Trugoy the Dove (David Jolicoeur), and Mase (Vincent Mason) were Long Island high school students. Their demo tape, "Plug Tunin'," was heard by fellow Islander Prince Paul, leader and producer for the popular rap band Stetsasonic, who pre-dated The Roots by a good decade. Paul would help De La ink a deal with Tommy Boy Records.

Prince Paul—the dude behind the once unique, now ubiquitous inclusion of skits on albums—produced De La's 1989 debut, *3 Feet High and Rising*. De La's ebullient sound was left of center and light-years removed from the dominant sound of hardcore rap. Native Tongues was now considered the future. "Me Myself and I" became a Top 40 pop hit in the United States (number one R&B) and the album went gold. With success came heat. The '60s pop act the Turtles sued De La for sampling without permission. The forces of fogeydom won the case, and it not only hurt De La Soul but hip-hop as a whole, since all samples had to be legally cleared. The legal issues resulted in numerous albums being held up until all samples were cleared.

De La Soul Is Dead finally came in '91. It earned mixed reviews, and its darker perspective (the album cover was a knocked-over daisy plant) didn't connect with many 3 Feet High fans. The album produced one hit, "Ring Ring Ring (Ha Ha Hey)." De La Soul's next move was the hard-hitting Buhloone Mindstate. Reviews were supportive, but sales were less so. The same fate awaited the overlooked Stakes Is High (1996), which featured Common and Mos Def.

Four years later, De La Soul dropped Art Official Intelligence: Mosaic Thump, the first in a proposed three-album series. The CD debuted top ten. Phase two, AOI: Bionix, also fared well. Following its release, De La Soul left Tommy Boy and signed with another indie and came through with 2004's The Grind Date. Two years later the third part of the trilogy, The Impossible Mission: TV Series—Pt.1, was released. De La Soul would enjoy a comeback of sorts when in 2005 they appeared on the Gorillaz hit "Feel Good Inc."

Naughty by Nature

It's not easy to be catchy enough for the pop charts but rugged enough for the street. Naughty by Nature managed to do just that.

Products of East Orange, New Jersey, NBN came together in '86 when MCs Treach (Anthony Criss), Vinnie (Vincent Brown), and DJ Kay Gee (Keir Gist) were all at the same high school. Their original name was New Style, and they were regulars at hometown talent shows. A few years down the road, the guys were spotted by local celeb Queen Latifah. She signed the group now known as Naughty by Nature to her management company, Flavor Unit, and helped them get a deal at her label, Tommy Boy. Their self-titled debut came in 1991 and immediately spawned the inescapable "O.P.P.," which sampled the Jackson 5's "ABC." Loaded with double entendres (what did you think "P" stood for?), "O.P.P." went top ten and made NBN stars. Gangsta Romeo Treach used his good looks to begin an acting career with credits that included *Juice*, *Poetic Justice*, and, in 2006, *The Sopranos*, as the rapper who's shot in the ass.

NBN took their popularity to new heights with 1993's *19 Naughty III*. It boasted another ghetto anthem, "Hip-Hop Hooray," and went platinum. *Poverty's Paradise* (1995) was NBN's last record on Tommy Boy, and while it didn't yield sing-along 'hood hits, it won the Grammy for Best Rap Album. The trio took some time off and in 1999 Treach married Pepa (Sandra Denton) of Salt-N-Pepa fame. Kay Gee concentrated on outside production duties, crafting hits for Zhané and Next.

On a new label, NBN came back with *Nineteen Naughty Nine: Nature's Fury*. "Jamboree," with Zhané, did pretty well, but just as things were back on track, Kay Gee left to work full-time on his label and production gigs. Treach and Vinnie regrouped and *IIcons* came in 2002. The CD sold well, but would be Naughty's hip-hop good-bye.

OutKast

André Benjamin (Dré) and Antwan Patton (Big Boi) went to the same high school in Atlanta's East Point district. While still teens they formed OutKast and became creatively aligned with ATL's Organized Noize Productions, whose members included Sleepy Brown and who were behind TLC's hit "Waterfalls." Along with their production skills, Organized Noize were at the core of the Dungeon Family, whose ranks included OutKast and fellow southerners Goodie Mob. Although all five of Goodie Mob's albums did respectable numbers, OutKast would overshadow the foursome. Yet even with their lower profile, Goodie Mob warrants love, if only because one of its founding members was Cee-Lo Green—one-half of Gnarls Barkley ("Crazy").

After getting in with Organized Noize, OutKast signed with LaFace, run by Kenneth "Babyface" Edmonds and LA Reid, and released "Player's Ball." The single climbed to the top spot on the rap charts, went gold, and whetted everyone's appetite for what was coming.

That was 1994's *Southernplayalisticadillacmuzik*. A top twenty hit, the album would sell a million copies, and in '95, OutKast nailed Best New Rap Group of the Year at The Source Awards. Hip-hop now had a new geographical laboratory—the Dirty South.

The year 1996 produced *ATLiens*. Also platinum, it hit number two and had the gold crossover single "Elevators (Me & You)" and the Top 40 title track. OutKast then dropped '98's *Aquemini*, which doubled the platinum status and hit number two. While there weren't huge hit singles, the CD was a critical fave.

OutKast's triumph was marred when their single "Rosa Parks" became the subject of a lawsuit instigated by the now deceased civil rights leader, who maintained that the rappers had hijacked her name in order to big up their music. After much to and fro, the suit would be dismissed sometime before Parks's death in October of 2005.

Dré changed his moniker to André 3000 and with Big Boi gave fans *Stankonia* (2000). Another critical and commercial explosion, the CD had two state-of-the-art singles, "B.O.B." and "Ms. Jackson"—their first number one pop. The album debuted at number two and went quadruple platinum. Now one of rap's biggest acts, OutKast landed a one-two punch with 2003's *Speakerboxxx/The Love Below*, a double album by separate artists: Big Boi's *Speakerboxxx* and André's *The Love Below*. The divide-and-conquer move fueled rumors that OutKast's days were numbered, but whatever was going on, it didn't affect sales. The double album was a multiplatinum sensation, grabbed the Grammy for Album of the Year in 2004, and generated two crossover number ones, Big Boi's "The Way You Move" and André's "Hey Ya." OutKast had become a hip-hop act that even people not into rap liked, which, depending on your point of view, can be a gift or a curse.

After obtaining mass appeal, Boi and André embarked on new creative ventures. Big Boi started a label, Purple Ribbon, and André did some films and, judging by his wardrobe, spent a lot of time shopping. In 2006 the guys came back together on *Idlewild*, a film and CD. Both the film and the CD received mixed reviews and died a quick death.

What was the name of OutKast's debut album?

a. Southernplayalisticadillacmuzik

b. Aquemini

c. Stankonia

d. ATLiens

POP quiz

The Fugees

Like OutKast and Naughty, The Fugees figured out a way to stay true while reaching out to potentially unexpected consumers—er, fans.

Lauryn Hill and Samuel Prakazrel Michel met while attending high school in New Jersey and started making music. Over time Pras's childhood friend Wyclef Jean, a BK resident by way of Haiti, came on board and the trio dubbed themselves Tranzlator Crew. Gigs were held, demos were recorded, then shopped, and in 1993 the crew signed to Ruffhouse, which was distributed through Columbia Records. Tranzlator Crew became The Fugees, a reference to Pras and Clef's "refugee" (a.k.a. immigrant) status. The Fugees released *Blunted on Reality* in 1994, and with its tough and intelligent vibe, it did quite well, mainly on the strength of singles "Nappy Heads" and "Vocab." The former song featured the trio's blend of rap, reggae, and Lauryn's sultry singing and rapping.

Whatever success The Fugees enjoyed paled in comparison to what was on the horizon, *The Score* (1996). The first single, "Fu-Gee-La," was released in January of 1996 and soon after reached gold status. "Ready or Not" was the second single off of the LP and featured an Enya sample, which almost caused yet another sampling-related lawsuit. Other standout tracks included a cover of Roberta Flack's '70s classic "Killing Me Softly," which showcased Lauryn's vocals. *The Score* became the must-have CD, hit number one pop, and would sell over five million copies. The Fugees were now one of rap's most successful groups, and the bigger they got the more folks began to wonder when the trio's obvious star, Lauryn, was gonna break out.

> **"THE FUGEES WERE NOW ONE OF RAP'S MOST SUCCESSFUL GROUPS, AND THE BIGGER THEY GOT THE MORE FOLKS BEGAN TO WONDER WHEN THE TRIO'S OBVIOUS STAR, LAURYN, WAS GONNA BREAK OUT."**

Ironically it was Clef, who wrote and produced most of The Fugees' songs, who jumped out first with '97's *The Carnival*. As for Lauryn? You know that story. Pras had the hit "Ghetto Supastar (That Is What You Are)" and Clef became the hitmaking go-to guy—witness Shakira's "Hips Don't Lie" (2006). His six solo CDs put The Fugees' tenure in question. A half-hearted attempt to regroup was bandied about in 2005, but outside of a single no one heard and a captivating appearance in *Dave Chappelle's Block Party* (2006), nothing jumped off.

The Black Eyed Peas

While ain't nobody mad at having a catchy little ditty (or watching Fergie drop it like it's hot), the Black Eyed Peas make '90s crossover king MC Hammer look gangsta.

Native Angelenos, BEP got their start in, yes, high school when will.i.am and apl.de.ap were in the break-dancing crew Tribal Nation. Over time they decided to stop spinning on their heads, go into rap, and became Atban Klann, which meant A Tribe Beyond a Nation—hello, biters. In '92 Eazy-E signed the Klann up, but not surprisingly, his staff at Ruthless didn't "get" the group, and while AK recorded an album, it never saw the light of day because their label had no clue how to market something that wasn't gangsta rap.

Atban Klann's deal essentially died when in 1995, so did Eazy. Yet will and apl pushed onward and with an added dancer/MC, Taboo, became the Black Eyed Peas. The guys started gigging around L.A., wowing the kids with their flow as well as their moves. They signed to Interscope Records and released their debut, *Behind the Front* (1998), which received great reviews. BEP was gathering steam and fans appreciated the group's affinity for live instrumentation and "positive" messages.

Now working full-time with background singer Kim Hill, BEP dropped *Bridging the Gap* in 2000. The album contained the single "Request Line" featuring Macy Gray as well as other guest spots from Jurassic 5, De La Soul, and Mos Def. While the respect continued, sales were flat. That is, until BEP decided to go in a "new" direction when they replaced Kim with singer Stacy Ferguson a.k.a. Fergie. Hot of bod and big of voice, Ferg took center stage on 2003's *Elephunk* and soon the combo of her star power and will's pop chops gave BEP a huge hit. They attacked the Top 40 with the ginormous singles "Where Is the Love?," "Hey Mama," and "Let's Get It Started," which rapidly became an all-purpose theme song/anthem. Just like that, BEP were major, though with much of the focus on Fergie, their rap cred was questionable. The Peas got even bigger (and more pop) with 2005's *Monkey Business*. Thanks to the not-so-subtle romp "My Humps" (which left little doubt as to the Peas' strong suit), the CD went multiplatinum and the foursome earned a slew of industry awards, including four Grammy noms and a win for Best Rap Performance by a Duo or Group. In 2006 Fergie released *The Dutchess*, a frothy pop treat that sold strongly. As for BEP's musical mastermind? Well, will released a solo album *Songs About Girls* in 2007 and continues to be one of the serious producer players, creating incredibly hot hits for everyone from John Legend to Busta Rhymes. The other two Peas? They continued to get paid for doing God knows what.

In 2000, the Black Eyed Peas single "Request Line" featured what singer?

a.   Jill Scott
b.   Macy Gray
c.   Erykah Badu
d.   Lauryn Hill

POP QUIZ

The Roots

Even though it isn't so, Philadelphia's The Roots are widely credited with bringing live instrumentation to hip-hop. Along with their own career, they've backed up numerous rap acts—most notably Jay-Z (he signed the band to Def Jam in 2005).

Rapper Black Thought (Tariq Trotter) and drummer ?uestlove (Ahmir Thompson) became friends in high school. Throughout the late '80s the team played in school and talent shows and started getting a rep in Philly. They soon linked up with bassist Hub (Leonard Hubbard) and rapper Malik B (Malik Abdul Basit-Smart) and became a hot underground act. The band recorded *Organix* in 1993 and signed with Geffen that same year. Their major-label debut, *Do You Want More?!!!??!*, came in '95, and thanks to constant touring, The Roots began to find an audience outside of traditional hip-hop circles. They also added beatboxer Rahzel and keyboardist Scott Storch, who after leaving The Roots (and being replaced by Kamal) would have himself a big ol' production/songwriting career.

The year 1996 brought *Illadelph Halflife*, whose first single, "What They Do," featured a music video in which the group parodied many of rap's stereotypical clichés. Although when compared to other platinum rap acts The Roots didn't fare well, their rep as a live act propelled them, and 1999's *Things Fall Apart* was a major success all around. It contained 2000 Grammy winner "You Got Me" (featuring Erykah Badu), their most commercial single to date. *Phrenology* arrived in 2002, but The Roots became bogged down with label drama—a situation that was fixed by forming Okayplayer. The imprint's first release was 2004's *The Tipping Point*, which like *Phrenology* had fantastic reviews but sluggish sales. The Roots then aligned themselves with Def Jam, the HQ of mainstream rap. Yet even the association with Jigga and company couldn't elevate *Game Theory*'s (2006) sales.

Wu-Tang Clan

The Wu-Tang Clan is equal parts business arrangement and meeting ground between nine solo stars. Consisting of RZA (Robert Diggs), GZA/The Genius (Gary Grice), the late Ol' Dirty Bastard (Russell Jones), Method Man (Clifford Smith), Raekwon the Chef (Corey Woods), Ghostface Killah (Dennis Coles), U-God (Lamont Hawkins), Inspectah Deck (Jason Hunter), and Masta Killa (Elgin Turner), the Wu made dark, idiosyncratic, and rugged music that was noncommercial and 'hood-approved. Oh, and dope as all get-out.

The members of Wu grew up in Brooklyn and Staten Island (a.k.a. Shaolin). In 1991 RZA, as Prince Rakeem, recorded "Ooh, I Love You Rakeem" for Tommy Boy. The experience at the label soured him on the industry, and with his own ideas, he decided to try doing things his way with some friends. Two of those friends—Genius and Ol' Dirty Bastard—had begun laying down the brick and mortar for what would eventually become the Wu. Soon after he heard about what was up, RZA was on board. Shortly afterward, a hodgepodge of various cousins and close neighborhood friends—Meth, Ghostface, Raekwon, U-God, Inspectah Deck, and Masta Killa—joined him. The guys all put their heads together and the end result of the think tank was to create—actually unfurl—an artistic hip-hop project that along with being musically on point would also serve as an industry unto itself.

The group took their name and a major portion of their vibe from classic kung-fu flicks, Eastern philosophy, numerology, Five Percenter teachings, Buddhism, mathematics, and comic books, among others. The jump-off of all those interests and thematic input was the 1993 indie single "Protect Ya Neck." The street anthem created much noise, but the Clan decided that the way to go and cash in with the greatest payoff was to hold out, stick to their guns, and wait until they found a record deal that would allow each member to sign to other labels, as well as let them record as Wu-Tang. Loud Records agreed to this radically unusual setup, and in '93 *Enter the Wu-Tang (36 Chambers)* appeared. Fans and the press dug it, and '94's single "C.R.E.A.M." made them serious players. Soon GZA, RZA, Raekwon, Method Man, and Ol' Dirty Bastard landed solo deals, most of which featured RZA handling production duties. He was first up with his newly formed group, the Gravediggaz. The group released an album in 1994 entitled *6 Feet Deep* that ended up going gold. Next, Meth went for his with '94's *Tical*. His thug appeal was later bumped up a notch with his 1996 Grammy-winning duet with Mary J. Blige, "You're All I Need/I'll Be There." Next up was ODB and *Return to the 36 Chambers* (1995). The CD had the off-kilter hits "Brooklyn Zoo" and "Shimmy Shimmy Ya" and went gold. That same year saw Raekwon's seminal *Only Built 4 Cuban Linx* (which featured Ghostface) and Genius/GZA's *Liquid Swords*. Both albums were instant classics. In 1996 Ghost finally went solo with *Ironman*.

As for the Clan, they reentered with '97's double album *Wu-Tang Forever*. It sold over 600,000 in the first week and yielded the hit "Triumph." The CD also introduced soon-to-be tenth member Cappadonna.

The Wu returned in 1998 with a flurry of solo joints, including *RZA as Bobby Digital in Stereo*, Method Man's *Tical 2000: Judgement Day* (which debuted at number two), and GZA's *Beneath the Surface*. In 1999, ODB unleashed *Nigga Please*, which hit stores while he was in rehab. Meth teamed up with former Def Squad associate, Wu affiliate, and crackup/stoner pal Redman on *Blackout!*—kicking off a lengthy recording and cinematic partnership based around a love of weed and Meth/Red's stoner comic à la Cheech and Chong timing. Ghost's brilliant *Supreme Clientele* marked Y2K.

Despite the love, the Wu franchise was in danger of getting dangerously overexposed, and perhaps that's why for most of 2000 they kept on the low. That same year ODB faced various legal woes. Things had appeared to be turning around for the beloved but troubled star, but then he escaped from a court-ordered rehab facility and went on the lam. Amazingly, he popped up (and avoided capture) in the fall of 2000 during an NYC show in support of *The W*. He was finally apprehended soon after in Philly, cut a deal, and in '01 went to prison.

Undaunted, Wu reunited for *Iron Flag* (2001). Yet the end of an era came in 2004 when ODB died of a heart attack. The group never disbanded, but clearly ODB's death had changed things up and put things in a new light. While various members continued to record (RZA in particular focused more on soundtrack work, most notably Quentin Tarantino's *Kill Bill* and Jim Jarmusch's *Ghost Dog: The Way of the Samurai*), outside of Ghostface's widely revered *Fishscale* (2006) and the follow-up *More Fish* (2006), the Wu-Tang Clan had lost their juice, but not for long. The group reunited in 2007 to record their fifth album, *The 8 Diagrams*, featuring previously recorded material from ODB.

Bone Thugs-N-Harmony

From the unlikely hometown of Cleveland, Ohio, hip-hop collective Bone Thugs-N-Harmony are more barbershop than they are standard hip-hop group. Known for their instantly recognizable style that includes insanely fast rhyming and unlikely harmonies, the group peaked early, but still remain classic despite their short-lived fame. Discovered in the early '90s by the late Eazy-E, under their original moniker, B.O.N.E. Enterpri$e, the group recorded and self-released their first album, *Faces of Death*. Consisting of "brothers" Krayzie Bone, Layzie Bone, Bizzy Bone, Flesh-N-Bone, and Wish Bone, the group soon changed their name to Bone Thugs-N-Harmony.

Their first release for Eazy's Ruthless Records was the EP *Creepin On Ah Come Up*, which introduced the group as something entirely different: dark, sinister, and wholly original. The eight-track EP featured "Thuggish Ruggish Bone," which helped the EP eventually go platinum.

Following the modest success of *Creepin*, Bone Thugs delivered their first full-length for Ruthless in 1995, *E. 1999 Eternal*, which debuted at number one on the Billboard 200 chart and featured more of Bone's now trademark dark, evil-inspired lyrics, as well as many an homage to one of their favorite pastimes: smoking weed. In addition to the dark lyrical content, the album's artwork was chock-full of cryptic symbols and occult-inspired images. Though the album did well upon its initial release, it was the death of Eazy-E that helped propel it into the sales stratosphere. Initially released with the song "Crossroad," the group rerecorded the track as "Tha Crossroads," a tribute to Eazy, which turned into a huge smash both in record stores and on MTV, as did tracks like "1st of tha Month."

After the huge success of *Eternal*, Bone Thugs' 1997 release *The Art of War* also debuted at number one on the Billboard charts, but quickly faded. The album was an ambitious double-disc release, focusing again on gloomy subject matter, but also making references aplenty of the Sun Tzu book of the same name. Also on the somewhat bloated album were straight disses of Chicago's Crucial Conflict, who were targeted for duplicating Bone's quick rhyming style.

The group's third offering, 2000's *BTNHResurrection*, debuted at number two on the Billboard charts, but again disappeared after excellent first-week sales. Rumors of a possible breakup were fueled by the obvious beef between Bizzy Bone and the rest of the group.

The year 2000 saw Flesh-N-Bone sentenced to eleven years in the pen following gun charges, and 2002 saw the release of *Thug World Order*, which did well at first, debuting at number twelve, but again disappeared quickly. Bizzy was asked to leave the group in 2002 but rejoined a year later, only to be asked to leave again in 2005.

The year 2007 brought a new Bone Thugs album, *Strength & Loyalty*. Bizzy Bone was the only member absent and the LP featured production from every producer you've ever heard of, including Jermaine Dupri and will.i.am. The first single, "I Tried," was produced by Akon, and the album featured guest spots from Mariah Carey, Bow Wow, Yolanda Adams, and Twista.

Which member of Bone Thugs-N-Harmony was asked to leave the group in 2002 and again in 2005?

    a. Krayzie Bone

    b. Wish Bone

    c. Layzie Bone

    d. Bizzy Bone

POP QUIZ

Cypress Hill

Ganja. Smoke. Weed. Pot. The Chronic. Hemp. Bud. Mary Jane. Dank. Herb. Reefer. Dro. Trees. Hydro. Cannabis. No matter what you call it or how you smoke it, there's no denying that marijuana has long been an integral component of hip-hop. Weed is such a central facet of hip-hop culture that it's considered newsworthy when a rap star *doesn't* hit the bong on the regular. These days the only people who smoke more weed than hip-hop fans are rappers and producers.

At hip-hop concerts not headlined by Will Smith or MC Hammer, the over-whelming odor of pot smoke can generally be smelled for miles around. In rap concerts, shout-outs to pot and enthusiastic plugs for the stoner lifestyle are nearly as ubiquitous and hoary a crowd-participation cliché as admonishing concertgoers to throw their hands in the air and wave them around in manner that suggests that they do not, in fact, nurse a strong opinion one way or another as to how said action is viewed or judged by others. News reports of rappers getting busted for pot are so common-place that they rarely cause much of an uproar or hurt rappers' careers.

Pot plays a number of crucial roles in the lives of hip-hop artists and fans. It smooths away the rough edges of an often heartless capitalist world. It enhances the sensual quality of listening to hip-hop—especially the production. For certain rappers it seems to enhance creativity. Tupac, for example, was famous for marathon recording sessions where, while drunk and high, he recorded songs in twenty minutes that would go on to sell millions and cement his legend. It's almost impossible to imagine the legacies of artists like Redman, Snoop Dogg, Dr. Dre, Devin the Dude, MF DOOM, and Madlib without their herb of choice, and no we're not talking about coriander, though that certainly has its fans within the hip-hop community as well.

Even in a genre as strongly associated with pot as hip-hop, the venerable Los Angeles trio Cypress Hill is legendary for its boundless enthusiasm for the deplorable practice of smoking marijuana. On "Smokefest 1999," by no less an authority on herbal relaxation than Tash of the Alkaholiks (a group that knows a little something about getting fucked up), Cypress Hill frontman B-Real was called "the smokiest cat in rap music." When De La Soul looked for a guest rapper to espouse the virtues of weed to a reluctant potential smoker on "Peer Pressure," it was B-Real (and to a lesser extent producer J Dilla) they sought out.

Yes, marijuana has been very good to Cypress Hill, and in return they've done everything in their power to promote the gospel of nature's healing leaf. But the group is noteworthy for much more than just its tireless campaign to promote illegal drug abuse among young people. They're also the top-selling Latin group in hip-hop history and the first Hispanic group to have platinum and multiplatinum albums. They've broken down doors for Hispanic artists and blazed paths as well as grass, serving as an inspiration for the flood of popular Hispanic hip-hop acts that followed. And though Cypress Hill couldn't maintain the popularity of their early-'90s heyday, they've managed to stay current by embracing numerous trends and altering their sound to suit the times. Lastly, they've smartly cultivated a loyal grassroots following (emphasis on the grass part) by touring constantly, often as the primary hip-hop act with big package tours like Lollapalooza and Smokin Grooves, where they have shared the stage with luminaries like The Fugees and A Tribe Called Quest.

"[CYPRESS HILL HAS] BROKEN DOWN DOORS FOR HISPANIC ARTISTS AND BLAZED PATHS AS WELL AS GRASS, SERVING AS AN INSPIRATION FOR THE FLOOD OF POPULAR HISPANIC HIP-HOP ACTS THAT FOLLOWED."

Cypress Hill formed in the mid-'80s, when Louis Freese, who rapped under the name B-Real, met Senen and Ulpiano Sergio Reyes, brothers who rapped under the names Sen Dog and Mellow Man Ace respectively. Mellow Man Ace would leave the group before its Columbia debut to embark on a solo career that included "Mentirosa," a bilingual hit single that taught an entire nation of clueless white boys very basic Spanglish. After dabbling in the street life as teenagers, Sen Dog and B-Real joined forces with producer DJ Muggs, whose dark, stormy production became the group's sonic trademark. Each member of Cypress Hill fulfills a crucial role within the group. B-Real is the charismatic frontman with the comically sinister lyrics and stylized nasal whine. Sen Dog is his loyal sidekick/hype man with a gruff, distinctive bark, while Muggs is the group's sonic architect and DJ.

Cypress Hill's self-titled 1991 debut album was a landmark in West Coast hip-hop history, a stone-cold classic that *The Source* named one of the top 100 hip-hop albums of all time. The album explored the dark, paranoid violent side of the stoner lifestyle in tense, aggression-filled hits like "Hand on the Pump" and "How I Could Just Kill a Man," an irresistible street anthem where B-Real contemplates some of the different scenarios that could lead him to indulge his inner mass murderer, from harassment from the fuzz to some fool breaking into his car. "How I Could Just Kill a Man" is one of those hip-hop classics that never stops ricocheting through popular culture. Throw it on at a party today and you're sure to have heads bopping while aging Gen-Xers with thinning hair wipe away a single perfect tear in fond, melancholy remembrance of raucous college parties past. DJ Muggs ends the song with a shout-out to punk band Suicidal Tendencies in the form of a cheeky reference to "All I wanted was a Pepsi," the famous catchphrase from the group's hit song "Institutionalized." Both DJ Muggs and Cypress Hill would go on to rock audiences aggressively with subsequent releases.

Cypress Hill went triple platinum and secured the trio's place in hip-hop history. The group's follow-up, 1993's *Black Sunday*, became an even bigger hit, going quadruple platinum largely on the strength of the monster hit "Insane in the Brain," a thoroughly tongue-in-cheek ode to mental illness driven by some of Muggs's most inspired, infectious production and a ubiquitous music video. Emboldened by the success of their first two albums, the group began branching out. DJ Muggs produced the sick bagpipe beats behind the House of Pain smash "Jump Around," yet another instant party-rocking classic from the man behind "Insane in the Brain" and "How I Could Just Kill a Man." The group also journeyed into the rock world by collaborating with Pearl Jam (on "Real Thing") and Sonic Youth (on the tellingly titled "I Love You Mary Jane," a fond tribute to, well, you can probably figure that out yourself) on the *Judgment Night* soundtrack. While the Emilio Estevez vehicle it accompanies has mercifully been forgotten, the *Judgment Night* soundtrack became a landmark in rap/rock fusion thanks to its historic pairings of everyone from Del tha Funkee Homosapien and Dinosaur Jr. to Sir Mix-A-Lot and Mudhoney.

Cypress Hill then joined the exclusive likes of Louise Lasser, Frank Zappa, Milton Berle, Sinéad O'Connor, and Adrien Brody in getting banned from *Saturday Night Live* thanks to the group's on-air pot-smoking and destruction of its instruments following a performance of "I Ain't Goin' Out Like That."

But such bad-boy antics did nothing to dim the group's popularity with fans, especially college students who shared the group's love of mind-altering substances. A backpack with a Cypress Hill sticker on it consequently has multiple meanings: it says the owner rocks out to Cypress Hill's gloomy brand of hip-hop, but it also asserts membership in the international fraternal order of pot smokers. To the uninitiated, a Cypress Hill poster on a college dorm room simply conveys enjoyment of the band's music. But to those in the know it sends out a more furtive message: "Hey, wanna smoke a bowl later?"

Cypress Hill helped build a fan base by touring with traveling alternative rock festival Lollapalooza in 1994 and 1995 alongside a veritable who's who of rock royalty. The trio also played the 1994 incarnation of that great granddaddy of American rock concerts, Woodstock, where they introduced Eric Bobo, a respected musician (and son of jazz legend Willie Bobo) who'd go on to tour extensively with the group and with the Beastie Boys. Cypress Hill also appeared on the legendary "Homerpalooza" episode of *The Simpsons* alongside fellow music-world luminaries Sonic Youth, the Smashing Pumpkins and, um, Peter Frampton.

Nineteen ninety-five's *Cypress Hill III: Temples of Boom* went platinum and sold one and a half million copies, but wasn't anywhere near as well-received as the albums that preceded it. The formula that had served the group so well on their classic first albums was starting to wear a little thin. Not surprisingly, they headed in different directions for solo outings. DJ Muggs produced a pair of *Soul Assassins* compilations featuring impressive rosters of hip-hop talent, including Dr. Dre, RZA, GZA, KRS-One, Xzibit, Wyclef Jean, Mobb Deep, and many more. Muggs also mentored in-demand producer the Alchemist and released a heavily rock-influenced solo album (2003's *Dust*) and a well-received album-length collaboration with GZA of the Wu-Tang Clan (2005's *Grandmasters*), which also led to a remix album.

Sen Dog, meanwhile, formed the rap-rock group SX-10 and recorded an album with older bro Mellow Man Ace as the Reyes Brothers (2006's *Ghetto Therapy*). Not to be left out, B-Real was briefly part of the rap group Psycho Realm and has turned in memorable guest appearances on high-profile songs like OutKast's "Xplosion," "East Coast/West Coast Killas," a Dr. Dre–produced 1996 New York/California posse cut with Nas, RBX, and KRS-One that set out to kill the intercoastal beef (needless to say, Tupac and Biggie could vouch that that turned out real well), and

Snoop Dogg's "Vato," a retro banger that casts a fond look back at the days back when *Cypress Hill* and *The Chronic* boomed defiantly out of every low-rider in L.A.

Nineteen ninety-eight's underrated *IV* found the trio exploring everything from surprisingly empathetic character studies about a corrupt cop and other outsiders ("Looking Through the Eye of a Pig") to bawdy sex raps ("I Remember That Freak Bitch") to gloomy fatalism ("Tequila Sunrise"). The disc was the group's weakest-selling album to date. By the time Cypress Hill released album number five, it was clear a change of sound was needed, so the fellas consummated their long-standing flirtation with rock and roll with *Skull & Bones*, a double album with one disc devoted to relatively straightforward hip-hop and another devoted to rap-rock. The project's first singles were tracks called "(Rock) Superstar" and "(Rap) Superstar" that took jaundiced, cynical looks at the starmaking machinery and the bleak, Darwinian world of major-label politics. Cypress Hill were battle-scarred veterans warning newcomers of the treachery of a music industry more snake-infested than air-bound Samuel L. Jackson vehicles.

Stoned Raiders (2001) returned the group to more solidly hip-hop ground while 1999's *Los Grandes Éxitos en Español* and 2004's *Till Death Do Us Part* found the group paying homage to their Latin American roots while simultaneously angling for the lucrative Spanish-language and Reggaeton markets. It's ultimately up to listeners to decide whether Cypress Hill is nobly expanding their horizons and bravely experimenting with new genres and sounds on albums like *Los Grandes Éxitos en Español*, *Till Death Do Us Part*, and *Skull & Bones* or cynically cashing in on passing trends.

But no one can deny that Cypress Hill has managed to stay relevant in a genre notoriously inhospitable to longevity and continued success. They've earned a hallowed place in hip-hop history as Latin pioneers, as evidenced by the release of a disappointingly skimpy greatest hits album (2005's *Greatest Hits from the Bong*) that ended, in a Reggaeton mix of "Latin Thugs," with a telling nod to Cypress Hill's sometimes strained efforts to stay current. Surely a group as venerable and influential as Cypress Hill deserves more than just nine old favorites and three new tracks.

Cypress Hill paved the way for the current Latin explosion and they're still deep in the game. As long as there are college kids smoking weed and listening to "Insane in the Brain" and "How I Could Just Kill a Man" (which is to say, forever), they'll be around, getting high, and playing your town.

From which television show was Cypress Hill banned?

a. Saturday Night Live

b. The Tonight Show with Jay Leno

c. MADtv

d. Late Show with David Letterman

ALL TOGETHER NOW:

'90S RAP GROUPS

GANG STARR PERFORMED WITH THE ROOTS AND MACY GRAY IN 1999 AT NEW YORK'S HAMMERSTEIN BALLROOM.

BB
BB

THE FUGEES COLLABORATED WITH CYPRESS HILL ON THE TRACK "BOOM BIDDY BYE BYE."

THE ROOTS TOURED WITH THE FUGEES IN 1996.

NJ → LA

NAUGHTY BY NATURE PREVIOUSLY USED DESIGNER/ILLUSTRATOR SKAM2 FOR ALBUM ARTWORK/LOGOS AS DID A TRIBE CALLED QUEST.

CYPRESS HILL WAS GIVEN A SHOUT OUT ON NAUGHTY BY NATURE'S "HIP-HOP HOORAY."

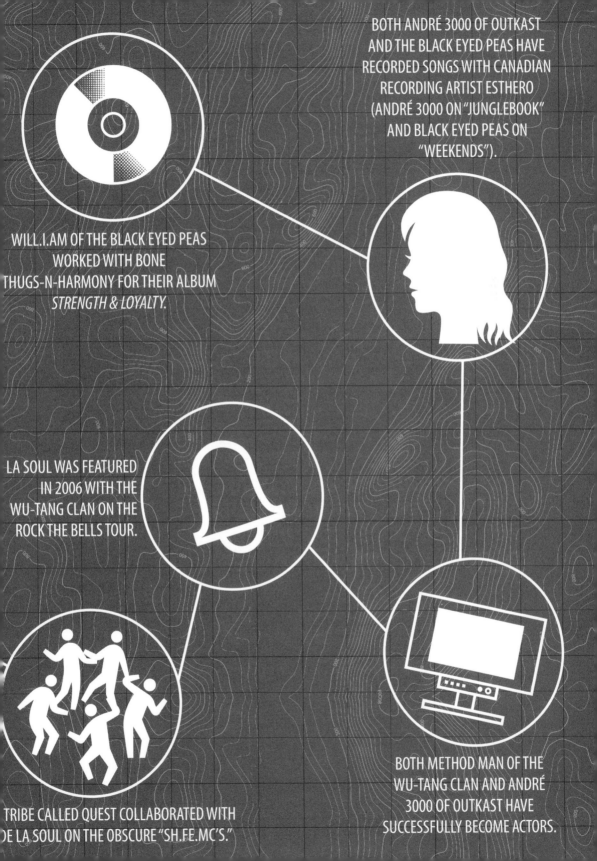

BOTH ANDRÉ 3000 OF OUTKAST AND THE BLACK EYED PEAS HAVE RECORDED SONGS WITH CANADIAN RECORDING ARTIST ESTHERO (ANDRÉ 3000 ON "JUNGLEBOOK" AND BLACK EYED PEAS ON "WEEKENDS").

WILL.I.AM OF THE BLACK EYED PEAS WORKED WITH BONE THUGS-N-HARMONY FOR THEIR ALBUM *STRENGTH & LOYALTY*.

LA SOUL WAS FEATURED IN 2006 WITH THE WU-TANG CLAN ON THE ROCK THE BELLS TOUR.

TRIBE CALLED QUEST COLLABORATED WITH DE LA SOUL ON THE OBSCURE "SH.FE.MC'S."

BOTH METHOD MAN OF THE WU-TANG CLAN AND ANDRÉ 3000 OF OUTKAST HAVE SUCCESSFULLY BECOME ACTORS.

CHAPTER 5

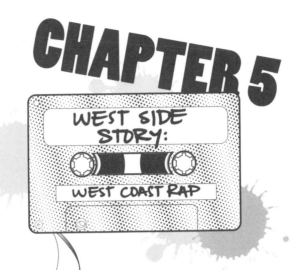

WEST SIDE STORY:

WEST COAST RAP

A wise man once said that East Coast hip-hop was meant for headphones and West Coast hip-hop was meant for car stereos. During 1992 and 1993, it was impossible to turn on MTV and *not* see a Dr. Dre–related video. No matter the time of day, Dre and Snoop's blurred-out marijuana leaf hats and that girl who gets her bikini top pulled down in the "Nuthin' but a 'G' Thang" video were corrupting minds nationwide. Similarly, it was damn near impossible to walk down the street and not hear some trunks rattling due to *The Chronic*'s G-funk bass lines, chilled-out guys reclined so low behind the wheel it looked like no one was driving. At the same time, Dre's former cohort from N.W.A., Ice Cube, was hanging out with the Bomb Squad and pissed off at the country, spitting some of the angriest rhymes heard to date. Though Tupac and Biggie's beef sometimes overshadowed the genre-changing music being created, shades of West Coast hip-hop can be heard in just about all production to this day, no matter its origin on the globe.

Dr. Dre

Dre's exit from N.W.A. was significant, and not only for him. Wasting no time, he formed Death Row Records with former bodyguard/overall dubious character Suge Knight—who over time would become as notorious a player as the music industry had ever come across. Among many of the nefarious acts attributed allegedly to him is that Suge threatened to kill Ruthless Record's Jerry Heller if Heller didn't let Dre out of his contract. However it happened, the issue was resolved and Dre was free to record. He hit the ground running with 1992's "Deep Cover." The moody song did double duty as it introduced Dre's patented "G-funk" grooves and gave the public its first taste of Dre's young protégé Snoop Dogg. With "Deep Cover" under his belt, Dre went to the studio and what he cooked up ushered in a new era.

> **"WITH 'DEEP COVER' UNDER HIS BELT, DRE WENT TO THE STUDIO AND WHAT HE COOKED UP USHERED IN A NEW ERA."**

With jewels like "Nuthin' but a 'G' Thang," "Dre Day," and "Let Me Ride," Dre's debut solo album, *The Chronic*, blew up. It was more than just a top ten charter—it was multiplatinum, one of the biggest-selling rap CDs ever. The CD was a challenge to every other rapper and producer. After *The Chronic* you simply couldn't hear a rap song that didn't have the G-funk groove. Dre was the Man, and from Snoop to Warren G to hook guy Nate Dogg, Dre and Death Row set the pace.

That pace and Suge's mind-set began to take its toll. By '96 Dre was finally fed up and left to form his own label, Aftermath Entertainment, under Interscope Records. At the time it seemed crazy to walk away from a winner, but Dre had the last laugh when Death Row fell off and Suge was jailed for a parole violation.

Dre roared back with 1999's *2001*, which had the monsters "Still D.R.E." (rumor has it that it was ghostwritten by Jay-Z) and "The Next Episode." The record was massive and that was all he wrote. Or rapped. Dre has been in the studio off and on over the ensuing years since *2001* working on the long-awaited follow-up, *Detox*. But even without his own album, Dre kept busy with production (insert name rapper here) and building his roster: Eminem, 50 Cent, Busta Rhymes, and The Game.

Ice Cube

Growing up in South Central Los Angeles, O'Shea Jackson a.k.a. Ice Cube started writing rhymes in his late teens. With Sir Jinx, Cube created the duo C.I.A. and often performed at parties hosted by relative luminary Dr. Dre. The connections to Dre lead to Cube meeting Eazy-E. Eazy dug Cube's vibe, asked him to cook up a rap, and Cube laced E with something he called "Boyz-N-the-Hood." Eazy dissed it, but despite the thumbs-down, he must have seen something, and soon enough Cube, Dre, and Eazy formed the first version of N.W.A. Yet just in case that didn't pan out, Cube had a fallback career. He left L.A. to study architectural drafting—a skill all aspiring rappers turned actors/directors need—obtained a one-year degree from the Phoenix Institute of Technology, and returned home in 1988. His arrival coincided with the release of *Straight Outta Compton*, and the rest is—you know the rest.

Like Dre, Cube was pissed at N.W.A.'s management. In 1989 he became the first member to jump ship, relocating to NYC with his new crew, Da Lench Mob. With them Cube recorded the fiery *AmeriKKKa's Most Wanted* (1990). Produced by Public Enemy's Bomb Squad production team, the CD was a charged fusion between East Coast and West Coast rap and instantly went gold—praised as a groundbreaker, but also dogged for Cube's raw anti-gay/anti-female lyrics. Cube then formed his own company, which, perhaps in response to the heat, was run by a woman. He also produced protégée Yo-Yo's 1991 pro-female debut, *Make Way for the Motherlode*. Both the album and artist enjoyed a brief but sweet moment in the spotlight. Also in '91, Cube made his big-screen debut with an acclaimed role in John Singleton's gritty *Boyz N the Hood*. Throughout his career, Cube would flip it up between music and movies and score in each medium, with some of his cinematic coups including the uproarious *Friday* franchise (which Cube wrote), *Three Kings* (alongside George Clooney), and 2002's blockbuster comedy *BarberShop*.

Death Certificate (1991) was more political and X-rated than Cube's first joint, and as a result ignited a firestorm—always good for sales. Among the more controversial cuts were the scathing "No Vaseline," an attack on N.W.A. manager Jerry Heller (seen as anti-Semitic), and "Black Korea," both of which were protested by civil rights groups. Cube's lyrics were so unrelenting that *Billboard* magazine took the unprecedented step of condemning them. *Death Certificate* might have ticked people off, but predictably it sold like crazy, going platinum and to number two on the charts. In 1992, Cube toured with Lollapalooza, which shored up the rowdy white-boy audience, and then he converted to Islam. That year he also came through with *The Predator*, which became the first album to debut number one pop and R&B/hip-hop. Among the high points were "It Was a Good Day," "Check Yo Self," and the title track, which laid the smackdown on *Billboard*'s editor in chief.

Acknowledging the impact of G-funk, Cube dropped '93's *Lethal Injection*. While it went platinum, the reviews weren't strong, making the CD Cube's last solo project for a minute. In 1994, he masterminded Da Lench Mob's *Guerillas in tha Mist*, and over the next few years would reunite with Dre on "Natural Born Killaz." Cube, along with Mack 10 and WC, became Westside Connection and released 1996's *Bow Down*, which eventually went platinum. In November of '98 Cube returned with *War & Peace, Vol. 1 (The War Disc)*. *The Peace Disc* arrived two years later.

With most of his energy focused on movies, it looked as though Cube had grown tired of rapping. Six years later, though, he managed to surprise the haters with 2006's *Laugh Now, Cry Later*, which was put out by his own independent label, Lench Mob Records, and soon reached platinum status.

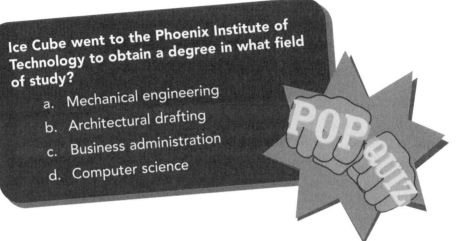

Ice Cube went to the Phoenix Institute of Technology to obtain a degree in what field of study?

a. Mechanical engineering

b. Architectural drafting

c. Business administration

d. Computer science

Snoop Dogg

It's hard to be mad at Snoop Dogg. High as three kites, laid-back, and gangsta, he is probably the most engaging and enduring figure to come out of the Westsiiiide. Calvin Broadus was raised in Long Beach, California, a.k.a. the LBC, and as a kid was nicknamed Snoop because of his resemblance to the *Peanuts* canine. From puppy puss to gangsta rapper—gotta love that. Running with the wrong crowd and gang-affiliated (to this day Snoop proudly rocks the Crips blue), Snoop often got into trouble with the man. Not long after he graduated from high school, he was popped for possession of coke. A teenager and in and out of detention, he needed to break the cycle, and he found that escape through music. He began making crude tapes with his boy Warren G, who as luck would have it was Dr. Dre's half brother. Warren slipped him a tape and Dre decided to work with Snoop. Don't worry—Warren would get his shine later with '94's "Regulate."

Dre invited Snoop Doggy Dogg to drop a verse or two on 1992's "Deep Cover," and Snoop's drawling flow made the track. The excitement escalated into hysteria when Snoop also did damage on Dre's *The Chronic*. Enjoying damn near as much wax time as Dre, Snoop shone. All of this laid the groundwork for Snoop's much-anticipated debut, *Doggystyle*. But because this is hip-hop, shit had to get f'ed up. While in the studio with Dre, Snoop was arrested in connection with the drive-by death of Phillip Woldermarian. Snoop was charged with being an accomplice to murder. Mr. Dogg claimed self-defense, saying that Woldermarian had a gun. After performing at 1993's MTV's Video Music Awards, Snoop turned himself in. A few years passed by as he awaited trial.

While all this was unfolding, *Doggystyle* (1993) became the very first debut album to come out at number one. It would eventually go four times platinum. Top ten singles "Who Am I (What's My Name)?" and "Gin and Juice" helped the CD hold down its high chart position, as did the hand-wringing over Snoop's legal mess and violent, sexist lyrics. And they were violent and sexist. Knowing that nothing sells like drama, Snoop exploited the impending trial with a short movie called *Murder Was the Case*, as well as an accompanying soundtrack. Both the film and soundtrack debuted at number one in 1994.

Much of 1995 was spent prepping for the trial, and one year later, in 1996, a jury found Snoop not guilty of all charges. No doubt relieved and focused, he went back to the studio—this time noticeably sans his producer mentor. Yet even though Dre wasn't on board, *The Doggfather* (1996) had that G-funk feel. Too bad for Snoop, it didn't garner the same love that *Doggystyle* had, and though it sold well (double platinum), there were no standout singles. Along with the disappointing sales, *The Doggfather* arrived just as "gangsta" rap was starting to lose some of its popularity, and adding to that, it came just weeks after the 1996 murder of new friend and labelmate Tupac Shakur and during Dre's departure from Death Row and the ascendancy of Doctor Doom, Suge Knight. All of which meant that Snoop got caught up in outside B.S., and that translated into bad promotion. Oh, and the album wasn't great.

Taking the slight snub as a hint, Snoop began to change up his steez, toning down the gangstarisms and reaching out to the rock crowd by joining 1997's Lollapalooza tour. *Da Game Is to Be Sold, Not to Be Told*, Snoop's first CD for Master P's No Limit, came in 1998—again yielding no massive hits, but selling respectably. In quick succession came *No Limit Top Dogg* (1999) and then *Tha Last Meal* in 2000, both of which saw Snoop mixing up his West Coast sound with P's southern roster. Even though Snoop's CDs were getting inconsistent reviews, it didn't matter because by 2000 he was as much a pop icon and personality as a rap star. So it wasn't unusual that he parlayed that persona into movie roles, e.g. *Soul Plane* and *Starsky & Hutch* where he played the role he was made for, '70s pimp Huggy Bear. Also on Snoop's cinematic CV, some self-produced, straight-to-DVD porn. Kids, don't try that at home.

> **"EVEN THOUGH SNOOP'S CDS WERE GETTING INCONSISTENT REVIEWS, IT DIDN'T MATTER BECAUSE BY 2000 HE WAS AS MUCH A POP ICON AND PERSONALITY AS A RAP STAR."**

In 2002 Snoop moved to Capitol Records. *Paid tha Cost to Be tha Bo$$* was very successful in great part because of The Neptunes-produced track "Beautiful." The single showed a softer, more female-friendly side, and it was greeted with raves and big sales, eventually going to the top of most music charts. Along with the sonic shift, Snoop had upped up his playa pimp thang and was frequently seen hanging out with former actual pimp the Archbishop Don "Magic" Juan. The flamboyant Bishop, who carried around a jewel-encrusted pimp goblet and dressed like a cross between Superfly and a Muppet, served as sidekick/spiritual advisor, and both he and Snoop were rarely photographed with out a harem of scantily clad girls.

Making moves and movies, Snoop took his "fo' shizzle, ma nizzle" act to another new label. His first Geffen CD was 2004's *R&G (Rhythm and Gangsta): The Masterpiece*, and it too had a very sweet Neptunes collabo, the sparse "Drop It Like It's Hot." That single was Snoop's first number one on the Billboard Hot 100 chart. But once again Snoop's professional life was being impacted by his personal nonsense. In 2003, Snoop and crew were accused by a makeup artist who worked with him for *Jimmy Kimmel Live* of drugging and sexually assaulting her during Snoop's guest-host spot. In December of 2004, one month before the makeup artist filed a lawsuit, Snoop filed a preemptive suit claiming extortion. Both suits were dropped. And the hits kept on coming.

In 2006, Snoop and posse were arrested at London's Heathrow Airport for "violent disorder and affray." That must be some English legal term for acting the fool when you get turned away from the first-class lounge. After everyone was escorted outside, they trashed a duty-free shop, injuring cops. The guys spent a night in the joint and were released on bail and subsequently banned from flying British Airways.

When Snoop returned to London to face the music, the British Home Office got together and decided to deny him entry to the UK for "the foreseeable future" owing to the fight and prior conviction back home.

Speaking of those convictions, Snoop added to his jacket in the fall of 2006. He was detained at a California airport (he doesn't have much luck there, huh?) and airport screeners found a collapsible police baton in his carry-on. The TSA took the baton and allowed Snoop to fly. Weeks later authorities decided to press charges and issued a warrant for his arrest. Bail was set at $150,000—and Snoop ponied up. A freaking *month* later, he was popped at another Southern California airport—it's sort of hard to have any sympathy—for possession of weed and a firearm. Again released on bond, he eventually entered a no-contest plea on these charges and received a suspended three-year sentence. Okay, and now for the insane. He was grabbed a *month* later following his appearance on *The Tonight Show*, for, you guessed it, drugs and a weapon. Bail was set at $60,000, which he posted. Then in March of 2007, Snoop was denied entry into the UK, stemming from his arrest in 2006. This forced the cancellation of British dates of his tour with Diddy. In April of 2007, he was banned from entering Australia to attend the MTV Australian Video Music Awards.

Somehow in between being a freaking idiot, Snoop managed to record and release *Tha Blue Carpet Treatment*. The CD got strong reviews and had a bit of a more serious tone—though not so serious as to keep Snoop from dueting with R. Kelly on the single "That's That."

Which record label has Snoop Dogg not been signed to?

a. Capitol Records

b. Geffen Records

c. No Limit

d. Def Jam

POP QUIZ

Tupac Shakur

Tupac Shakur lived each day like his death was imminent, but his words would live forever. An unmistakable strain of fatalism runs throughout his music, a dogged, unshakable conviction that the only possible outcomes for uncompromising young black men are early deaths or long prison bids. It's tempting to imagine what Tupac's music might have sounded like if he had ever overcome his adolescent fixation with the glamour of dying young and leaving a thugged-out corpse, but a big part of the rapper's enduring appeal stems from dying beautiful and pure and rife with unfulfilled promise.

Like all great pop martyrs, Tupac mastered the tricky science of being something to everyone. To underground hip-hop heads he was the socially conscious son of a Black Panther and the living heir to everything Huey P. Newton and Angela Davis fought for. To teenage girls he was the ultimate fantasy boyfriend, a fragile soul whose thuggish exterior masked a sensitive inner poet. To gangstas and drug dealers he was the archetypal thug, an O.G. whose commitment to living the Thug Life (a nebulous concept if ever there was one) was literally tattooed on his chiseled flesh. To the countless rappers who followed in his footsteps Shakur left behind an endlessly recycled blueprint on how to achieve massive pop stardom without losing the streets. For moralistic busybodies like C. Delores Tucker and William Bennett, Tupac symbolized the society-destroying recklessness of gangsta rap's warped moral compass.

Tupac was a man divided against himself, a prophet of black power who waged warfare against a veritable army of powerful and not-so-powerful black men and women. He was a man who recorded hopeful, pro-woman anthems like "Keep Ya Head Up" and "Dear Mama" when not fighting off sexual assault cases or disparaging groupies and enemies as bitches and hos. He was a goofball New York theater kid who relentlessly antagonized the New York hip-hop establishment. He was both demonized and lionized by a press corps he manipulated with guile and cunning.

Tupac was a seething mass of contradictions we're still trying to figure out today, over a decade after he was gunned down in Vegas. It's no exaggeration to call Shakur the hip-hop Elvis, and like the King of Rock, Tupac is far bigger in death than he ever was in life.

Tupac's story is forever linked with that of the Black Panthers and their thwarted dream of racial, social, and economic equality for African-Americans. His mother, Afeni, was a proud member of the Panthers and gave birth to the future icon not long after being acquitted of over a hundred charges of "conspiracy against the United States government and New York City landmarks." Shakur's godfather, meanwhile, was legendary Black Panther Geronimo Pratt, while his stepfather, Mutulu Shakur, spent several years on the FBI's Most Wanted list. So you could say that revolutionary political activism was in Tupac's blood.

Born June 16, 1971, in Harlem, Shakur developed an early love of music, words, and performing. While still a preteen, he joined the 127th Street Ensemble, a troupe of young African-American actors, where he snagged a plum role in Lorraine Hansberry's classic *A Raisin in the Sun*. Shakur's family then moved to Baltimore, where he enrolled in the Baltimore School for the Arts.

In 1988 the Shakurs heeded Horace Greeley's famous admonition to "Go West!" by moving to Marin County, California. But by the time Shakur transferred to Tamalpais High School, his mother had sunk into crack addiction that Shakur would go on to document indelibly on "Dear Mama," where he rapped, with disarming sweetness, "Even as a crack fiend, mama/You always was a black queen, mama."

After high school Shakur hooked up with Digital Underground, a heavily P-funk-inspired Bay Area hip-hop group that scored big crossover hits with infectious party anthems like "The Humpty Dance" (in honor of front-man Shock G's Groucho-glasses-sporting alter ego, Humpty Hump) and "Dowhatyalike." Shakur toured with the group as a dancer and roadie and secured his first big national attention when he was prominently featured on "Same Song," a track from Digital Underground's *This Is an EP Release* that was later used in the woeful Dan Aykroyd/Chevy Chase comedy *Nothing but Trouble*. Tupac made the most of his "Same Song" turn by performing the song in the film alongside the rest of the group. It would be hard to envision a less auspicious cinematic debut.

In 1991 Shakur recorded his solo debut, *2Pacalypse Now*, an angry, incendiary, politically charged album far removed from the unthreatening goofiness of Digital Underground. The disc scored a minor hit in "Brenda's Got a Baby," a grim story song about a twelve-year-old daughter of a junkie father and absent mother who becomes pregnant with her cousin's baby. Needless to say, "Brenda's Got a Baby" would have been an awkward fit on a Digital Underground album like *Sex Packets*. Though it never reached the heights of future Tupac singles, the track deftly illustrated Pac's ability to get inside characters' heads and write empathetically about the female experience.

"THOUGH IT NEVER REACHED THE HEIGHTS OF FUTURE TUPAC SINGLES, [BRENDA'S GOT A BABY] DEFTLY ILLUSTRATED PAC'S ABILITY TO GET INSIDE CHARACTERS' HEADS AND WRITE EMPATHETICALLY ABOUT THE FEMALE EXPERIENCE."

Between the release of 1991's *2Pacalypse Now* and 1993's *Strictly 4 My N.I.G.G.A.Z.*, Shakur snagged the role of a lifetime as a mercurial aspiring kingpin in *Juice*, a gritty hood drama directed by longtime Spike Lee cameraman Ernest Dickerson. Shakur helped make the film a hip-hop classic that's regularly referenced by contemporary rappers. He turned in a much less memorable performance in July of 1993 as an unassuming mailman in John Singleton's muddled romantic drama *Poetic Justice*.

Shakur had a thriving career in multiple media, but his out-of-control behavior was starting to affect his work. He was famously fired from the Hughes Brothers' noir-styled 'hood classic *Menace II Society* after he physically assaulted director Allen Hughes. Shakur also reportedly auditioned for the role of dimwitted shrimp enthusiast Bubba in *Forrest Gump*, but the part ultimately went to Mykelti Williamson.

Shakur's propensity for trouble grew with his rising fame. In 1991 he filed a $10 million lawsuit against the Oakland Police Department for excessive force and brutality and settled for a much smaller sum. In '93 he was busted for shooting at two police officers reportedly harassing an African-American driver. Usually shooting police officers leads to lengthy jail sentences and/or the death penalty, but both officers were inebriated when Shakur shot them and the charges against him were dropped.

But the most serious charges against Shakur arose later in 1993 when the rapper was charged with sexually abusing a female fan. He insisted that the sex was consensual but was convicted of sexual abuse and sentenced to a lengthy prison sentence. For most pop stars constant run-ins with the law and physical altercations with potential collaborators would be the kiss of death, but Shakur's considerate arrest record and reputation for violence only strengthened his street cred. His stints in prison let fans know that he was no studio gangster who hollered bloody murder on tracks but spent his free time sipping tea, petting his cats, and leafing through poetry books.

No, Tupac seemed intent on living his music even if it killed him. In the crazy, mixed-up world of '90s major-label gangsta rap, his antisocial tendencies and bad-boy persona were sizable commercial assets.

Shakur's life had become a bloody, lurid melodrama complete with constant drug and alcohol use—the rapper regularly recorded while drunk and high on marijuana—frequent clashes with Johnny Law, battles with societal gatekeepers like Dan Quayle (who famously insisted that there was no place in society for Tupac's music, a statement history has rendered wildly ironic), and brutal fights with friends turned enemies.

On November 30, 1994, Tupac was shot five times in an apparent robbery attempt at a studio in New York. Shakur believed the heist was orchestrated by former friend Notorious B.I.G. and Bad Boy capo Sean "Puff Daddy" Combs. Despite being shot in the head, groin, arm, and thigh, he left the hospital against doctor's wishes only three hours after surgery, a remarkable feat of will and determination that helped cement his growing legend as an indestructible gangsta rap god.

Seemingly everything that happened in Shakur's life found its way into his music, so it surprised no one when he released "Hit 'Em Up," an explosive diss track that accused B.I.G. and Combs of being behind his recent shooting. In the song, Shakur boasts of fucking B.I.G.'s wife (R&B singer Faith Evans) and extends the beef to East Coast artists like Mobb Deep and Chino XL.

Bad Boy, Notorious B.I.G., and Combs went out of their way to downplay the Death Row/Bad Boy rivalry, especially once the media began to depict it as a rivalry not just between rappers or labels but between entire coasts. When at the 1995 Source Awards Suge Knight infamously mocked Combs's predilection for hogging the spotlight and appearing in his artists' videos, Combs graciously insisted he was proud of everything Death Row, Dr. Dre, and Snoop Dogg had accomplished.

Tupac was playing a dangerous game, but fans and the media couldn't get enough. The rapper began his prison sentence on Valentine's Day 1995 and watched his album *Me Against the World* shoot straight to the top of the charts while he rotted away in the big house. He was living a schizophrenic existence, on top of the world professionally even as he was mired in the belly of the beast. *Me Against the World* reflected the rapper's bleak fatalism during this time with its alternating currents of rage, self-pity, sentimentality, and empathy. The title said it all: Shakur was at war with the world, himself, enemies real and imagined, and the system. It's an extraordinarily angry album whose mind-set can best be described by the song title "Fuck the World." Yet the pro-woman anthem "Dear Mama" illustrated that Shakur was still capable of inspiring others while bogged down in hopelessness himself.

In the mid-'90s, Shakur faced one very big problem. He'd appealed his conviction but couldn't afford the $1.4 million bail that would earn him at least temporary freedom. Suddenly a solution appeared in the hulking form of a former college football player with an incongruously unthreatening nickname. Even in the brutal, violent world of gangsta rap, Death Row head Marion "Suge" Knight was a notorious figure infamous for running his label like a street gang and for allegedly dangling Vanilla Ice out of a hotel balcony until he signed away his publishing rights. Knight was undoubtedly the baddest motherfucker ever named Marion.

Death Row had emerged as a major musical force in the early '90s thanks to the stunning work of Dr. Dre, the sonic genius behind N.W.A.'s albums, Snoop Dogg's *Doggystyle*, and his own seminal solo debut, *The Chronic*. By the time Knight began eyeing Shakur as the potential savior of Death

Row, Dre's relationship with Suge was broken beyond repair. Dre had one foot out the door, so Knight needed a new marquee star. He found one in Shakur, one of rap's biggest names and an icon whose dangerous, violent persona perfectly meshed with Death Row's equally thugged-out, nihilistic ethos.

Knight was an ominous figure straight out of Shakespeare or the Bible and he offered Shakur one hell of a Faustian bargain: freedom in exchange for his soul. Knight agreed to put up the bail to spring Shakur from jail in exchange for Shakur signing with Death Row Records. With the benefit of hindsight, it's clear that this solution to Shakur's problems was probably worse than the problems themselves, but at the time Knight must have looked like the answer to all of his hopes and dreams.

> **"DRE** HAD ONE FOOT OUT THE DOOR, SO **KNIGHT** NEEDED A NEW MARQUEE STAR. HE FOUND ONE IN **[TUPAC] SHAKUR,** ONE OF RAP'S **BIGGEST NAMES** AND AN **ICON** WHOSE DANGEROUS, VIOLENT PERSONA PERFECTLY MESHED WITH **DEATH ROW'S** EQUALLY THUGGED-OUT, NIHILISTIC ETHOS.**"**

Shakur couldn't have known that when he inked his contract with Death Row he was officially entering a treacherous endgame phase in his career and life. Death Row brought out the worst in him, inflaming the rapper's paranoia and sense of persecution and downplaying the social consciousness and political anger that had always been one of his greatest strengths.

Upon his release from prison, Shakur made up for lost time by writing and recording songs in marathon sessions that would eventually yield material for the rapper's double-disc Death Row debut, *All Eyez on Me*, his follow-up, *The Don Killuminati: The 7 Day Theory*, and a never-ending stream of posthumous releases. These recordings were filled with eerie premonitions of Tupac's death, though anyone who spends much time with Knight is bound to end up speculating about their imminent demise.

All Eyez on Me went on to become one of the top-selling rap albums of all time. The smash hit single "California Love," produced by Dr. Dre—which was supplemented by a popular *Mad Max*–themed video—was a joyous celebration of the rapper's adopted home. Dre also produced "Can't C Me," another standout track, but bad blood between the rapper/producer—who was soon to leave Death Row to start his own Aftermath label—and Knight and Tupac kept collaborations between Tupac and Dr. Dre to a minimum. The rest of the album was produced by soundalike producers like Daz Dillinger who could offer a passable imitation of Dre's patented G-funk sound for a fraction of the price.

All Eyez on Me was recorded in just two weeks. Its follow-up, as its title suggests, was written and recorded in just seven days. Tupac clearly sensed that he was running out of time. He was correct. On September 7, 1996, he was shot four times by an unknown assailant after attending a Mike Tyson fight with Knight in Vegas. He was rushed to the hospital and placed on life support, but it was too late. Six days later Shakur was officially pronounced dead. He was just twenty-five. His friend turned enemy Notorious B.I.G. was murdered the following year under similarly mysterious circumstances. In the span of a single year hip-hop lost two of its strongest voices to senseless violence.

Shakur's cult has flourished in his absence. Death has done little to slow down his output. Death Row has put out an album of unreleased Tupac material damn near every year following the rapper's death, generally to mixed reviews but impressive sales. In death as in life, Tupac has been Suge Knight's cash cow.

Ja Rule, 50 Cent, Master P, The Game, and DMX are just some of the hip-hop icons whom fashioned themselves unashamedly in Tupac's image. Even rappers like Jay-Z and Nas, whom Tupac disparaged in song, have paid homage to him with covers, remakes, and posthumous collaborations. Since his death, the Tupac business has become an entire industry, complete with poetry collections (1999's *The Rose That Grew from Concrete*), remix collections (*Nu-Mixx Klazzics*), compilations inspired by Tupac's poetry, and enough documentaries to fill a decent-sized video store, most notably Nick Broomfield's cheeky, wildly entertaining *Biggie & Tupac* and 2003's *Tupac: Resurrection*, which gave an impressionistic account of the rapper's life through his own words. Then there's the fairly popular conspiracy theory that Shakur faked his own death and is chilling complacently on an island somewhere, a deluded line of reasoning that speaks to the hip-hop community's unwillingness to acknowledge the irrevocable passing of arguably its greatest icon.

Today Tupac's influence and importance are discussed and debated by everyone from street-corner hustlers to tweedy Ivy League academics. In dying young, Shakur became one of the music world's true immortals. He will never be forgotten.

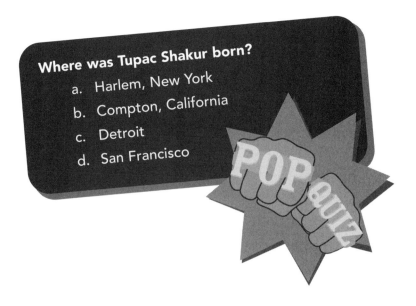

Where was Tupac Shakur born?

a. Harlem, New York

b. Compton, California

c. Detroit

d. San Francisco

POP quiz

CHAPTER 6

HEAVY HITTERS:

2000s SOLO RAP

T hough it started early on with *Paid in Full* and went to the next level with No Limit Records, materialism didn't really peak until this decade, when videos started to cost millions and chains started to cost more than cars. Although this sort of mind-set has dominated the media and airwaves, with artists bragging about how much they own, there's been a steady uprising of rags-to-riches success stories, stemming from Jay-Z and moving on with Young Jeezy and The Game. Which is not to say that intellect has been lost from hip-hop, as Kanye West (as rich as he may be) still rhymes about personal struggles and takes the time to speak out against the president on national TV. All of the subgenres of hip-hop are still there, with MCs like Nelly keeping the clubs open late and Bow Wow holding down the teenage girls. The decade is still incomplete, though, so there's no telling what else may come.

50 Cent

As everyone and their mama knows, 50 Cent was raised in rough-ass Southside Jamaica, Queens. The neighborhood was a virtual drug dealer's paradise back in the day and the scene of many infamous shootings and nefarious characters, including Kenneth "Supreme" McGriff of the notorious Supreme Team. Naturally the danger and dealing helped make Jamaica an almost ideal lab for hip-hop. It certainly shaped young Curtis Jackson's life: so much so that he may be one of the few rappers whose subject matter closely mirrors the reality of his upbringing.

Fiddy hit the ground struggling. His mom (who birthed him when she was just fifteen) was a hustler and addict and passed when he was just a kid. With Pops also out of the picture, Curtis was reared by his grandmother. Grandma's love couldn't keep him off the streets, and as a teen, 50 also hustled. Selling crack was a good look, until 50 got busted—repeatedly—and did some jail time. It was during one of his street-to-jail round trips that he started thinking there must be a better way and that way was rap music. That and the fact that he was now a father to a son, Marquise Jackson. In 1996, 50 met local luminary Jam Master Jay, and Run-D.M.C.'s DJ gave 50 some beats to rap over. Liking the results, Jay signed 50 to his label, JMJ Records, but nothing much jumped off and 50 aligned himself with the popular NYC-based production team the Trackmasters. Poke and Tone had crafted hits for, among others, Nas and Jay-Z, and signed 50 to their imprint, which was distributed by the almighty Columbia

"GRANDMA'S LOVE COULDN'T KEEP HIM OFF THE STREETS, AND AS A TEEN, 50 ALSO HUSTLED. SELLING CRACK WAS A GOOD LOOK, UNTIL 50 GOT BUSTED— REPEATEDLY— AND DID SOME JAIL TIME."

Records. Together work began on 50's debut, *Power of the Dollar*—the release of which was preceded by "Your Life's on the Line," "Thug Love" (featuring a then on the come-up Destiny's Child), and "How to Rob." It was that song that lit a spark in NYC's rap community. Loaded up with antagonistic rhymes about how this new jack would hijack some of hip-hop's heavyweights, "How to Rob" set into motion both admiration and hostility.

While fans might have dug the new kid's willingness to name names, some of those names, it appeared, did not. Shortly after "How to Rob" came out, 50 was stabbed at a midtown NYC recording studio. A few months later in 2000, there was more violence and mythmaking when right before 50's album was set to be released, the young rapper was shot in his neighborhood. Not just shot—shot nine times. Even though the bullets didn't hit any vital organs—he did get shot in the cheek, but obviously that didn't slow things down too much—50's life was clearly in peril. So was his career. Soon after the attempted murder, Columbia decided to cut their losses, severed ties with 50, and shelved *Power of the Dollar*.

Let's face it—after getting nine slugs in you, losing a label deal is peanuts, and 50 took the diss from Columbia in stride. He went back to the under-ground and formed G-Unit, whose membership consisted of local dudes Lloyd Banks and Tony Yayo. As time went on and 50 was an established star, G-Unit's lineup would change. Because of his incarceration on weapons possession charges (the motivation for the "Free Yayo" shirts Eminem and 50 once rocked), Tony was replaced temporarily by former Cash Money associate and Nashville homie Young Buck.

With 50, G-Unit was responsible for a string of hugely popular self-produced and -marketed mixtapes, which not only led to 50's eventual deal with Interscope Records, but G-Unit's as well. As GGGGG-Unit!!, the guys recorded their Interscope debut, 2003's *Beg for Mercy* (double plat-inum), and its lead single, "Stunt 101." Banks's solo debut for G-Unit/Interscope Records, *Hunger for More*, came a knocking in 2004, followed two years later by *Rotten Apple*. The first did significantly better numbers than the second, reaching double-platinum status. Tony came out of jail in 2004, but after presenting a fake passport to his PO *one day later*, he landed his ass back inside. Genius. After being sprung a few weeks later, Tony could begin work on his own thing, and after a few more mixtapes laid some more groundwork for his major-label debut, 2005's *Thoughts of a Predicate Felon*. As for new kid Buck, his first G-Unit CD was 2004's *Straight Outta Cashville*, followed by 2007's *Buck the World*.

Okay. Enough about those clowns. Back to the saga of Curtis Jackson. After forming G-Unit, 50 started working closely with producer Sha Money XL. The end result was the series of mixtapes, many hosted by DJ Whoo Kid, that helped put the Columbia debacle way behind him. Fiddy's street rep was back in full force thanks to a bunch of street hits that mocked other rappers—in particular fellow Queens resident and then big dawg Ja Rule, who not surpringly became one of 50's archrivals. From 2000 to 2002, 50's mixtapes were unstoppable and his rep grew, as did the mythology behind his shooting. That street love got even louder when supposedly during a radio show Eminem mentioned his admiration for 50. Soon a bidding war broke out among the major labels, and as the numbers reached seven figures, Eminem came out on top, and for his troubles and cash got to sign 50 to a joint deal with Shady/Aftermath. Both of his new label bosses, Em and Dre, would work side by side with 50 on his much-anticipated debut.

Yet before that debut could hit the streets, 50 appeared on the *8 Mile* soundtrack with former underground hit "Wanksta." This new version was a big old smash in 2002, and so was the next joint. Produced by Dre, "In Da Club" was the first official single off of 50's major-label debut, *Get Rich or Die Tryin'*. The track hit number one and set the stage for 50's finally available CD, which arrived in 2003. He was hot, controversial, and a star. *Get Rich* clocked an astounding 872,000 units in just five days—smashing SoundScan records.

Not only was 50 the man to beat, sales-wise, he was in the news for everything. Topping that list, he was tied to the 2002 murder of Jam Master Jay, the FBI investigation of rap label Murder Inc.'s dealings with

Kenneth "Supreme" McGriff, and also a shooting at 50's management company, Violator. To top that off, 50 was thrown into jail in 2002 for gun possession. The combo of street tough, creative genius—okay, maybe not genius—escaping death, and making money made 50 an irresistible figure, in and out of the media. And 50 milked it and made millions.

In 2004, 50 added another rapper to his G-Unit clique, but by the time The Game's solo joint appeared a year later, he and Mr. Cent weren't BFF anymore. Just as 50 and Game's collabo "How We Do" was making its way up the charts, 50 let it be known, during an interview at NYC's HOT 97, that The Game had to turn in his G-Unit membership card. The dismissal wasn't handled well by either camp, and after the on-air "you're fired," some of 50's dudes and Game's dudes got into it outside HOT 97 a.k.a. SHOT 97. Things got so out of hand that one of Game's boys got a bullet in the leg. The beef would continue and in fact escalate to the point where even those outside of hip-hop circles were getting concerned. Within a few weeks or so of the 2005 shooting, 50 and The Game kissed and made up, the former obviously not literally, at a NYC news conference that was about as staged as a Broadway show. Shortly after that public display of unity, Game started yapping off again, sometimes showing up at shows sporting a gorilla mask to further mock his on-again, off-again rival.

While all this extracurricular crap was unfolding, bootleg copies of 50's second CD, *The Massacre*, were all over the Internet and the street. The leakage forced Interscope to speed up the official release of the much-anticipated CD and *The Massacre* arrived in the spring of 2005. Shock of shocks, it sold 1.15 million copies in its first week of release, spawning several hit singles, among them the suggestive "Candy Shop." Later that same year, 50 took his thuggish appeal to gaming with *50 Cent: Bulletproof* (clearly a shooting game, right?) and then, just in time for the holidays, he made like his mentor Eminem and starred in the serious and semi-biopic *Get Rich or Die Tryin'*. Unlike *8 Mile*, which was both a commercial and critical achievement, 50's thespian turn got less enthuastic returns and reviews. The soundtrack for the film featured Mr. Jackson along with new G-Unit signees Mobb Deep (Prodigy and Havoc), a veteran Queens duo who, outside of '95's certified classic "Shook Ones Pt. II," never did much of anything anyone outside of the hardcore fans cared much about. Mobb Deep's first and often delayed G-Unit CD was 2006's *Blood Money*. It sank like the *Titanic*.

As for 50? To round out his media domination, he "wrote" his autobiography, *From Pieces to Weight: Once Upon a Time in Southside Queens*, introduced a book publishing imprint focusing on modern-day street fiction, bought a major share of vitaminwater (beats drinking Pimp Juice), and oversaw his popular, if not particularly interesting, clothing line, the G-Unit Clothing Company. In 2007, the winter of 50's discontent centered around yet another slab of beef—this time a lame-ass, totally made up for the bloggers and radio brouhaha with Cam'ron, a man who clearly would start a fight with his own reflection if he thought it would get him attention.

50's third album *Curtis* (2007) revealed a softer side to the Teflon Don, featuring collaborations with everyone's favorite blue-eyed R&B singers, Justin Timberlake and Robin Thicke. Released on the same day as Kanye West's *Graduation* amid a much-hyped marketing campaign, it debuted at number two, proving that hip-hop's Superman was no longer invincible.

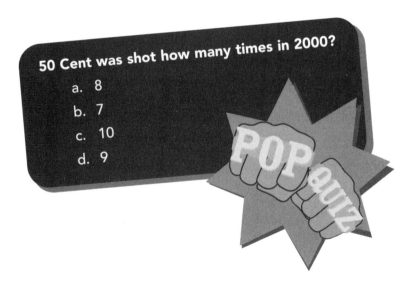

50 Cent was shot how many times in 2000?

a. 8
b. 7
c. 10
d. 9

POP QUIZ

Kanye West

Kanye West would have had his fifteen minutes of fame, as well as a nice paycheck, even if he had never grabbed the mic. After all, before 2004's *The College Dropout* dropped in, West had an impressive career, producing hits for, among others, Alicia Keys, Brandy, and Jay-Z.

Born in Atlanta in 1977, Kanye and his mother moved to Chicago when he was three, after his parents divorced. Unlike a number of MCs who hustle their way (most of the time illegally) up the MC ladder, West attended both the American Academy of Art and Columbia College Chicago before dropping out to focus on music. Starting out with production duties for local Chicago talent, he also appeared on songs from Monica, Do or Die, and Consequence.

By the late '90s, Kanye's signature trademark production techniques (which included speeding up R&B hooks) coupled with his strong work ethic helped him catch fire. He soon joined up with Roc-A-Fella Records, which was run by Kareem "Biggs" Burke, Damon Dash, and Jay-Z. K soon became the Roc's go-to guy, with his biggest moves being "Takeover" and "Izzo (H.O.V.A.)" off Jay's *The Blueprint* (2001).

Soon Kanye let it be known that he planned on making his own rap album. The project was repeatedly delayed, with the chief and most compelling reason arising in 2002. That's the year that Kanye came *this* close to dying in a very nasty car accident. The event understandably rocked K's world, but along with needing to recover, he had his debut CD on his mind. His strong survival instincts, along with a dogged insistence on getting back to work, would become the thematic basis for "Through the Wire." The title referred to West's decision (both brave and typically attention-grabbing) to record with his jaw wired shut. The song would eventually be the first single of 2004's *The College Dropout*, but as that CD kept getting bumped back, K. West kept busy cooking up smashes for, among others, Lil' Kim ("Came Back for You"), Jay-Z ("'03 Bonnie and Clyde"), and Alicia Keys ("You Don't Know My Name"). Just as "Through the Wire" was really blowing up in late '03, another Kanye joint, "Slow Jamz," a collabo with

Twista and Jamie Foxx, also exploded. Kanye now had tons of production credits, two slamming singles, and all eyes on him as the world (okay, the music world) awaited his debut.

"[KANYE WEST'S] STRONG SURVIVAL INSTINCTS, ALONG WITH A DOGGED INSISTENCE ON GETTING BACK TO WORK, WOULD BECOME THE THEMATIC BASIS FOR 'THROUGH THE WIRE.'"

Wordy and at times witty and bristling with fiery beats, *The College Dropout* quickly went from hot CD to phenom. Fans loved it, it went multi-platinum, and the critics raved. For his part, West became a media darling by simply being one of the biggest egomaniacs in rap history. Impressive. That aside, he got himself a sweet ten nominations for the 2005 Grammys. *The College Dropout* won the Best Rap Album award, the triumphant "Jesus Walks" won Best Rap Song, and West shared a writing credit (and Best R&B Song) for Alicia Keys's "You Don't Know My Name." But the big news wasn't what West won, but what he lost, specifically Album of the Year. He licked his wounds and fired back with 2005's *Late Registration*. With the sexy smash "Gold Digger" (featuring Jamie Foxx), the album lived up to the hype and sidetracked the sophomore jinx—debuting at number one, selling over 900,000 copies in its first week of release, and earning Kanye three more Grammys in 2006. The album wasn't all radio fluff, though. "Diamonds from Sierra Leone" spoke bluntly about the topic of conflict diamonds in, you guessed it, Sierra Leone, and "Crack Music" focused directly on West's idea of crack cocaine being one of the black community's biggest problems.

The album didn't fare as well at MTV's European Music Awards, and upon losing Video of the Year (for his "Touch the Sky") to Justice vs. Simian,

West hopped up onstage and berated the crowd, claiming that he should have won, despite his later admission that he had never even seen the winning video. West's video, which depicts him as an Evel Knievel–like daredevil, got the attention of the real-life Knievel, who sued in December of 2006 for trademark infringement.

Post–*Late Registration* saw Kanye not only being showered with accolades and awards for his album, but in the middle of a number of controversial situations. First, in the *All Eyes on Kanye West* MTV special, West blatantly spoke out against the rampant homophobia in hip-hop music. Comparing African-American struggles to those of gays, he urged his fellow rappers to "stop it." Later, citing his own defamatory slang in years past, he stated that his "consciousness [had] since been raised," and that there's no difference between calling a man a "fag" and a woman a "bitch."

Less than a month later, West appeared alongside former *Saturday Night Live* cast member Mike Myers during a benefit concert for Hurricane Katrina that aired on NBC. Obviously straying from the script, Kanye went off on post-Katrina efforts, how badly blacks were being portrayed in the media (stating that blacks were shown "looting," while whites were shown "looking for food"), and, of course, that "George Bush doesn't care about black people."

Recently, West has collaborated with a number of artists, including Japan's Teriyaki Boyz, Fall Out Boy, and Timbaland. He is working on a television show directed by Larry Charles, and released an exclusive track for Nike's Air Force 1 anniversary. Kanye was also seen at a party for Italian fashion designer Fendi with the company's logo shaved into his hair. In addition to all of that, he started his own label imprint, G.O.O.D. (Getting Out Our Dreams), in 2004, and released Common's *Be* as well as John Legend's *Get Lifted*, both of which received a number of Grammy nominations and wins. 'Ye proved that he was not only the critics' favorite, but also the people's champ when his third album, *Graduation*, beat 50 Cent's *Curtis* to debut at number one in 2007. With the first week sales of close to a mil, the fashionable MC cemented his spot alongside hip-hop's elite.

Nelly

With a flow that was one part southern drawl, one part midwest twang, Nelly was commercial as hell and proud of it.

The superstar, who started out life as Cornell Haynes Jr., came up in the greater St. Louis area and got into hip-hop as, yes, a teenager. It was then that Nelly, who had serious aspirations to be a professional baseball player (word has it that he had some real talent), hooked up with some of his high school friends—Ali, Kyjuan, Murphy Lee, and City Spud. Together the fivesome became the St. Lunatics (the name no doubt a shout-out to their hometown)—one that didn't enjoy much of a hip-hop profile, at least not outside of the city limits. As a unit the Loonies had a regional hit in 1996 ("Gimmie What U Got"), but after trying to snag a record deal, the guys took a vote and figured that Nelly might have a better chance as a single act.

That strategy would pay off in a few years, not just for Nelly, but for the Lunatics' individual members. When Nelly landed his deal and became ultra-large, that success afforded him clout, which he used to set his boys up. Each enjoyed modest solo deals, no doubt helped by their connection to a superstar.

Soon after Nelly signed with a major label his star began to rise and there was an audible buzz in the air about this cute kid from the heartland with the tricked-up flow. In 2000, Universal Records released Nelly's *Country Grammar*. More catchy than a cold, the title track ruled the charts and became a hands-down summer anthem. The album celebrated multiple chart-topping singles, including "E.I." and "Ride Wit Me." In 2002 Nelly came back with *Nellyville*, which was even bigger than its predecessor. The CD topped, at various times, a mind-blowing ten Billboard charts and for all intents and purposes gave every impression of being an unstoppable source of hit after hit. High on the list of Nelly's hits was the number one stunna "Hot in Herre." Produced by The Neptunes, "Hot in Herre"—his first number one hit—was another sexy anthem and had women everywhere "tak[ing] off all [their] clothes." The success and the stats erased any doubts that Nelly was just some one-hit wonder novelty artist.

"THE SUCCESS AND THE STATS ERASED ANY DOUBTS THAT NELLY WAS JUST SOME ONE-HIT WONDER NOVELTY ARTIST."

Nelly kept cranking out hits like "Iz U" and "Shake Ya Tailfeather" with Murphy Lee and Diddy, dueted with Destiny's Child's Kelly Rowland ("Dilemma")—for which he won a Grammy in 2003—and then simultaneously dropped two CDs, *Sweat* and *Suit*, in September of 2004. With party tracks ("Flap Your Wings") and sweet songs ("My Place") and even a duet with country superstar Tim McGraw, the CDs kicked Nelly back to the top of the charts. Since then he has been conspicuously on the low musically, concentrating on other business ventures, although he did pop up on Janet Jackson's '06 stinker "Call on Me." Some of his successful side projects include his women's clothing line, titled Apple Bottoms, his energy drink Pimp Juice, and part ownership of the NBA expansion team the Charlotte Bobcats. While involved in a high-profile relationship with R&B hottie Ashanti, Nelly managed to find time to release his fifth studio album, *Brass Knuckles*.

T.I.

Pharrell called him the "the Jay-Z of the South," but it wasn't until *King*—one of a mere handful of rap CDs to go platinum in 2006—that T.I. really lived up to the hype and the honorific. Equal parts rough and relaxed, T.I. (born Clifford Harris Jr.) has carried the mantle for the ATL, all the while proving that having dope beats doesn't have to also mean dopey lyrics. The good-looking, slick-talking T.I. first came outta the box with 2001's *I'm Serious* (Arista), and while it didn't quite blow him up, he kept grinding, and in 2003 started upping his profile and sales with the single "24's." After that, T.I. was unstoppable. That same year he dropped *Trap Muzik* (which had the breakout hit "Rubber Band Man"), and then a year later he claimed the throne with *Urban Legend*, featuring the top ten singles "Bring Em Out" (which featured a vocal sample of Jay-Z's "What More Can I Say") and "U Don't Know Me."

After coming out of the big house due to an earlier run-in with the po-po, T.I. made up for lost time with a vengeance. *King* exploded and went number one, selling 522,000 copies in its first week. T.I. dominated radio thanks to the Grammy-nominated "What You Know"—his highest charting single. Not only did T.I. rule the radio and charts, he also made a splash with his lead role in the coming-of-age flick *ATL*, which came out the same week as *King*. T.I.'s new royal status only increased the demand for his flow, and he popped up on several hot records, most notably Justin Timberlake's "My Love." In 2007, he got himself a Best Rap Solo Performance Grammy for "What You Know" and another for his collabo with J. Timberlake. The King was unstoppable, once again claiming his spot atop the Billboard 200 in 2007 with his fifth effort, *T.I. vs. T.I.P.*, and landing a role in *American Gangster* alongside Denzel Washington and Russell Crowe. However, T.I.'s ride in the fast lane slowed that October when he faced federal weapons charges after ATF agents arrested the father of five in Atlanta for allegedly trying to purchase machine guns and silencers.

T.I.'s hit single "Bring Em Out" featured a sample of what Jay-Z song?

a. "Encore"

b. "Hard Knock Life (Ghetto Anthem)"

c. "What More Can I Say"

d. "Girls, Girls, Girls"

POP QUIZ

Ludacris

Before Ludacris (Christopher Bridges) hit the mic as a rapper, he worked the mic—logging lots of airtime as a popular ATL radio jock. In the mid-'90s, that gig would be a major factor in helping Luda develop poise, professionalism, a hyper (on-air) persona, witty verbiage, and a serious rep in the South—one that helped him make his way all the way from the control booth to the studio. After appearing on Timbaland's LP *Tim's Bio* in 1998, he began to hone his own thang, which made its first real impression on *Incognegro* (2000). The CD was on Luda's label Disturbing tha Peace and became the talk of Atlanta. Soon after the CD and single "What's Your Fantasy" became regional hits, Scarface (of the Geto Boys) came calling. Scarface was the head of Def Jam South—an imprint the label formed to tap into the growing Dirty South scene—and Luda became the first act on that imprint. Later in 2000, a repackaged version of *Incognegro* entitled *Back for the First Time* arrived. The first single was Luda's former hit "What's Your Fantasy," but its salacious subject matter met with resistance from radio. Eventually the song broke through and helped usher in an era of nasty singles for the Dirty South. The choice is yours.

Luda followed up his success with more, releasing The Neptunes-produced "Southern Hospitality." Next, "Area Codes," featuring Nate Dogg, the Timbaland-produced "Rollout (My Business)," and "Move Bitch!" were released off of Luda's follow-up, *Word of Mouf* (2001). The album hit number three on the charts and went quadruple platinum. Luda's way with a double entendre made him a popular collaborator (e.g., Missy Elliott's "One Minute Man" and Mariah Carey's "Loverboy"). Album number three came in 2003, and like the joints that preceded it, *Chicken-N-Beer* was a smash, as were the singles "Stand Up"—Luda's first Billboard Hot 100 chart-topper—and "Splash Waterfalls." Not taking time to slow down, 'Cris then came back a year later with *The Red Light District*, which featured the single "Get Back." That same year Ludacris seized the spotlight on Usher's ubiquitous "Yeah!" That song topped the Billboard Hot 100 for twelve weeks.

Off the mic, Luda also made an impact. In 2005 he starred in two highly acclaimed films, *Hustle & Flow* and the Academy Award–winning *Crash*. Fresh from his cinematic splash and strong reviews, Luda hit the number one spot in 2006 with *Release Therapy*. While the CD showed a more thoughtful side (e.g., the "Brenda's Got a Baby"–esque "Runaway Love"), the single "Money Maker" (a collabo with Pharrell) proved that Luda could still make it sexy—and also scoop up the Grammy for 2007's Best Rap Song. Along with being one of the handful of rap CDs to hit number one and go platinum in 2006, *Release Therapy* got serious industry validation when Luda earned the Grammy for Best Rap Album. The 2007 awards also afforded Luda much airtime and further pumped up his cross-generational appeal.

Lil Wayne

Lil Wayne (Dwayne Michael Carter Jr.) first gained notice in the late '90s as the youngest member of Cash Money Millionaires' Hot Boys, which also featured next big things Juvenile, Turk, and B.G. After making a name with that crew, Weezy grew up and into his skills, becoming one of the hottest MCs in the game. He made his solo move in '99 with a big ol' hit off his debut album, *Tha Block Is Hot*. The single "Tha Block Is Hot" was a southern smash. In 2000, Wayne came with *Lights Out*, featuring the single "Shine," and in 2002 *500 Degreez*. During that two-year period, Cash Money got rid of every other Hot Boy, but stayed true to Wayne—in great part no doubt because of the almost familial connection between Wayne and his boss/mentor Baby. That alliance motivated the duo's 2006's *Like Father, Like Son*.

In 2004, Weezy F. Baby came correct with *Tha Carter*, fueled by the hit single "Go DJ." In 2005, he was named president of Cash Money Records, and also began to pop up more frequently on other rappers' tracks. In 2006, he hit critical and commercial mass with *Tha Carter II*, which was so well-received and more focused that many in the game whispered loudly that Wayne—who had always been good, but never great—had enlisted a ghostwriter. True or not, Wayne was at the top—even having the cojones to call out big dawgs like Jigga in print. Rap fans everywhere anxiously waited for Wayne's future albums to drop, all part of *Tha Carter* series.

The Game

There is no rapper more 'hood, more street, more down, more all-around hardcore than The Game. Okay, that's not even true, but damn the Compton homie tries to hammer that point home every time he opens his mouth—that is, when he isn't beefing with everyone shy of the pope.

Government name Jayceon Taylor, The Game lived a hard-knock life, including gangbanging. After getting shot, Jayceon had a much-needed epiphany, and, inspired by the greats of rap (Tupac, Biggie, Jay, Dre, N.W.A.), turned to music in 2002. With a tough-as-nails delivery and equally bleak rhymes, The Game made his name on mixtapes. By 2003 Dr. Dre, who knew how to find and nurture young guns, signed him to Aftermath. After many starts and stops, *The Documentary* was released in 2005, executive-produced by Dre and featuring significant input from the good doctor as well as 50 Cent. The CD was a joint project of Aftermath and G-Unit Records, and it was an immediate triumph. The album was number one, went platinum-plus, and contained the hits "How We Do," "Hate It or Love It," and "Dreams."

Suddenly the West Coast had a new champion, but all the love soon dissipated as Game entered into a series of public and on-wax feuds. His wrath seemed to have no limits—among those he jumped on was East Coast mixtape maestro and former next big thing Joe Budden. But the beef that really brought the drama to its peak was between The Game and boss/mentor 50 Cent. The war of words brought bad memories of a similarly unproductive war between the late Tupac Shakur and Biggie Smalls. The main differences? That Game seemed to be too eager to start shit and, despite some incidents, no one ended up dead. The battle between Game and 50 reached such absurd heights that in March of 2005 they were coerced into a press conference where they metaphorically kissed and made up. Either way, Dre found himself caught in the middle, and while he never spoke out, he was conspicuously M.I.A. from 2006's *Doctor's Advocate*—whose title spoke volumes about The Game's connection to Dre. The CD also debuted at number one, but it failed to catch fire in quite the same manner as his previous release.

"SUDDENLY THE WEST COAST HAD A NEW CHAMPION, BUT ALL THE LOVE SOON DISSIPATED AS GAME ENTERED INTO A SERIES OF PUBLIC AND ON-WAX FEUDS."

Young Jeezy

Along with the Clipse, Young Jeezy is a leading proponent of what critics dubbed "coke-rap." And we ain't talking about the soft drink.

At first Jeezy (Jay Jenkins) harbored ambitions of being not an artist, but an industry executive—you could say, judging by his limited lyrical focus, that he's achieved his goal. Years before releasing any of his own muic, Jeezy had already created Corporate Thugz Entertainment and promoted New Orleans's successful Cash Money crew. In 2003, Jeezy's second indie effort, *Come Shop Wit' Me*, sold more than 50,000 copies. He also made noise as a member of the ATL-based act Boyz N Da Hood (Bad Boy Records), who released their self-titled CD just weeks before J's solo joint entered the top ten.

That success begat more, and soon Jeezy was one of his label's premier stars with his platinum-plus Def Jam CD *Let's Get It: Thug Motivation 101* (2005). Driven by the street banger "Soul Survivor," the album was a big smash, snuggling into the number two spot on the charts. Jeezy would come through a year later in late 2006 with the equally commercially, though not critically, successful *The Inspiration* ("I Luv It" and "Go Getta"), which confirmed his role as a big dog.

Dipset a.k.a. The Diplomats

Dipset (a.k.a. The Diplomats) barely sell any records, but the streets—at least in NYC—and the critics love them. The Harlem-based crew/lifestyle revolves around chief Cam'ron, Juelz Santana, Jim Jones (who can't rap to save his life but, go figure, had 2006's smash "We Fly High"), J.R. Writer, Hell Rell, and Diplomat Records president Freekey Zekey. As a unit, Dipset have dropped two volumes of *Diplomatic Immunity* ('03 and '04), which did okay, but not as well as their barrage of mixtapes.

Cam'ron

Cameron Giles played b-ball with Mason "Ma$e" Betha—whose fifteen-plus minutes included being Puffy's shiny-suited sidekick on "Mo' Money

Mo' Problems." Although Killer Cam was a good enough hoopster to get scholarship offers, he didn't have the grades and ended up at a small college, which he attended for less than a minute. Cam came back to Harlem and decided to switch his major to drug dealing before he moved into hip-hop.

Through Ma$e, Cam linked up with the Bad Boy posse, yet didn't sign with Puffy. He opted to go with Lance Rivera's Untertainment, which had a deal with Epic Records. Cam's first joint was '98's "Pull It," and the pop-rap hit "Horse & Carriage," featuring Ma$e. The single went top ten R&B and Cam'ron's debut album, *Confessions of Fire*, reached gold status.

After 2000's *S.D.E. (Sports, Drugs, and Entertainment)*, Cam shifted to Roc-A-Fella Records and appeared in the Dame Dash–produced dramatic film *Paid in Full*. On the musical tip, 2002's "Oh Boy" was a big radio smash and the album *Come Home with Me* also sold nicely. Following the CD, Killa Cam concentrated on Dipset, yet found time in '04 to bring the critically beloved *Purple Haze*. A year later, C made news—the bad way, when he escaped a carjacking in D.C. (though he did get shot in the arm). In 2006, he directed the DVD *Killa Season* and released the album of the same name, which hit number two. It was also in 2006 that Cam waged a wax battle with former boss Jay-Z on "You Gotta Love It." A mixtape fave, the eight-minute rap blasted Jigga for such crimes against rap as wearing sandals and looking like Joe Camel. Ouch.

For what sport was Cam'ron offered a college scholarship?

    a. Football

    b. Basketball

    c. Baseball

    d. Track

POP QUIZ

Juelz Santana

Juelz (LaRon James) got his break when fellow Harlemite Cam'ron gave him a chance to shine in 2000 on the track "Double Up" off of Cam's release *S.D.E. (Sports, Drugs, and Entertainment)*. From there, Juelz signed on to become a full-time Diplomat and made his solo debut with 2003's *From Me to U*, featuring the single "Santana's Town." He remained active with The Diplomats' mixtapes and then dropped his second CD, *What the Game's Been Missing!*, in 2005. It featured the hit single "There It Go (The Whistle Song)," which hit number six on the Billboard Hot 100 chart, and eventually made its way to platinum certification.

Bow Wow

Lil' Bow Wow (born Shad Moss) proves you can grow old in hip-hop—as long as you begin your career when you're just out of underoos. An Ohioan, Bow Wow (he lost the "Lil'" when he hit his teens) got his big break at a very tender age by being discovered by Snoop Dogg (who gave the pint-sized rapper his name). After doing some spot gigs here and there, Bow's talent caught the attention of Jermaine Dupri, who, having overseen and guided the kiddie duo Kris Kross (1992's ubiquitous "Jump"), knew about working with juvies. Jermaine signed Bow to his So So Def roster and co-wrote and produced a now preteen Bow's debut CD, *Beware of Dog* (2000). The album held the warm-weather anthem "Bounce with Me," along with "Ghetto Girls."

Freshly established as the new kid—literally—Bow Wow and Dupri went back to the lab and came out with the poppy *Doggy Bag* (2001). Once again the little girls not only understood, they bought the CD, and Bow's star power translated easily to the big screen when he starred in the comedy *Like Mike* in 2002. Bow Wow also had a sizable hit with "Take Ya Home." Soon after, he lost the "Lil'" and left So So Def for Columbia Records. The shift in labels also meant that Bow was leaving his mentor and ersatz father figure, Dupri. Feel free to insert Freudian analysis here.

Unleashed (2003) was a bit more grown-up, though still PG, yet perhaps due to JD's absence, it didn't do amazing numbers. Bow took time out of the studio to appear in *Johnson Family Vacation* (2004) alongside Cedric the Entertainer and Solange Knowles and *Roll Bounce* (2005). That same year he went back to his day gig, as well as reunited with JD. The partnership produced Bow's fourth album and top ten hit *Wanted* (2005). The album, which featured contributions from Snoop Dogg, Ciara (whom he was briefly romantically linked to), and Omarion, with the top five singles "Let Me Hold You" and "Like You"—his highest-charting release—helped to reignite Bow's career. The fire kept burning in 2006. Still under the legal drinking age (though judging by a flurry of interviews, more than capable of talking shit), Bow kicked off with *The Price of Fame*, featuring the number one jam "Shortie Like Mine," featuring the even younger Chris Brown. In late 2007, Bow Wow teamed up with his Scream tour buddy Omarion for a *Best of Both Worlds*–type album called *Face Off*.

Chamillionaire, Mike Jones, and Paul Wall

Every year has the song you just can't escape. In 2006, it was "Ridin'." A platinum number one hit, "Ridin'" made Houston's Mixtape Messiah a.k.a. Chamillionaire a star.

A first-generation Nigerian, Cham (Hakeem Sediki) was originally associated with Houston's independent rap record label Swishahouse, also home to future platinum stars Paul Wall and Mike Jones. Jones would go on to hit the pay dirt with 2005's *Who Is Mike Jones?* and "Still Tippin'" (which featured Paul Wall). Wall was a DJ and rapper and closely creatively aligned with the late Houstonian DJ Screw—who pioneered the druggy, speed-altered remixing technique called chopped and screwed.

Wall, like Jones and Cham, first made his bones in the mixtape scene and would come to join up with his childhood friend Cham to form the Color Changin' Click. Together they recorded 2002's *Get Ya Mind Correct*, which moved more than 100,000 copies and rocketed to regional and then national attention. Wall would follow that up with the solo album

Chick Magnet. Cham and Wall grouped together again for 2005's *Controversy Sells*, which came out a few months before Wall's major-label jump-off, *The Peoples Champ*, which eventually reached platinum status. By then Wall (who enjoyed a side career making platinum grills) and Cham had parted ways both professionally and personally. Wall stuck with Swishahouse, while Cham made independent moves. In the spring of 2007, Wall released his sophomore solo LP, *Get Money, Stay True*.

In 2005 Chamillionaire formed his own label, Chamillitary Entertainment, and became one of the first rap acts to actively use the Web to promote himself. The majors came around, and in late 2005 Cham presented *The Sound of Revenge*. The CD went top ten and then erupted when the second single, "Ridin'" (which inspired the "Weird Al" Yankovic parody "White & Nerdy"), hit. Cham joined an elite group when the Grammys handed him an award for Best Rap Performance by a Duo or Group in 2007. With the release of his second album, *Ultimate Victory*, it was really clear that this kid was ridin' real pretty.

HEAVY HITTERS:
2000s SOLO RAP

CAM'RON RELEASED HIS SINGLE "TOUCH IT OR NOT" FEATURING LIL WAYNE.

LIL WAYNE AND JUELZ SANTANA BOTH WORKED WITH CHRIS BROWN ON HIS SELF-TITLED DEBUT ALBUM.

JUELZ SANTANA AND T.I. WERE TWO OF THE TWENTY ARTISTS FEATURED ON THE GAME'S "ONE BLOOD (REMIX)."

BOTH YOUNG JEEZY AND BOW WOW HAVE BEEN ROMANTICALLY LINKED WITH TWO OF R&B'S MOST POPULAR ARTISTS, KEYSHIA COLE AND CIARA.

THE GAME'S "HATE IT OR LOVE IT" WAS PRODUCED BY COOL & DRE, WHO ALSO PRODUCED YOUNG JEEZY'S "STREETS ON LOCK."

BOW WOW'S MENTOR, JERMAINE DUPRI, PRODUCED JANET JACKSON'S SINGLE "CALL ON ME," WHICH FEATURED RAPPER NELLY.

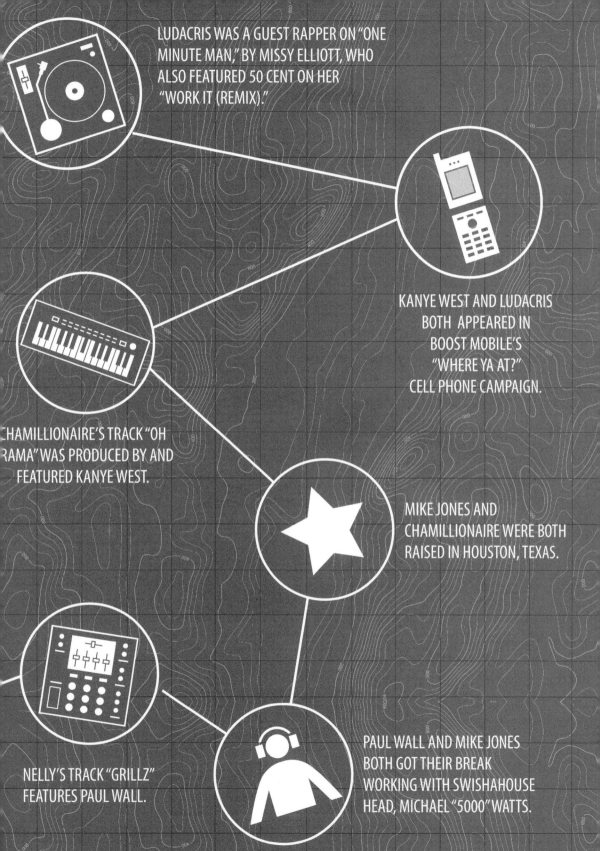

LUDACRIS WAS A GUEST RAPPER ON "ONE MINUTE MAN," BY MISSY ELLIOTT, WHO ALSO FEATURED 50 CENT ON HER "WORK IT (REMIX)."

KANYE WEST AND LUDACRIS BOTH APPEARED IN BOOST MOBILE'S "WHERE YA AT?" CELL PHONE CAMPAIGN.

CHAMILLIONAIRE'S TRACK "OH RAMA" WAS PRODUCED BY AND FEATURED KANYE WEST.

MIKE JONES AND CHAMILLIONAIRE WERE BOTH RAISED IN HOUSTON, TEXAS.

NELLY'S TRACK "GRILLZ" FEATURES PAUL WALL.

PAUL WALL AND MIKE JONES BOTH GOT THEIR BREAK WORKING WITH SWISHAHOUSE HEAD, MICHAEL "5000" WATTS.

CHAPTER 7

WHERE'S THE BEEF?

When the East Coast vs. West Coast feud took off in the '90s, "beef" for a lot of people started to mean more than just that stuff you eat on sandwiches. Silly as they may seem sometimes, beefs are as part of hip-hop as the 808 and gold rope chains. Where would the genre be if Kool Moe Dee hadn't put LL's trademark Kangol under the wheel of his Jeep on the cover of *How Ya Like Me Now*? If Ice Cube hadn't penned "No Vaseline"? If there was no "The Bridge," "South Bronx," or "The Bridge Is Over"?

FROM B-BOYS CHALLENGING THEIR OPPONENTS WITH SPINE- twisting poses to NYC's five boroughs symbolically duking it out for musical supremacy—in some form or another, there's always been a warrior mentality when it comes to hip-hop. Nowhere is that more clearly heard than in rap music's beefs. Back in the day—we mean baaaack, like in the late '70s—many believed that allowing city kids to work out their teenage frustrations—which in NYC included rampant unemployment, drugs, street violence, and a city that was all but going down the tubes— would reduce the chances of them actually beating the crap out of each other, or worse. In a perfect world, rappers settle their differences not with guns, knives, or rock-paper-scissors, but rather by using what God gave them—words.

Just like punk rock did for disaffected English kids, early hip-hop gave city kids a chance to relapse and express themselves, and maybe find some light at the end of a very bleak tunnel. So instead of stabbing that dude who pissed you off, you threw down, by break-dancing or more commonly battling—but with words, not weapons. Not only did it help keep folks alive, always a positive element to any experience, but rap battles became an art form unto themselves and provided fans some of the greatest moments on wax. Sure, before hip-hop was a recorded medium and was strictly a street-corner, park-playground activity, these mano a mano verbal fisticuffs remained a secret among ciphers and friends in the 'hood. But once rap went from the street to the studio to the airwaves and beyond, everyone had the chance to listen in, and rappers, maybe because they knew they had a real audience, stepped up their warrior game. Some will tell you that the relative innocence of the hip-hop battle dissipated with the rise of gangsta rap. Suddenly it wasn't enough to cut someone down with metaphors. Now you just capped the guy. While hip-hop battles continue to this day—as this goes to press, somewhere Cam'ron is finding someone to vent at—it ain't just nostalgia that tells you that the level of skills and real one-upmanship ain't what it once was. It might be fun for the fans and a major boom for the mixtape market and hip-hop radio, but a rapper simply calling out a rival by mocking him, without using rhymes, or simply making derogatory statements, doesn't constitute a battle. That's more like a drunken bar fight or a diss fest. A real memorable hip-hop battle has got to be more than naah-na-na-naaah-na! Yeah, Jay-Z wears sandals, but since Jay didn't respond, no battle. It's some dude whining. And as we've all seen, sometimes whining isn't enough for today's breed of knuckleheads. As soon as you draw a weapon, you ain't battling. You're committing a felony. This isn't the mafia, boys and girls. It's music. Okay, lecture over. But more importantly remember this: along with all the uplifting socioeconomic cultural blah-blah-blah, for fans the chief and best end result of any hip-hop clash of the titans is some really cool and often plain-out classic duels. Here are some of them.

N.W.A. vs. Ice Cube, 1990–1991

As is often the case, the inspirational source of this beef was very personal. That's because Ice Cube was not only a founding member of N.W.A., but also the first to bail and the first to point fingers at Eazy-E, Ruthless Records, and the group's not well-liked manager, Jerry Heller.

Opening shots: N.W.A.—"100 Miles and Runnin'" and "Real Niggaz"
Back at ya: Ice Cube—"No Vaseline"

Juice Crew vs. Boogie Down Productions, 1986–1987

Possibly one of the greatest of all time. This beatdown between Marley Marl's Queenbridge-based Juice Crew (of which MC Shan was a key member) and the Bronx's Boogie Down Productions headed up by the loquacious KRS-One was the hip-hop equal to the Ali vs. Frazier fight. Both crews gave as good as they took, and hip-hop ultimately won because all of the bullets fired hit their targets and were dope as shit. This was nothing less than interborough crew fight to the finish, a turf war for true lyrical supremacy and bragging rights for nothing less than the invention of hip-hop. As it was then, this remains a classic.

Opening shot: MC Shan—"The Bridge"
Back at ya: BDP—"South Bronx"
Third round: MC Shan—"Kill That Noise"
And again: BDP—"The Bridge Is Over"

Kool Moe Dee vs. LL Cool J, 1987–1991

Kool Moe Dee had a long-standing hip-hop pedigree. As one-third of old-school faves Treacherous Three (one of the first rap groups to actually make records), he was behind party jams like "Body Rock" and "Feel the Heartbeat"—all recorded before 1982. Moe Dee went solo and had three pretty popular albums in the late '80s, marked by his nimble, sped-up flow. It was around this time that a young kid from Queens, LL Cool J, was starting to catch on fire, and Moe Dee, with the cockiness that it seems rap stars are just born with, declared that this new jack had swagger-jacked Moe's attitude and, most important, his rapping technique. Not nice. The feud kept Kool Moe Dee in the public eye for a nice chunk of time and also made for even nicer entertainment as these two all-stars went shell toe to shell toe.

Opening shot: Kool Moe Dee—"How Ya Like Me Now"
Back at ya: LL Cool J—"Jack the Ripper"
Third round: Kool Moe Dee—"Let's Go"
Next: LL Cool J—"To Da Break of Dawn"
And again: Kool Moe Dee—"Death Blow"

Antoinette vs. MC Lyte, 1987–1988

The long-forgotten Antoinette was the self-proclaimed "gangstress of rap," managed by Hurby "Luv Bug" Azor, who would also guide Salt-N-Pepa. MC Lyte was a Brooklyn teen on the come-up. It's unclear what actually started the drama, but to many who were there it seemed like the issue between the two girls was not just creative differences, but full-out hatred, stemming in good part from Antoinette's public dissing of Lyte's brother Milk. In quick succession, the insults were met by insults, making this one of the few hardcore and no-holds-barred girl-on-girl hip-hop actions.

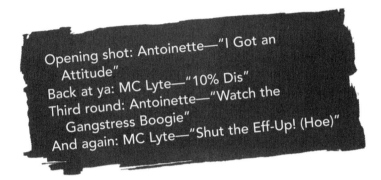

Opening shot: Antoinette—"I Got an Attitude"
Back at ya: MC Lyte—"10% Dis"
Third round: Antoinette—"Watch the Gangstress Boogie"
And again: MC Lyte—"Shut the Eff-Up! (Hoe)"

U.T.F.O. and the Real Roxanne vs. Roxanne Shanté, 1984–1985

It goes a little something like this. Lolita Gooden (a.k.a. Roxanne Shanté) overheard that the then hot BK trio U.T.F.O. had just canceled a gig. The group had made their name with "Roxanne, Roxanne" about a girl who was too good to talk to the fellas. Lolita was pissed and decided to ask her fellow Queensbridge friends, who included DJ Mister Magic and Marley Marl, to help her cook up a 12-inch answer. Naming herself Roxanne Shanté in response to the U.T.F.O. track, Gooden dropped "Rox-

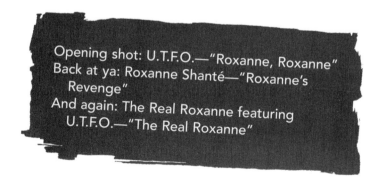

Opening shot: U.T.F.O.—"Roxanne, Roxanne"
Back at ya: Roxanne Shanté—"Roxanne's Revenge"
And again: The Real Roxanne featuring U.T.F.O.—"The Real Roxanne"

anne's Revenge," which was just a pure slice of in-your-face, almost profane venom. The single actually was responsible for a huge number of answer singles. At some point, U.T.F.O. also got angry, mainly because Marley Marl had copped U.T.F.O.'s music to help make Roxanne's record. They threatened to sue, and soon after, Roxanne Shanté made nice and would redo her song with alternate music. While this war lasted, it was a beautiful thing as Brooklyn's master production team/rap group fought the Juice Crew's female fury to determine who was the real real Roxanne.

LL Cool J vs. Canibus and Wyclef Jean, 1997–1998

After defeating Moe Dee, LL's rep as king of the battles was intact. So in 1997 he invited the then next big thing (who went nowhere) Canibus to join a posse cut. Canibus was a protégé of Wyclef and was being talked about in rap circles. The new guy entered the studio and must have done something very right, or as LL saw it, very wrong, because after hearing Can's verse, LL reentered the studio to rerecord his verse to top his guest. It was on. A war of the words ensued between the master (hey, he doesn't have that mic tattoo for nothing), a newcomer, and some guy who has no business battling.

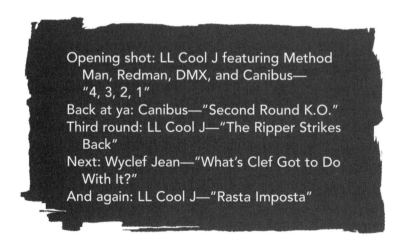

Opening shot: LL Cool J featuring Method Man, Redman, DMX, and Canibus—"4, 3, 2, 1"
Back at ya: Canibus—"Second Round K.O."
Third round: LL Cool J—"The Ripper Strikes Back"
Next: Wyclef Jean—"What's Clef Got to Do With It?"
And again: LL Cool J—"Rasta Imposta"

3rd Bass vs. Vanilla Ice, 1991–1994

Known as much for their lyrical talent as their short fuses, 3rd Bass took it upon themselves to defend hip-hop's honor as well as disassociate themselves—like anyone would think otherwise—from flavor of the week the hapless Vanilla Ice. Lyrically, this was clearly a no-brainer, no contest, and all it did was pretty much allow 3rd Bass, who were serious artists, to go for a quick and obvious kill. If Mr. Van Winkle had won, this world would have stopped spinning.

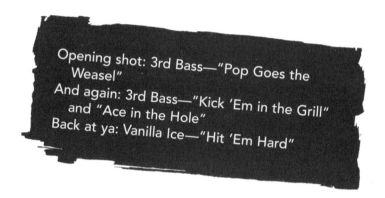

Opening shot: 3rd Bass—"Pop Goes the Weasel"

And again: 3rd Bass—"Kick 'Em in the Grill" and "Ace in the Hole"

Back at ya: Vanilla Ice—"Hit 'Em Hard"

Tim Dog vs. DJ Quik, Dr. Dre, and Snoop Dogg, 1991–1992

Holding it down for the BX, Tim Dog set the already bubbling under East/West war into high gear with 1991's *Penicillin on Wax*. The major ammo? The single "Fuck Compton," which, wow shock, didn't make the kids in Compton too happy. Tim's regional pride helped make his single and album underground hits and also spurred a flurry of politely worded retorts from his West Coast counterparts. After doing battle with B-listers, Tim decided to up the ante by going after Dr. Dre's then boo, R&B singer Michel'le. Just like that everyone was in on the fun and games.

Opening shots: Tim Dog—"Fuck Compton" and "Step to Me"
Back at ya: DJ Quik—"Way 2 Fonky" and "The Last Word"
Third round: Tim Dog—"Michel'le Conversation"
And again: Dr. Dre featuring Snoop Dogg—"Fuck Wit Dre Day (and Everybody's Celebratin')"

Jay-Z vs. Nas, 2001–2005

Onetime "friends" but longtime rivals, Jay and Nas set new standards for bringing the beef with this war of wit and words. Kicking things off was "Takeover." The song, which was on Jay's *The Blueprint* and premiered at a HOT 97 concert, put Nas (whose status had receded a bit) seriously on blast for not having a dope album since his debut, *Illmatic*. "Takeover" took great pains to remind Nas just how many hot CDs Jay had dropped (it was no secret that Jay was bigger commercially), and then for extra insurance went for Nas's baby mama, who just happened to be an ex of Jay's. Ouch.

Nas fired back with "Ether," the first cut off his "comeback" CD *Still-matic*. "Ether" pulled no punches and was painfully direct (i.e., "Fuck Jay-Z"). The song was raw and on point, and Jay returned fire with "Super Ugly," which took the insulting to such a new low (way too many details about sex with Nas's ex) that Jay later admitted on the radio that his mom had scolded him for going over the line. Admitting that "weakness" didn't go well with fans who loved the beef between two of the all-time greats. Although the songs are considered jewels, popular opinion has it that Nas had the better song and the stronger comeback. Jay and Nas's relationship would remain strained until 2005, when Jay brought Nas out onstage at a New York radio concert, and then stunned fans by signing his once archenemy and subject of some of his most vicious rhymes to Def Jam. See? We all can get along.

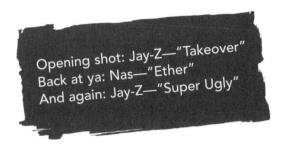

Opening shot: Jay-Z—"Takeover"
Back at ya: Nas—"Ether"
And again: Jay-Z—"Super Ugly"

Eminem vs. Benzino, 2000–2001

Has a beef ever been so one-sided? It began after Benzino's *The Source* (of which he was then editor) gave Em's classic *The Marshall Mathers LP* a two-mic rating (which was later changed to four after reader outcry). Benzino was so soundly defeated in both this beef and his professional life that one almost feels bad for him.

After he claimed that Eminem was responsible for black and Latino MCs only being able to rap about money and material things due to Em's supposed support and control from and by big business such as MTV, it was fairly obvious from the get-go that Benzino had some jealousy issues due to the white rapper's success. Initially silent on the subject, after repeated baiting from Benzino, Em finally responded, both on record and on HOT 97, where he called Benzino the "worst rapper in the world" and reminded listeners that he had never even met him. Further angered by this, Benzino threatened to fight Eminem and was subsequently dropped from his label, Elektra.

For some reason Benzino continued to bait Eminem by releasing some potentially damaging tracks Em had recorded years before, but the action did nothing but make him look overly vengeful, and after ignoring a court order to limit publication of the lyrics to said tracks, he was forced to pay Em's label a substantial amount of money.

After Benzino eventually turned his beef with Eminem toward Em's extended label family in 50 Cent and Busta Rhymes by publishing a less than favorable piece on G-Unit, Interscope withdrew advertising from *The*

Source, and the magazine's reputation was further damaged. Eventu[ally] removed from his position at *The Source* due to the insane amount [of] trouble he had caused the magazine, Benzino has finally learned to sh[ut] his mouth regarding the Eminem situation.

> Opening shots: Benzino—Mixtape freestyle and "Pull Ya Skirt Up"
> Back at ya: Eminem—"The Sauce" and "Nail in the Coffin"

50 Cent vs. Ja Rule, 2003–2006

Well before even signing with Interscope, 50 Cent had beef with both Ja Rule and his label, Murder Inc., after one of 50's friends supposedly stole some of Ja's jewelry, which led to a confrontation outside the Hit Factory in New York, where 50 suffered a minor stab wound to the back. The beef existed strictly on mixtape level until 50's debut album was released, which is when all hell broke loose.

> Opening shots: 50 Cent—*Get Rich or Die Tryin'* ("Wanksta" and "Back Down")
> Back at ya: Ja Rule—"War Is On," "Guess Who Shot Ya," and "Loose Change"
> Third round: Eminem featuring 50 Cent and Busta Rhymes—"Hail Mary 2003"
> Next: Ja Rule—*Blood in My Eye* ("The Crown" and "Clap Back")
> Back at ya: Ja Rule featuring Jadakiss and Fat Joe— "New York"
> And again: 50 Cent—"Window Shopper"

50 Cent vs. The Game, 2004–present day

Beginning before the release of Game's debut album, *The Documentary*, this beef started with Game supposedly recording with G-Unit rival Joe Budden, which 50 didn't take kindly to. Differences were put aside for the release of Game's album, though, but soon arose again after Game went on record saying that he had no interest in preexisting G-Unit beefs, and even expressed interest in working with some of those artists.

Fiddy wasn't too fond of this, and went on the radio stating that he had kicked Game out of G-Unit, and that Game's record wouldn't have sold as well without 50's input. Reaching its peak, the feud got ugly when Game and his entourage confronted 50 while on the radio in New York, which resulted in a member of Game's posse being shot outside of the beef epicenter, HOT 97.

The beef went languid for a minute, but 50 reemerged in the media claiming responsibility that Game's record did so well only because 50 appeared on it. Game responded with the huge diss track "300 Bars and Runnin'," as well as his battle cry of "G-UNOT."

Opening shot: The Game—"We Are the Champions"
Back at ya: The Game—"300 Bars and Runnin'"
Third round: 50 Cent—"Piggy Bank" video
Next: The Game—"Stop Snitchin', Stop Lyin'"
    DVD/mixtape
Back at ya: 50 Cent—"Not Rich, Still Lyin'"
Yet again: Spider Loc—various tracks
And another: The Game—"240 Bars (Spider Joke)"
It's not over: The Game—"The Funeral (100 Bars)"
One more time: The Game—"SoundScan"
And again: Lloyd Banks—"Show Time (Killing Game)"

Despite a peace offering from Game toward 50, the beef continued well into 2006. In March of 2007, G-Unit's Tony Yayo was arrested for allegedly assaulting the fourteen-year-old son of Game's manager and Czar Entertainment CEO, Jimmy "Henchmen" Rosemond. Along with other members of G-Unit, 50 Cent was detained and questioned.

CHAPTER 8

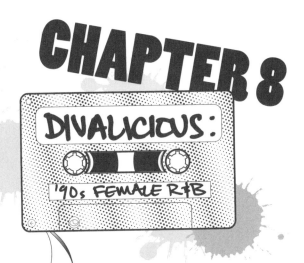

DIVALICIOUS:

'90s FEMALE R&B

nspired by classics like the Supremes and Martha and the Vandellas, women in the '90s R&B scene surely fueled many a night of lovemaking with their soaring voices and smooth backing tracks. Vocalists such as Whitney Houston (pre– Bobby Brown) and Mary J. Blige are, at this point, the obvi- ous mothers of the current R&B scene, but in addition to those ladies' numerous hits, the '90s gave birth to a number of classic R&B jams. Janet Jackson's *Rhythm Nation 1814* (technically released late in 1989, but it kept people dancing for years with its eight singles) and the late Aaliyah's *One in a Million* are just two of the records that had the current generation's R&B singers awkwardly dancing at the freshman homecoming dance. Just start- ing to cross over to more hip-hop-based beats, '90s R&B has a dis- tinct sound, with more focus on vocal delivery than straight-up sexiness to sell records.

Mary J. Blige

In the beginning there was Mary J.

Okay, obviously there were always female R&B singers going for theirs, but things in the game done up and changed as soon as Mary J. Blige arrived. With her 1992 debut, *What's the 411?*, R&B was instantly remixed, remodeled, and totally readjusted, and just like that, it had a distinctly hip-hop flow. With a Kangol pulled down low over her eyes, rocking a baseball jersey and Timbs, Mary was a tattooed, trash-talkin' goddess who repped for the 'hood and sang from the gut. Fierce but still laced with vulnerability, she was an around-the-way girl next door, able to love her man do or die, but not afraid to kick his trifling ass to the curb or cut any encroaching chicken heads without batting a false eyelash or breaking an acrylic nail tip.

> **"WITH A KANGOL PULLED DOWN LOW OVER HER EYES, ROCKING A BASEBALL JERSEY AND TIMBS, MARY WAS A TATTOOED, TRASH-TALKIN' GODDESS WHO REPPED FOR THE 'HOOD AND SANG FROM THE GUT."**

Like her single said, Mary was about "Real Love." Real hurt. Real life. And as the uncontested Queen of Hip-Hop Soul (a title given to her by the artist then known as Sean "Puff Daddy" Combs), Mary J. Blige with her rugged grooves bridged the gap between R&B and rap.

Mary Jane Blige was born in the Bronx and raised in Yonkers, New York. In 1989 a teenage Mary went to a local shopping center and recorded Anita Baker's "Caught Up in the Rapture" into a karaoke machine. Andre Harrell, who had just launched Uptown Records, heard it and signed nineteen-year-old Mary as a backup singer. Working with Combs, an ambitious Uptown intern, Mary began work on her solo album, which dropped in 1992.

It wasn't long after *What's the 411?*'s success that damn near every girl singer had a thug busting a verse on the hook, and just like that, the seemingly oxymoronic term "hip-hop singer" became a straight-up fact and mainstay of the industry. Of course Mary wasn't the first to fuse hip-hop and R&B—that honor goes to Chaka Khan's "I Feel for You" (1984), which featured Melle Mel. Then there was Jody Watley and Rakim's "Friends" in 1989. But Mary J. Blige made hip-hop soul much more than a gimmick. And there was no better example of that than her 1996 Grammy-winning duet with Method Man, "You're All I Need/I'll Be There."

In 1994 came *My Life*. Where *What's the 411?* was all swagger and sass, *My Life* was darker, with a markedly bluesier, more introspective feel. Rumor had it that the album was motivated by Mary's then tumultuous relationship with Jodeci's K-Ci Hailey. With songs like "I'm Going Down" and "Be Happy," the album's intensity exposed Mary's inner torment and, because misery loves company, became a touchstone for her female fans. *My Life* was close to the bone, raw, and remains Mary's most popular— not in terms of sales, but appeal—CD. It is also the record against which all future efforts are compared.

After *My Life*, Mary continued to put out CDs (1997's *Share My World* and 1999's *Mary*), each further reinforcing her status but also increasingly focusing on Mary's struggle (and eventual triumph) over a messy life and her demons. Mary's philosophy was bolstered by a renewed spirituality, a clear head, and that old standby, "a good man" (she married longtime BF Kendu Isaacs on December 7, 2003), and was summed up by 2001's *No More Drama*. The album featured Mary's first number one single, "Family Affair," produced by Dr. Dre, and the emotionally charged "No More Drama." Yet while album sales were holding steady and climbing, Mary's sound was getting a little predictable. Even a much-hyped reunion with Puffy on 2003's *Love & Life* failed to resonate in the way it used to. She was still the Queen, but the hardcore waited for a studio experience that rivaled the in-the-moment—as if her life depended on it—fire Mary brought live.

That moment came with 2005's *The Breakthrough*—originally intended to be a greatest hits release. Don't call it a comeback, but *The Breakthrough* lived up to its title because it felt like a new beginning—or at least a return to form. The CD, which debuted at number one and sold 727,000 copies in its first week of release (the biggest first-week sales for an R&B female in chart history), was soul deep. Typified by the gorgeous "Be Without You"—the biggest and longest-charting hit of her career—the album earned Mary an astounding eight Grammy nods in 2007, including Record of the Year and Song of the Year. She ended up taking home three awards that night, all in the R&B category. Mary returned to the spotlight in late 2007 when she released her eighth studio album, *Growing Pains*. Still to this day, Mary is taking her imitators to school and is a superstar who has defined a generation.

What was the longest-charting single of Mary J. Blige's career?

a. "Family Affair"

b. "I'm Going Down"

c. "Be Without You"

d. "Real Love"

POP QUIZ

Whitney Houston

If you spent any time peeping 2005's train wreck/reality TV series *Being Bobby Brown*, it's understandable that your perception of Whitney Houston might be skewed. Blame the show's fair share of "oh no, they didn't" moments and Mizz Whitney's (who divorced Brown in 2007) behavior, which basically boiled down to being ghetto without the fabulous. Lost in all the gossip and bad behavior was the talent that got Whitney Houston into the spotlight in the first place. Even her harshest critics know that when she was good, she was very very good, and to that end, Whitney can saaang her ass off.

That much has been evident since her jump-off way back in 1985. Sleek, sexy, and groomed to within an inch of her then young life, Whitney—the New Jersey–born daughter of noted session singer Cissy Houston and cousin of the illustrious Dionne Warwick—displayed a talent that made critics weak in the knees and fans eager to cough up the bucks. She was so influential and such a force in the industry that even if you didn't totally dig her (many pop music writers loudly complained that she wasn't "soulful," i.e., black enough), she dominated pop/R&B, so much so that in the mid-'80s through the mid-'90s you could basically sum up the sound of that music as BW and AW—before Whitney and after Whitney. She became what other singers strived to be—even 2006's comeback queen, Mariah "call me Mimi" Carey, was first introduced as a variation on the Whitney theme. Whitney's vocal style could be over the top, but the sheer power of those vocals, even when the material was cheesier than Kraft single slices (e.g., "Greatest Love of All"), Whitney managed to make it feel honest. Dropping hit after hit with songs like "I Wanna Dance with Somebody (Who Loves Me)" and "So Emotional," Ms. Houston was certainly on top.

By 1993, Whitney had shimmy shimmy ya-ed from chart-topping Grammy-winning singer to chart-topping Grammy-winning singer/actress, thanks to a standout lead role in the tearjerker drama *The Bodyguard*. Not merely content to have her name above the title, Whitney also delivered the film's theme song, a tonsil-rattling cover of Dolly Parton's "I Will Always Love You" that stayed at the number one spot for weeks on end and whose ubiquity reached "make it stop!" status.

Whitney followed up that mega-smash with another, 1995's "Exhale (Shoop Shoop)" from her follow-up film project *Waiting to Exhale*. As the '90s moved on, there came a crop of new female singers, each more than eager, and in some cases prepared, to dethrone La Houston.

Like most facets of the music industry, R&B is a tough game and the players are constantly changing up and getting younger in order to satisfy a public with the attention span of a crack-addicted fly with ADHD. The late '90s saw Whitney struggling to stay relevant, as more and more R&B

singers started taking their cues not from the comparatively mature stylings of her or Toni Braxton, but from Mary J. Blige. Yet never count a champion down. While Whitney might not have been number one, she was far from washed up and still had that ability to come up with a hot joint. Which is just what she did in 1998 when after an eight-year hiatus she dropped the slinky "My Love Is Your Love." The collabo with Fugees mastermind Wyclef Jean was not only unexpected and "urban," but also kinda hot. It proved to be one of her last significant chart successes. By the time the millennium rolled up, Whitney was spending more time in the tabloids and, sadly, rehab than in the studio or, more importantly, on the radio. Although she inked a massive contract with her then label Arista for a whopping $100 million, outside of a few greatest hits type packages, nothing major has come from the Houston camp in a minute. Or two.

> ## "WHILE **WHITNEY** MIGHT NOT HAVE BEEN **NUMBER ONE,** SHE WAS FAR FROM WASHED UP AND STILL HAD THAT ABILITY TO COME UP WITH A **HOT JOINT."**

Reality check, one, two, one, two. Whitney's now in her forties, not the optimum age for doing a hot remix with anyone in Dipset. Killer pipes or not, it's going to take nothing short of a full-out miracle (or the class of the twenty-first century a.k.a. Beyoncé, Ciara, Keyshia Cole, and Alicia Keys simultaneously calling it quits or getting fat and ugly) for Whitney Houston to stage the comeback her fans know she's got the talent to pull off. But even though the odds are against her, you'd be foolish to sleep on Whitney.

Mariah Carey

If Whitney repped for the old guard and MJB held it down for hip-hop, then Mariah split the difference. In 1990, the former background vocalist for Latin singer Brenda K. Starr (MC would later cover Starr's "I Still Believe") released her self-titled debut LP. Massively hyped—perhaps due to Mariah's relationship with label head Tommy Mottola—it sold almost ten million copies in the United States, yielded four number ones, "Vision of Love," "Love Takes Time," "Someday," and "I Don't Wanna Cry," and earned Grammys for Best New Artist and Best Female Pop Vocal Performance. *Emotions* (1991) also knocked one outta the park, and by 1992 Mariah was so huge that she could go and release an EP (*MTV Unplugged*) and make it, uh, happen.

By 1993, Mariah was Mrs. Head of Label (a.k.a. Mottola) and presented her third full-length CD, *Music Box*, which also sold like crack. Except that crack is, as we all know, whack. Actually the critics also held the same opinion of MC—okay, not that she was whack, but that her grandstanding, melismatic five-octave range was a bit much. The public gave the crits the middle finger and Mariah kept charting and hitting insanely high notes all the way to the bank. In 1994, she released the requisite holiday album, *Merry Christmas*, and the following year gave her fans *Daydream*. The first single, "Fantasy," was all good, but with the remix—featuring the late Ol' Dirty Bastard—Mariah got a lil' nasty. Even though Mariah followed up "Fantasy" with the typically maudlin "One Sweet Day" (a duet with the equally ginormous Boyz II Men), there were signs that her sound, much like her cup size, was "evolving."

That much became obvious with 1997's *Butterfly*. The first single was "Honey," and its action-flick-themed video was widely perceived as a kiss-off to her now ex-hubby, Tommy Mottola. The album's title was some sort of metaphor for MC's newfound freedom to spread her wings, blah blah. Whatever. The CD sold like crazy and was her most hip-hop-flavored to date. Also dope was the first single off 1999's *Rainbow*, "Heartbreaker," featuring Jay-Z. With it, Carey became the first artist in every year of the '90s to top the charts. She also broke a long-held record previously owned by the Beatles for the most cumulative weeks spent atop the Billboard Hot 100 chart.

But as fabulous as the '90s were, the jump to the new millennium sucked. It started out swell. MC switched labels and inked an $80 million deal with Virgin Records, but a year later all hell broke loose as she sort of lost it personally (rambling suicide messages on her Web site, inappropriate *TRL* behavior, and the capper, her movie debut *Glitter*, which tanked and the soundtrack tanked squared). Needless to say, Virgin and MC said buh-bye, though Mariah did get to keep $28 million—not bad. In 2002, Mariah signed to Def Jam and released *Charmbracelet*, which did alright. Proving that old adage that the tenth time is the, uh, charm, in 2005 Mariah gave us *The Emancipation of Mimi*, which would become not only her most successful and commercially well-received album in eons, but also, thanks to hits like the ubiquitous "We Belong Together," the top-selling CD of 2005 and earner of multiple Grammy nominations, scooping up three wins. "We Belong Together" had enormous success, becoming the first song to simultaneously hold the number one spot on nine Billboard charts. "Don't Forget About Us" was MC's seventeenth chart-topping number one hit and tied her with Elvis for the most number ones by a solo act. Please call it a comeback. Please.

Which single gave Mariah Carey the record of holding the number one spot on nine Billboard charts simultaneously?

a. "One Sweet Day"

b. "We Belong Together"

c. "Honey"

d. "Don't Forget About Us"

POP QUIZ

Janet Jackson

The "normal" Jackson better known as Janet—Miss Jackson, if you're nasty—was born to sing. So after establishing herself as a child actress (most notably on '70s sitcom *Good Times*), Janet entered the family business. In 1982 she delivered her self-titled debut, then followed that up a year later with *Dream Street*. There's a reason why you've never heard of these albums—no one bought them.

Three years later, Janet linked up with producers/writers Jimmy Jam and Terry Lewis, who repped hard for the then explosive Minneapolis sound. The result was the five-times-platinum *Control*, and if it wasn't Janet's debut, it was something mo' betta. Namely, it was the leadoff to a stratospheric series of albums that took Janet all the way to the top. *Control*'s dominance was no fluke, which was proven with the six-times-platinum follow-up, 1989's *Rhythm Nation 1814* and number one hits like "Miss You Much," "Escapade," and "Love Will Never Do (Without You)," which made Janet the first singer with seven top five singles off of one album. Even Michael couldn't do that! The hits kept coming and so did the paychecks. In 1991, Janet made a label move from A&M Records to Virgin Records and signed a massive deal worth millions. That same year she secretly married choreographer and "collaborator" René Elizondo.

> **"THE HITS KEPT COMING AND SO DID THE PAYCHECKS. IN 1991, JANET MADE A LABEL MOVE FROM A&M RECORDS TO VIRGIN RECORDS AND SIGNED A MASSIVE DEAL WORTH MILLIONS."**

Janet got '92 started right with a duet with the late great Luther Vandross, "The Best Things in Life Are Free." The next year she went back to her roots, starring in the 'hood drama *Poetic Justice* opposite Tupac Shakur. She also dropped *janet.* and got the party going with the sultry "That's the Way Love Goes," which spent eight weeks at number one and emerged as her biggest hit ever. Then, like clockwork, the top ten hits kept coming: "If," "Again," "Because of Love," "Any Time, Any Place," and "You Want This." It all culminated in Janet's third straight number one album and sales of a sweet seven million copies.

JJ and MJ did the duet thing in 1995 with the somewhat scary "Scream," which featured an insanely expensive futuristic video that did the impossible—made Janet look bad. The single initially did well, but soon faded away. Two years later came *The Velvet Rope*, which was hugely hyped as Janet's most personal recording to date. Translation? It was about sex. With reviews mixed, yet four big singles ("Together Again," "Got 'Til It's Gone" featuring Q-Tip, "I Get Lonely" featuring Blackstreet, and "Go Deep"), *The Velvet Rope* failed to rack up the nosebleed sales of its predecessors, though let's be fair, it did sell three million CDs, which ain't shabby.

In 1999 Janet scored with "What's It Gonna Be?!," a duet with Busta Rhymes, and the next year hit the big screen in the semi-lame *Nutty Professor II: The Klumps*. The year 2000 also saw the end of Janet's secret marriage. In 2001 she came back with "All for You," and while the title song/single was fun and reached number one on the charts, the album didn't *completely* catch the public's attention.

That would happen in 2004, when while appearing at the Super Bowl XXXVIII halftime show with Justin Timberlake, an allegedly unplanned move from JT resulted in Janet's costume being ripped and her breast (pierced, thank you very much) being exposed to a live audience of unsuspecting innocent children! Oh, and hundreds of millions of drunk football fans. The incident resulted in massive mea culpas from Justin and Janet (though to be fair, she caught the brunt of the blame as if she had ripped her own shirt off), massive outrage, even more massive fines from the FCC, and the introduction of the term "wardrobe malfunction" into the lexicon. The upside? We all got to see Janet's tit. The downside? She was promoting her latest release, *Damita Jo*, and had suddenly gone from sexy singer to smut peddler. Blame the breast or just not a great CD, but *Damita Jo* didn't do big numbers and Janet disappeared from the spotlight, holing up with boyfriend/megaproducer Jermaine Dupri.

In the summer of 2006 and in fighting shape (meaning she'd lost some of the pounds she packed on during the downtime), Janet reemerged just in time to push her new CD *20 Y.O.*, the age that the now forty-year-old Jackson said she felt. Or looked. Or maybe wished that she still was, since today's R&B fans might not want to dance along to some lady old enough to be their mom. Janet said goodbye to Virgin in 2007 and signed with Island Records, home to boyfriend Jermaine Dupri and the hitmaker responsible for Mariah's comeback, LA Reid.

Toni Braxton

Chief among Whitney's up-and-coming competition was Toni Braxton, the first solo female artist signed to then powerhouse label LaFace Records, which was founded and run by musician/songwriters/producers Antonio "LA" Reid (currently CEO of Def Jam Records) and Kenneth "Babyface" Edmonds, the man whose melodic R&B triumphed as one of the '90's defining and most commercially successful sounds. With a husky delivery reminiscent of Anita Baker (herself an R&B/adult contemporary star in the '80s), Toni's 1993 self-titled debut straddled the gulf between old- and new-school R&B. With hits like the aching "Another Sad Love Song," the dramatic "Breathe Again," and the rip-your-lungs-out power ballad "Un-Break My Heart" (off her sophomore disc, *Secrets*), Toni's distinctive alto and her predilection for moody material ruled. Yet by the late '90s, a very public battle with LaFace over, among other issues, money, Toni's career slowed to a grinding halt. She made a tentative comeback with the sexy "He Wasn't Man Enough," but the new sound—and new image, thanks in great part to well-publicized plastic surgery—only took Toni so far, and by 2006 she was reduced to playing Vegas.

Faith Evans

You gotta feel a little bit sorry for Faith Evans. Not just because her life had more than its fair share of sadness and drama, but also because that sadness and drama did a lot to overshadow a career that should have been bigger.

Jersey girl Faith was a classically trained singer who left college to make it in the music biz. In the early '90s she racked up credits as a background singer and, thanks to work on Mary J. Blige's *My Life*, met Puffy, who signed her to Bad Boy, which released *Faith* in 1995. The CD went platinum thanks to "You Used to Love Me" and "Soon As I Get Home." The same year, Faith met labelmate the Notorious B.I.G. and, inexplicably, they got hitched after dating for nine days. Mrs. B.I.G. kept writing for other artists, as well as singing, and had a baby. But by 1996 the marriage was—shock—strained, and adding another layer of tension were rumors about Faith and her estranged man's archrival Tupac—which Pac respectfully alluded to in "Hit 'Em Up." The war of words helped set into motion the East/West turf wars. By March 1997, Faith and Biggie were separated, but that didn't numb the pain of his murder, and the widow added a level of true pathos on Puffy's tribute song "I'll Be Missing You," which became one of the year's biggest hits.

Keep the Faith (1998) also had hits, including the Puffy-produced "Love Like This." In 2001 came *Faithfully*, which contained the Grammy-nominated "Can't Believe." It was her Bad Boy swan song, and in 2005 Faith dropped *The First Lady*, which failed to do much of anything sales-wise.

Aaliyah

Defined as much by scandal and tragedy as by her talent, Aaliyah was a promising, innovative artist and muse to Missy Elliott and Timbaland. A former *Star Search* contestant (she lost) and child of the industry (her uncle/manager was at the time married to R&B legend Gladys Knight), Aaliyah's break came when her uncle introduced her to another of his clients, a then up-and-coming R&B singer named R. Kelly. Liking what he either saw or heard, Kelly took the teen under his uh, wing, and began cooking up tracks for what would become Aaliyah's 1994 debut, *Age Ain't Nothing but a Number*, the title of which would take on a whole 'notha meaning.

With a cool as crap image, low-slung baggy jeans, dark shades, and her hair almost covering her pretty face, Aaliyah garnered attention and then some. On the back of the Kelly-penned "Back & Forth" and an Isley Brothers cover, "At Your Best (You Are Love)," her debut went double platinum. Yet that took a backseat to the drama that was about to unfold. Rumors began to spread that R. Kelly, more than ten years her senior, had not only produced but also seduced and married the fifteen-year-old. Her people and his people kept their respective lips sealed, but that didn't stop the fans and media from talking. Indeed a few years down the road, documents confirmed that the couple had done the deed but annulled the union after a few months. The former Mr. and Mrs. Kelly's creative hookup was also over, but Aaliyah proved that she didn't need her old (literally) man when it came to making music.

Teaming with, among others, Timbaland and Missy Elliott, Aaliyah dropped *One in a Million* in 1996. Hits such as "If Your Girl Only Knew" and "One in a Million" signaled a new edgier sound and the CD went double platinum. In 1998 Aaliyah and Timbo teamed up again for the quirky smash "Are You That Somebody?" off the *Dr. Dolittle* soundtrack. Aaliyah decided to try her hand at acting, co-starring with martial arts hero Jet Li and rapper DMX in *Romeo Must Die*. "Try Again," from the film's soundtrack, became A's first pop number one and resulted in a Grammy nomination for Best Female R&B Vocal Performance.

In 2001, Aaliyah worked on the vampire film *Queen of the Damned* and was cast in the as yet unfilmed *Matrix* sequels. She also released *Aaliyah*, again working primarily with Timbaland and Missy. The CD boasted the hit "We Need a Resolution," which, like the album, got terrific reviews. That August the singer flew down to the Bahamas to film the video for her second single, "Rock the Boat." The shoot would end tragically when on the 25th, she and several crew members died in a plane crash. Stunned, the R&B community expressed its grief by making Aaliyah's CD double platinum and her only number one LP. "Rock the Boat" and "More Than a Woman" both became posthumous top ten R&B hits. In 2002, *I Care 4 U*, a blend of hits and unreleased material, entered at number three, with "Miss You" topping the R&B charts in 2003. Baby girl would forever be missed.

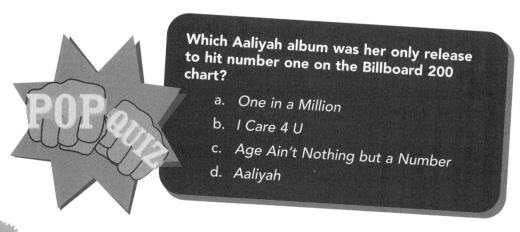

POP *QUIZ*

Which Aaliyah album was her only release to hit number one on the Billboard 200 chart?

a. One in a Million

b. I Care 4 U

c. Age Ain't Nothing but a Number

d. Aaliyah

Brandy

Like many of her peers, Brandy Norwood grew up under the spell of Whitney Houston. Guided by her mother/manager—who also oversaw the markedly less successful career of younger brother Ray J—Brandy got her start as a teenager and became not just a singing star, but with *Moesha*, which aired for six seasons, a TV star as well. Brimming with upbeat chaste charm, Brandy's eponymous debut dropped in 1994, containing the hits "I Wanna Be Down" and "Baby." In '96 Brandy struck big again with "Sittin' Up in My Room," off the Babyface-produced soundtrack to *Waiting to Exhale*. Instead of recording a follow-up, Brandy concentrated on *Moesha* and the starring role (opposite Whitney) in 1997's *Cinderella*. In 1998 came *Never Say Never*. The CD contained the Grammy-winning megahit "The Boy Is Mine," a duet with the ATL's Monica that topped the Billboard Hot 100 chart for an astounding thirteen weeks.

Brandy eventually outgrew her teenybopper image, a point driven home by the birth of her daughter and a "marriage" (which was later revealed to have never been legally recognized) to a producer. Her new grownness was revealed on 2002's *Full Moon*, which failed to sell as well as prior CDs but featured the chart-topping Rodney "Darkchild" Jerkins–produced "What About Us?" *Afrodisiac* (2004), featuring the Kanye West–produced "Talk About Our Love," got great reviews, but like the song said, Brandy had come to the end of the road. The majority of the album was produced by Timbaland, yet it still couldn't achieve Brandy's previous levels of success. Her semi has-been status was reinforced in 2006 when she became a celebrity guest judge on the reality show *America's Got Talent*. But joy turned to tragedy on December 30, 2006, when Brandy's Land Rover struck another vehicle, causing a chain reaction on the Interstate 405 freeway in Los Angeles. The impact from her vehicle killed a woman driving one of the four cars involved in the accident. Brandy turned back to music to comfort her during this tough period, recording tracks for her fifth album.

Monica

Another girl singer hitting high notes before she hit high school was Monica Arnold. Monica worked with the innovative producer Dallas Austin and her 1995 debut, *Miss Thang*, spawned the platinum top ten singles "Don't Take It Personal (Just One of Dem Days)" and "Before You Walk Out of My Life." After dropping "The Boy Is Mine" with Brandy, Monica released an album of the same name and then disappeared from view, returning with 2003's *After the Storm*, which, as is usually the case with post-teen singers, focused more on mature themes. Monica came back again, now older, a mother, and more street, with 2006's *The Makings of Me*, which did not do well sales-wise, becoming Monica's lowest-selling release to date.

Mýa

A D.C. native, Mýa Harrison seriously studied dance as a young'un and could not only bust a move, but had musical skills too. When her musician dad caught wind of those skills, he helped her shop demos. She caught the ear of a local manager and got a major-label deal in the late '90s. Like many of her fellow teen R&B stars, Mýa wasn't exactly a belter, but her sweetness—hitched to a subtle vibe that signaled she might not be all that innocent—worked. She blew up from the jump, as her self-titled debut went platinum and yielded three hit singles, "It's All About Me," "Movin' On," and "My First Night with You." She continued to shine when "Ghetto Supastar (That Is What You Are)" and "Take Me There" (*Bulworth* and *The Rugrats Movie* soundtracks respectively) also charted.

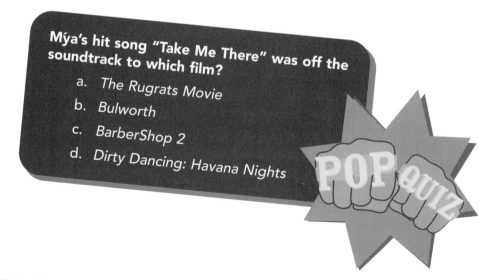

Mýa's hit song "Take Me There" was off the soundtrack to which film?

a. The Rugrats Movie

b. Bulworth

c. BarberShop 2

d. Dirty Dancing: Havana Nights

POP QUIZ

Mýa's sophomore CD, *Fear of Flying* (2000), also went platinum and featured "Case of the Ex" and the "Best of Me." In 2002 she starred in the acclaimed film *Chicago*, which earned the Screen Actors Guild award for Outstanding Performance by a Cast in a Motion Picture. The next year, *Moodring* went gold. After focusing on film for a while, Mýa dropped *Liberation*, which showcased—surprise—a sexier sound.

Jennifer Lopez

Jennifer Lopez had already racked up credits as a dancer and actress by the time she released 1999's *On the 6*. The album went triple platinum and spawned the hits "If You Had My Love" and "Waiting for Tonight." The Nuyorican hottie wasn't technically an R&B singer—in record company lingo, Lopez, much like early Mariah, was "worked" pop. But "Jenny from the Block" (to quote her 2002 hit) still got love from the streets. Helping J.Lo earn that cred was a splashy and ultimately messy relationship with Sean "Puff Daddy" Combs, which famously culminated in a 1999 shootout at a NYC nightclub, an incident for which Combs was tried and acquitted. The resulting bad publicity ended the affair between the two. Post her stint as a gun moll, Lopez enjoyed the 'hood-friendly hit "I'm Real (Murder Remix)" (2001), a thug duet featuring Ja Rule that stirred up controversy due to Jen's use of the N-word, off of her 2001 sophomore album, *J.Lo*. She released two more albums, *This Is Me . . . Then* in 2002 and *Rebirth* in 2005. Unsurprisingly, all albums enjoyed great success. Jenny also reclaimed her 'hood cred with a sizzling cameo in LL's 2006's smash "Control Myself." Jenny from the Block worked double shifts in 2007, releasing her first all-Spanish album, *Como Ama Una Mujer*, in the spring and her sixth English album, *Brave*, in the fall. J.Lo announced her pregnancy in 2007, taking a break from showbiz to focus on motherhood the following year.

DIVALICIOUS:
'90s FEMALE R&B

FAITH EVANS MARRIED THE NOTORIOUS B.I.G., WHO MARY J. BLIGE ENLISTED FOR HER "REAL LOVE" RECORD.

BOTH AALIYAH AND FAITH EVANS GREW UP SINGING IN CHURCH.

MARY J. BLIGE GOT HER START AT UPTOWN RECORDS WORKING WITH DIDDY, WHO IS THE EX-BOYFRIEND OF JENNIFER LOPEZ.

JENNIFER LOPEZ STARRED IN THE MTV REALITY SHOW *DANCELIFE*, AND WHITNEY HOUSTON STARRED IN THE BRAVO REALITY SHOW *BEING BOBBY BROWN*.

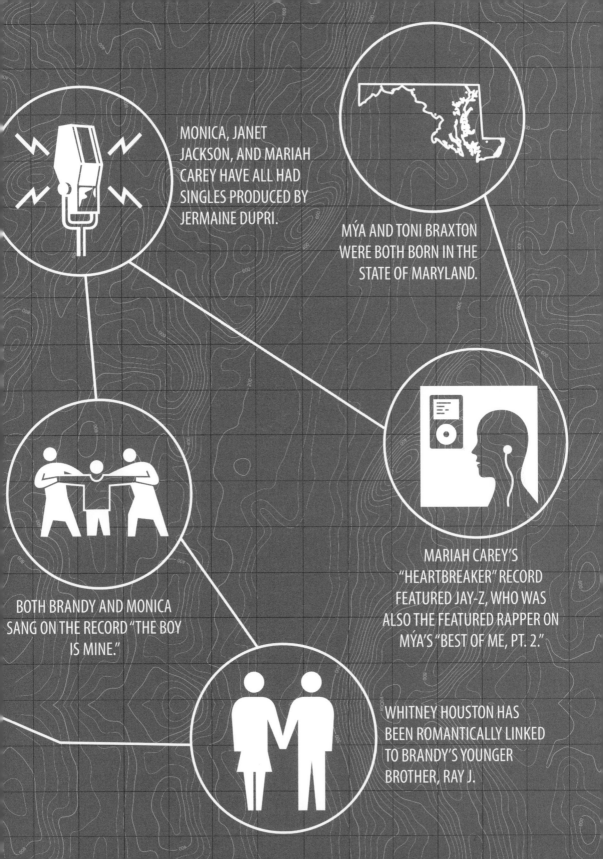

MONICA, JANET JACKSON, AND MARIAH CAREY HAVE ALL HAD SINGLES PRODUCED BY JERMAINE DUPRI.

MÝA AND TONI BRAXTON WERE BOTH BORN IN THE STATE OF MARYLAND.

BOTH BRANDY AND MONICA SANG ON THE RECORD "THE BOY IS MINE."

MARIAH CAREY'S "HEARTBREAKER" RECORD FEATURED JAY-Z, WHO WAS ALSO THE FEATURED RAPPER ON MÝA'S "BEST OF ME, PT. 2."

WHITNEY HOUSTON HAS BEEN ROMANTICALLY LINKED TO BRANDY'S YOUNGER BROTHER, RAY J.

CHAPTER 9

BABY MAKIN' MUSIC:

'90s MALE R&B

Although to the casual fan most R&B album covers featuring men from the 1990s are interchangeable (think silk shirts and abs), the music most definitely was not. Sure, there are some singers that might make you say "who?" but people say the same thing about classic vocalists from Motown's heyday that might have only had one or two hits heard regularly on the oldies station. The '90s began the long careers of Chicago's own weirdo/hitmaker R. Kelly, apparent cybersex fan Usher (you know you've heard that "Dot Com" song on the radio), and producer/singer Babyface. Although their good looks didn't hurt, none of the men who found success in the '90s would have sold many records or remained in the spotlight if it weren't for their undeniable vocal skills.

R. Kelly

Love him, hate him, or just hope he doesn't get anywhere near your kid sister, but there's one profound fact: R. Kelly is one of R&B's biggest stars. Equal parts gangsta and gentleman, he can write soaring anthems of self-empowerment, crank out a banging love song so sex-drenched you need a condom just to listen to it, or cook up a completely loony epic—all with the same level of intensity. Does he write the same five songs over and over again? Possibly, but on the flip side you could say that Robert Kelly's style is one of the most recognized and imitated of the last decade. Either way you cut it, the dude rules.

> **"EQUAL PARTS GANGSTA AND GENTLEMAN, [R. KELLY] CAN WRITE SOARING ANTHEMS OF SELF-EMPOWERMENT, CRANK OUT A BANGING LOVE SONG SO SEX-DRENCHED YOU NEED A CONDOM JUST TO LISTEN TO IT."**

He's been doing so since 1992, when, backed by his where-are-they-now group Public Announcement, he kicked things off with *Born into the 90's*. R&B heads ate it up and "Honey Love" and "Slow Dance (Hey Mr. DJ)" went to number one. Sensing that fans liked him (they really liked him), R. decided to drop Public Announcement and go solo, starting with '93's *12 Play*. Seeing as how the CD sold over five million units, it was a smart move. The album's singles "Sex Me, Pts. 1–2," "Bump N' Grind" (number one pop and R&B, staying on the latter chart for twelve weeks), and "Your Body's Callin'" set Kelly's thematic steez—sex, and lots of it. The next year was a busy year for R. Not only was he enjoying *12 Play*'s success, but he produced Aaliyah's *Age Ain't Nothing but a Number*, and as it would later be revealed, up and married the fifteen-year-old as well. That little bit of cradle robbing sparked some controversy and set into motion the widely held perception that Mr. Kelly had a thing for the niñas. But even whiffs of pedophilia couldn't slow R.'s career down. In 1995, he worked with another sexually suspect singer, handling Michael Jackson's "You Are Not Alone," and then later that year came through with an eponymous album. Said CD sold over five million copies, was Kelly's first to top the pop charts, and produced the platinum singles "You Remind Me of Something," "Down Low (Nobody Has to Know)," and "I Can't Sleep Baby (If I)"—all of which hit number one R&B and reached the pop top ten.

Kelly crossed over for sure with 1996's "I Believe I Can Fly," written for the Michael Jordan vehicle *Space Jam*. With the sex-you-up vibe muted to inaudible and filled with that faux gospel feel-good crap suitable for grad-uations and A.A. meetings, "I Believe I Can Fly" was ubiquitous and earned Grammys for Best Male R&B Vocal Performance, Best R&B Song, and Best Song Written Specifically for a Motion Picture or for Television. Who knew that category even existed? After making housewives happy, Kelly returned somewhat to his raunchy form with '98's double-disc *R.*, which, even with a scary duet with Celine Dion (the number one "I'm Your Angel") became Kelly's biggest-selling project to date, going eight times platinum-plus. Kelly was on the path to racking up more chart-topping hits in the '90s than any other male artist, but, not content to rule just one decade, he kept keeping on in the next. *TP-2.com* spent three weeks at number one and he scored two more huge singles, "I Wish" and "Fiesta," which featured Jay-Z.

Digging the whole "Fiesta" experience, R. and Jay came together for the heavily hyped *The Best of Both Worlds* (2002), but serious sales were eclipsed by more serious drama. In the winter of 2002, news broke that there was a videotape showing Kelly having sex with a fourteen-year-old girl. Copies of the video were bootlegged, some radio stations dropped him, and *The Best of Both Worlds*, which had entered the charts at the number two spot, sank like a stone, weighed down by the scandal.

Adding insult to self-inflicted injury were numerous civil suits involving alleged former conquests as well as a new round of sex videos (Kelly denies it is him on the tapes) and accusations from Sparkle, a former Kelly protégée (1998's "Be Careful"), who announced that the girl in the original tape was in fact her underage niece. In 2003, Kelly was officially charged by Chicago police with twenty-one counts of child pornography–related offenses. Kelly pleaded not guilty and in response to the furor released "Heaven I Need a Hug." One would think hugging would be the *last* thing on homeboy's mind. Kells's case finally headed to court in September 2007.

Kelly scrapped *Loveland*, his next scheduled project, and went back into the studio and came back with *Chocolate Factory* (2003). "Ignition" went to number two on the Billboard Hot 100, followed by his next album, *Happy People/U Saved Me*. Despite the accusations, R. Kelly was on a roll—one that temporarily slowed down following his reunion with Jay-Z on the lackluster *Unfinished Business*. A subsequent tour imploded when the obvious issues between the superstars boiled over to the stage. In 2005, weeks before his trial was to begin, Kelly roared back from the debacle with *TP.3 Reloaded*, the highlight of which was the strange even by Kelly standards "Trapped in the Closet" series. The songs featured videos that became almost as infamous as that *other* one. Not one to downplay his sexual adventures, Kells continued to get his freak on with 2007's *Double Up*, with raunchy lyrics such as, "Like *Jurassic Park*, except I'm your sexasaurus."

Which is R. Kelly's biggest-selling album to date?

a. 12 Play

b. TP-2.com

c. Chocolate Factory

d. R.

POP quiz

Usher

Few child singers have the goods to sustain a career—let alone get larger (musically, not physically) as they mature. Ladies and gentlemen: Usher! Spotted by a label executive at an ATL talent show, the then fourteen-year-old Usher Raymond auditioned for LaFace Records co-founder Antonio "LA" Reid. We all know the rest of the story. In classic showbiz style, the last name was kicked to the curb. His 1994 debut was simply *Usher*. Co-executive-produced by Sean "Puffy" Combs (that's what he was forcing others to call him back then), Usher's single "Think of You" went gold and voilà! A star (almost) was born.

Actually, things really started to heat up after Usher graduated from high school. *My Way* (1997) featured producers Jermaine Dupri, Babyface, and Puffy as "You Make Me Wanna" blew up, topping the R&B charts for a mind-melting eleven weeks and selling two million copies. Also charting and selling quite nicely were follow-ups "My Way" and "Nice & Slow," which became Usher's first number one on the pop charts, meaning that white folks were starting to dig him as well. *My Way* ended up with a six-times-platinum certification and resulted in Usher's first Grammy nomination for Best Male R&B Vocal Performance for "You Make Me Wanna." Ush kept in the public eye with a few minor film roles, dropped a live CD (1999), and then unleashed the big guns with *8701*, released on August 7, 2001, a.k.a. 8/7/01. The CD was preceded by "U Remind Me," which hit number one on the Billboard Hot 100 and stayed put for four weeks.

Also large was "U Got It Bad," a slinky slow jam that also took up residence at the top spot, while The Neptunes-produced "U Don't Have to Call" (is it egomania to have the first letter of your name in every song?) made its way into the top three as *8701* sold more than eight million copies worldwide. The love didn't stop there. In 2002, "U Remind Me" won the Grammy for Best Male R&B Vocal Performance, while due to eligibility cutoffs, "U Don't Have to Call" won the same award one year later. Only Stevie Wonder and the late Luther Vandross could say they'd achieved that Grammy one-two punch.

In 2004, *Confessions* arrived. It sold 1.1 million copies in its first week, the highest SoundScan numbers ever for a male R&B artist, and went on to move more than fifteen million copies worldwide. The CD contained some of the most personal and intimate songs of Usher's career—again singing about sex, specifically cheating on then girlfriend Chilli of TLC. Less intimate but more party-jumping was the first single, "Yeah!" Produced by Lil Jon and featuring Ludacris, "Yeah!" went to number one, as did "Confessions Part II." In September 2004, "My Boo," Usher's duet with Alicia Keys, included on the *Confessions Special Edition*, which came out six months after the original unspecial version, also was number one. That same year, "Caught Up" went top ten and in 2005 Usher won three Grammys, including Best R&B Performance by a Duo or Group with Vocals ("My Boo" with Alicia Keys), Best Rap/Sung Collaboration ("Yeah!"), and Best Contemporary R&B Album (*Confessions*). In August of 2006, Usher took a stab at Broadway, joining the musical *Chicago*. It seemed there was truly nothing this man couldn't do. Usher broke the hearts of girls around the world when he wed his stylist and longtime boo, Tameka Foster, in August 2007 in a private ceremony in Atlanta. The couple had their first child later that year.

Babyface

Although most of the public knew him for his fly and finessed songs and production, Kenneth "Babyface" Edmonds started as a performer. The former member of the marginally popular '80's R&B band the Deele (whose ranks also included Antonio "LA" Reid, the La of LaFace Records and now chairman of the Island Def Jam Music Group), Face made his first serious stab at solodom with '89's *Tender Lover*. After that album went double platinum and kicked off four hit singles, Face went back to his day gig, cranking out hits for half the free world. With ruling the charts and running LaFace, it's a wonder that Babyface had time for his own CDs, but he did.

The year 1993 begat *For the Cool in You*. It was an even bigger hit than its predecessor, going triple platinum and producing Babyface's first top five pop hit, "When Can I See You" (which won him his first Grammy as a performer for Best Male R&B Vocal Performance) and introduced the concept of the R&B power ballad. In 1996, Babyface released *The Day*. The album was loaded with guest appearances including Mariah Carey, Stevie Wonder, and LL Cool J and resulted in another chart-topper, "Every Time I Close My Eyes." In 1996, Babyface won the Grammy for Producer of the Year and also Record of the Year with Eric Clapton for "Change the World."

Nineteen ninety-seven saw *Babyface MTV Unplugged NYC*, and four years down the road *Face2Face*, which had the bad luck to be released on September 11, not an optimum time to hype a CD. Four years after that? *Grown & Sexy*, which, even without a national tragedy impeding its potential, made little impact.

In 1996, Babyface shared the Grammy for Record of the Year with which artist?

a. Mariah Carey
b. Eric Clapton
c. Stevie Wonder
d. TLC

Ginuwine

Collaborating with a then relatively unknown Timbaland, Ginuwine cooked up sex-drenched and grinding R&B hits that, when combined with sinewy dance moves and incredibly well-groomed eyebrows, were the szzz-hit.

Born Elgin Baylor (after the ex-NBA star) Lumpkin—that name does *not* bring sexy back—Ginuwine grew up digging himself some Michael Jackson. He dug the superstar so much and apparently so well that along with singing in a few local hip-hop acts around D.C., he earned spending cash as an MJ impersonator. After a short spell in another D.C. vocal act, he decided to get himself a fallback career and earned his paralegal degree.

It was just around this time, as he was making plans for his future, that Elgin—now answering to his new stage name—met and was somewhat discovered by R&B quartet Jodeci in 1996. Soon after that fateful connection, G linked up with Timbaland, a producer with some Jodeci connects. T and G cooked up the futuristic, space-age "Pony" and Ginuwine landed at Sony. In 1996 came *Ginuwine . . . the Bachelor*. With the single "Pony" at number one, Ginuwine was a multiplatinum star and Timbaland got to increase his day rate.

In '99 the dynamic duo returned with *100% Ginuwine*, which also went double platinum, pushed by the crossover appeal of "So Anxious." Two years later, G decided to work without his Timbaland safety net. Like his previous work, *The Life* went platinum, while the ballad "Differences" became his biggest pop single to date. Later in 2001, Ginuwine was featured on P. Diddy's top ten "I Need A Girl, Part II," following that up with the popular *The Senior* (2003) and 2005's *Back II Da Basics*.

Montell Jordan

If you're gonna be a one-hit wonder, then make damn sure it's a freaking great one hit. Incorporating rap legend Slick Rick's timeless tale "Children's Story," "This Is How We Do It" was the jam, presenting an upbeat, party-hearty, "positive" POV of the then ultraviolent and controversial L.A. music scene. The display of hometown love from newcomer Montell Jordan got loved right back and the Def Jam artist saw his party anthem go to number one and sell over a million copies. Jordan then dropped *More . . .* in 1996. Although it didn't match the success of *This Is How We Do It*, it was nevertheless a hit. But things sort of went downhill after that. In '98 Jordan released his third album, *Let's Ride*, followed a year later by *Get It On . . . Tonite*. None experienced the same success of his past albums.

Joe

Joe used his seductive delivery, no-frills charm, and romantic songs to make the girls go crazy. Even if he was so anonymous you couldn't pick him out of a lineup. Sorry. It's true.

He grew up in Georgia and sang in church, and after high school, Joe Thomas made his way to the music capital of the world—or rather New Jersey, across the river from the music capital. While there, he met a producer, recorded a demo, and eventually landed at PolyGram Records. In '93 Joe debuted with *Everything*. Four years later, he found greater success when he moved to Jive Records and recorded *All That I Am*. His single "Don't Wanna Be a Player" topped charts and had a second life when he teamed with the late Big Pun. Together the laid-back Joe and the Boogie Down Pun cooked up a hip-hop remix of the track entitled "Still Not a Player," which helped forge a unity between Puerto Rican and black artists as well as injecting the somewhat bland Joe with a little flavor. In 1999, Joe got even more love. He appeared on Mariah Carey's "Thank God I Found You" and recorded "I Wanna Know." The ballad slow-burned its way to the top five spot in 2000 and helped launch his next LP, *My Name Is Joe*. The album also spawned Joe's biggest single yet, the remix to "Stutter" featuring rapper Mystikal, which spent four weeks atop the Billboard Hot 100 chart.

BABY MAKIN' MUSIC: '90s MALE R&B

GINUWINE FEATURED R. KELLY ON HIS SONG "HELL YEAH."

BABYFACE AND MONTELL JORDAN BOTH HELD CAREERS AS RECORDING ARTISTS AND SONGWRITERS FOR OTHER ARTISTS.

USHER IS SIGNED TO BABYFACE'S LAFACE RECORDS.

R. KELLY AND JOE ARE BOTH SIGNED TO JIVE RECORDS.

BOTH JOE AND USHER BEGAN THEIR SINGING CAREERS IN CHURCH.

CHAPTER 10

FAMILY AFFAIR:

'90S R&B GROUPS

ith New Edition laying the groundwork in 1980 for all "boy bands" to come, many others found success by slightly tweaking the formula and releasing some classic records. Undoubtedly the zenith of the R&B groups, the '90s introduced the public to Boyz II Men, Jodeci, and Dru Hill. And that's only the men! If you're reading this, you most likely remember En Vogue's video for "Free Your Mind" that had that fashion-show-from-the-future vibe and a bunch of guys stage-diving for some reason. You also probably remember TLC's video for "Ain't 2 Proud 2 Beg" where they were all dressed like cartoon characters and Left Eye had that egg on her glasses. These groups not only influenced the genre musically and in fashion (save for those wet-suits Jodeci are wearing on the cover of *Diary of a Mad Band*), but took the torch from New Edition and passed it to a later generation of much more vanilla groups like the Backstreet Boys and the Spice Girls.

Boyz II Men

In the '90s Boyz II Men were the, uh, men. Their singles broke chart records previously held by Elvis and the Beatles. Mainstream, baby. These weren't just boyz in the hood—these were boyz in your face. Wanya Morris, Nathan Morris, Shawn Stockman, and Michael McCary brought their own steez while mixing and matching key ingredients from those before them. First among the homages was their name, which for those of you playing the at-home version was a New Edition song. In fact Boyz II Men were discovered at a Bell Biv DeVoe show. BBD (Ricky Bell, Michael Bivins, and Ronnie DeVoe) did their own thing in 1990 when, after taking a break from the insanely big boy group New Edition (think Jackson 5—with Bobby Brown), dropped *Poison* and the single "Do Me!" The multiplatinum hits brought some hip-hop into the relative calm of R&B. And to keep the BBD/NE connect going, Michael Bivins, one-third of BBD and one-fifth of NE, originally managed Boyz II Men. But back to BIIM.

Calling their 1991 debut *Cooleyhighharmony* (a nod to a '70s comedy), Boyz II Men created a sound they labeled "hip-hop doo-wop." They scored right away with "Motownphilly," a shout-out to their label and hometown.

The guys followed up with "It's So Hard to Say Goodbye to Yesterday." It didn't hurt that along with having talent, BIIM worked with some of the best—notably Jimmy Jam and Terry Lewis and Babyface. It was Mr. Face who handed them their 1992 monster single "End of the Road."

Boyz II Men kept on keeping on with their second CD, *II* (1994), which contained more mega-smashes, including the Babyface-penned "I'll Make Love to You"—which spent a record fourteen weeks at the number one spot on the Billboard Hot 100. Like "End of the Road," the ballad broke more of those Elvis-level sales records, played constantly on radio and

MTV, and became an "our song" for homeboys and housewives alike. The guys then dropped another chart-topper in the form of the Jam and Lewis confection "On Bended Knee," and its success tightened BIIM's stranglehold on the charts.

By 1995 *II* had sold over twelve million copies and BIIM were, without question, one of the biggest pop/R&B acts going. In November of 1995, the Boyz joined Mariah Carey on the record-breaking "One Sweet Day," which ended up being nominated for Record of the Year at 1996's Grammys. While 1997's *Evolution* enjoyed good reviews and did well, the numbers weren't nearly as mind-boggling as before and the momentum began to swing away from BIIM's sound. By 2000's *Nathan Michael Shawn Wanya*, BIIM were all but coasting on goodwill, making 2002's *Full Circle* and their covers collections, 2004's *Throwback, Vol. 1* and 2007's *Motown: A Journey Through Hitsville USA*, mere blips on the R&B radar.

What was the name of Boyz II Men's debut CD?

a. *Evolution*

b. *II*

c. *Cooleyhighharmony*

d. *Nathan Michael Shawn Wanya*

POP QUIZ

Dru Hill

Tamir "Nokio" Ruffin, Mark "Sisqó" Andrews, Larry "Jazz" Anthony Jr., and James "Woody" Green grew up in B-More, met in middle school, and began singing together in 1992. Taking their name from their neighborhood (Druid Hill Park), the quartet created a youthful, vigorous sound that attracted the attention of a local manager, who arranged for them to perform at a record industry convention. From there word started to spread and in 1995 that buzz reached the ear of then president of Island

Black Music Hiram Hicks. He enlisted Dru Hill to record "Tell Me," which was featured on the *Eddie* soundtrack. The song went platinum, became a pop hit, and landed at the top of the R&B charts. Suddenly the teens from Maryland were huge. Dru Hill's eponymous CD hit stores in 1996 and exploded, selling over a million copies and producing the hits "In My Bed" (*Billboard*'s number one R&B single for 1997), "Never Make a Promise," and "We're Not Making Love."

In 1998 they released *Enter the Dru*. The CD debuted at number two, went double platinum, and contained the smash singles "How Deep Is Your Love" and "These Are the Times." In 1999 each member decided to work on solo efforts. The first out the gate was Sisqó. His *Unleash the Dragon* (1999) would morph from a one-off side project to a full-out sensation driven by the hits "Thong Song" and "Incomplete."

As Sisqó's star ascended, Dru Hill's status was called into question. The remaining three members used the "hiatus" to continue exploring their own music, and by 2002, one year after his platinum sophomore CD *Return of Dragon*, Sisqó was back in the mix. In 2002 Dru Hill reentered the game with *Dru World Order*, which introduced a fifth member, old Baltimore friend Rufus "Scola" Waller. Produced primarily by the group, *Dru World Order*'s sales failed to scale the heights of their previous outings and the group disappeared.

112

ATL's 112 had the distinction of being one of Bad Boy's most successful vocal acts, as well as the first. Marvin "Slim" Scandrick, Daron Jones, Quinnes "Q" Parker, and Michael Keith linked up in high school (oh my, this pattern is getting predictable) and started doing talent shows that helped them land management. Said management hipped Puffy to the quartet and Combs not only inked 112 to a deal but executive-produced their 1996 eponymous debut. With Puffy handling some of the songwriting duties, 112's album went platinum and "Only You" peaked at number three on the R&B charts. The next single, "Come See Me," was a little further down the charts, but the group had made their mark and in 1998 dropped *Room 112*, which also went platinum and upped their profile—even if you'd be hard-pressed to name anyone in the group. Taking their sweet time, 112 came through with 2001's *Part III*, which featured the hit singles "It's Over Now" and "Peaches & Cream," but they were starting to have issues with the notoriously controlling Combs and by 2003's *Hot & Wet* they had one foot out the door and left Bad Boy on less than fabulous terms. They landed at Def Soul and released *Pleasure & Pain* in 2005—which maybe fourteen people paid attention to. The group basically went AWOL and Daron became a noted producer (Jamie Foxx and Keyshia Cole) in the mid-2000s.

Total

Another Puffy project was the as-ghetto-as-they-wanna-be girl group Total. Loaded with teeth-sucking, acrylic nails, and weave-rocking sex appeal (if girls who look like they'll cut you is sexy), Kima, Pam, and Keisha initially blew up backing the Notorious B.I.G. on "One More Chance" and "Juicy." That led to their own single, "Can't You See," off the *New Jersey Drive* soundtrack. The trio's self-titled debut followed in 1996 and gave fans the hits "No One Else," "Kissin' You," and "Do You Think About Us?"—all of which were big R&B hits. As popular as Total were, their whole steez might have been a bit too "urban" for the mainstream, and soon after their second CD, 1998's *Kima, Keisha & Pam*, the bad girls of Bad Boy stepped off.

SWV

You can't miss if the inventor of New Jack Swing has got your back. So it's not that shocking that SWV (Sisters With Voices) exploded in the early '90s, thanks to their Teddy Riley–produced 1992 debut. The CD yielded a mess of top ten R&B/pop hits and made the girls very popular.

The three childhood friends Coko (Cheryl Gamble-Clemons), Taj (Tamara Johnson-George), and Lelee (Leanne Lyons) came up in the church. Years after finding God, they found a producer and mentor in the form of Riley, who thanks to his own group Guy, Bobby Brown's solo jam "My Prerogative," and Jodeci, changed R&B by giving it hip-hop's beats and balls. Riley hit the mark again with SWV's double-platinum *It's About Time*.

It's About Time contained several hit songs, including "Right Here" and the crossover "I'm So Into You." SWV topped that with a pair of number one R&B singles, "Weak" and "Right Here/Human Nature," a remix that sampled Michael Jackson's hit "Human Nature." "Weak" topped the Billboard Hot 100 chart, and then there was another R&B success, "You're Always On My Mind" in 1994. That same year the ladies dropped the gold-selling EP *The Remixes*.

SWV came back in '96 with *New Beginning* and the number one R&B song "You're the One." Following the pattern of many huge R&B acts, they seemed unable to keep the momentum going much past their third CD, 1997's *Release Some Tension*.

Which producer helped SWV get their start?

a. Raphael Saadiq
b. Dallas Austin
c. Babyface
d. Teddy Riley

POP QUIZ

TLC

If someone hadn't cooked up *Behind the Music*, it would have been invented purely for TLC. During their run as the biggest-selling female act of the '90s, TLC experienced the highest of highs and the lowest of lows, but throughout it all, they were always crazy, sexy, cool.

Tionne "T-Boz" Watkins, Lisa "Left Eye" Lopes, and Rozonda "Chilli" Thomas formed TLC in 1991, and soon the three Atlantans caught the ear of former '80s star Pebbles—then married to Antonio "LA" Reid, co-head of LaFace Records. Pebbles became their manager and TLC began working primarily with Dallas Austin, who along with producing many of their songs would later produce a son with Chilli.

TLC came outta the box blazing with "Ain't 2 Proud 2 Beg" off their 1992 debut, *Oooooooohhh . . . On the TLC Tip*. TLC's no-shame-in-their-game message was driven home by Left Eye's habit of rocking a condom over her—you got it—left eye. The group then dropped "Baby-Baby-Baby," yet as cool as the songs were, TLC's vibe took center stage because they embodied girl power.

That U.N.I.T.Y., combined with killer songs from Organized Noize, Baby-face, and Austin, made 1994's *CrazySexyCool* seriously great. TLC set it off with the first single, "Creep," which became the girls' first number one on the Billboard Hot 100. Also hitting the top of the chart was the socially conscious "Waterfalls." *CrazySexyCool* would sell over eleven million copies and earn a Grammy for Best R&B Album.

Yet despite the success, all was not well. Right before *CrazySexyCool* dropped, Left Eye, in a drunken rage, burnt down the house of her boyfriend, NFL star Andre Rison. She avoided jail time with probation and rehab. Then in '95, TLC filed for bankruptcy, claiming they'd been robbed of royalties. After a prolonged battle with their label and manager, they made peace with the former and split from the latter.

By 1999 there was nothing but love and TLC unveiled *FanMail*, which debuted at number one. The CD boasted the smashes "No Scrubs" and "Unpretty," which helped the Grammy-winning *FanMail* sell over six million units. Yet despite that, breakup rumors surfaced when Left Eye dissed her bandmates and announced plans for a solo CD. Miraculously, in 2001 TLC once again came together to record—but the joy was short-lived. In 2002, while on retreat in Honduras, Left Eye was killed in a car accident. Containing some contributions from their late partner, *3D* was met with positive reviews, but the praise was drowned out by sadness. While TLC has never officially broken up (in 2005 the remaining two-thirds even went the reality show route to find a new member with *R U the Girl*), TLC as fans once knew it was over. What remains is a legacy of dope songs delivered by ladies not too proud to be themselves.

What was TLC's first number one on the Billboard Hot 100 chart?

a. "Ain't 2 Proud 2 Beg"

b. "Creep"

c. "Waterfalls"

d. "Baby-Baby-Baby"

POP quiz

Jodeci

Jodeci were the anti–Boyz II Men. While BIIM wore coordinated outfits, Jodeci came to award shows rocking Hannibal Lecter's face guards and wielding machetes—seriously. If BIIM were the boys next door, Jodeci were the boys next door that you kept your daughter away from. In short, Jodeci oozed nasty sex.

"IF BIIM WERE THE BOYS NEXT DOOR, JODECI WERE THE BOYS NEXT DOOR THAT YOU KEPT YOUR DAUGHTER AWAY FROM."

The group came from North Carolina and consisted of two sets of brothers, Joel "JoJo" Hailey and Cedric "K-Ci" Hailey, and Donald "DeVante Swing" DeGrate and Dalvin DeGrate. As kids, each set of brothers toured throughout the South singing gospel (they all came from religious homes) and would hear the others' songs on the radio before they all met up as teens. After becoming friends, the Haileys and DeGrates decided to make an R&B group, calling themselves Jodeci, after three of the four members' nicknames.

With DeVante handling production, the foursome started assembling a demo, which they then brought to the attention of Uptown Records. The guys came close to being shown the door, but Uptown artist Heavy D dug the demo and persuaded label president Andre Harrell to do the right thing and check the group out. Harrell must have dug them, because Jodeci landed a deal and in 1991 burst through with *Forever My Lady*. The album went three times platinum and featured the single "Come & Talk to Me," which hit number one on the R&B charts.

In 1992 Jodeci delivered *Diary of a Mad Band*, but were feuding with the label and even went so far as to toy with leaving Uptown for the notorious Death Row. Even with the drama, Jodeci's sophomore album also went platinum, but the drama didn't let up when in '93 DeVante and K-Ci (the group's lead singer and sex symbol) pleaded guilty to charges involving groping, threatening, and pointing a gun at a female fan. Not great for the image—actually, perfect for Jodeci's bad-boy image.

Taking it in stride, Jodeci kept making music, taking a break to allow K-Ci to drop his sizzling remake of Bobby Womack's "If You Think You're Lonely Now" in '94. The next year Jodeci regrouped with *The Show, the After-Party, the Hotel* and then went on hiatus to work solo. DeVante would continue to do production for, among others, Al Green. But it was the Hailey boys who really scored. First they supplied background vocals for Tupac's smash "How Do U Want It" (1996). Then they decided to take the duo thang to the next phase with *Love Always* (1997). The album contained several hits—none bigger than the gorgeous "All My Life," which went to number one on both the R&B and pop charts—a first for the brothers. The CD sold four million copies and naturally K-Ci and JoJo decided to see if two was the charm. It was, since '99's *It's Real* went top ten and contained the smash "Tell Me It's Real." The hits kept coming for the Haileys with *X* (2000), which became their third straight platinum album. In 2002, they came back with *Emotional*, which failed to move the units like before.

En Vogue

By the time of En Vogue's *Funky Divas*, they were one of R&B's rising stars. Their 1990 debut, *Born to Sing*, had gone platinum and the pre-fabricated foursome—Cindy Herron, Maxine Jones, Dawn Robinson, and Terry Ellis—were loved by critics and fans alike.

That love swelled to huge proportions with their '92 sophomore disc. Flipping it between rap, reggae, rock, pop, and R&B, *Funky Divas* exploded with hits "My Lovin' (You're Never Gonna Get It)," "Giving Him Something He Can Feel," and "Free Your Mind." Sassy and sexy, *Funky Divas* went top ten—as did a collabo with Salt-N-Pepa, "Whatta Man."

As En Vogue geared up for album number three, Dawn Robinson split and eventually ended up working a little with Dr. Dre, as well as being one-third of R&B group Lucy Pearl. The other gals carried on, even dropping a single, "Don't Let Go (Love)," which went to the number two spot on the Billboard Hot 100. A few months after that success came *EV3*, which did pretty well, but clearly things had changed, and by 2000's *Masterpiece Theatre*, En Vogue was dropped from their label.

Destiny's Child

Beyoncé Knowles seems to have been bred from birth to be a pop star. Actually it probably goes further than that. Considering father Mathew Knowles's stage-dad tendencies, it wouldn't be surprising if he subjected partners to a rigorous screening process to determine the hotness, pipes, and all-around bootyliciousness of potential offspring. In that sense, Beyoncé's superstardom appears both inevitable and preordained. It seems like the only constants in this world are death, taxes, and Beyoncé's stardom. She's ascended to the level of celebrity where she requires only one word to be instantly recognizable, like Cher, Madonna, or Godzilla.

Born September 4, 1981, to future Svengali Mathew and a mother of French Creole heritage, Tina, Beyoncé was taking dance lessons and soloing in the church choir while barely out of diapers. Competitive and ambitious even at an early age, she won some thirty singing and dancing competitions. But it wasn't until the up-and-comer snagged a spot in an all-girl group called Girl's Tyme that Knowles entered *Star Search* with the group. And lost.

Clearly Beyoncé's career was going to need full-time guidance if the aspiring superstar was to get sweet revenge on Ed McMahon and his gaggle of haters. To help realize his lifelong dream of worldwide domination, father Mathew quit his six-figure job with Xerox and devoted himself full-time to making his talented little daughter a star.

From the ashes of Girl's Tyme, a troubled group with an ever-shifting lineup, arose Destiny's Child, a troubled group with an ever-shifting lineup. The group initially consisted of Knowles; Kelly Rowland, a childhood friend who eventually moved in with the Knowleses and had Mathew make her legal guardian; LaTavia Roberson; and LeToya Luckett. Being

> **"FROM THE ASHES OF GIRL'S TYME, A TROUBLED GROUP WITH AN EVER-SHIFTING LINEUP, AROSE DESTINY'S CHILD, A TROUBLED GROUP WITH AN EVER-SHIFTING LINEUP."**

the group's manager and the legal guardian of half its lineup, Mathew maintained an unusual level of control over his young charges, who practiced for hours every day.

Destiny's Child diligently set about winning a following in the Houston club scene by opening for touring acts like Immature and Dru Hill. In 1995 the group received a huge potential break when they were signed to Elektra, but they left the label without releasing an album.

By the time DC released their self-titled debut in 1998, Beyoncé was a grizzled vet at the ripe old age of sixteen. Finally Papa Knowles's dreams were starting to come true. *Destiny's Child* featured a veritable smorgasbord of hip-hop and R&B styles courtesy of big-name producers like Wyclef Jean, Jermaine Dupri, and D'Wayne Wiggins of Tony! Toni! Toné! fame. The disc scored a hit with the confusingly titled Wyclef collaboration "No, No, No Part 2" (for the record, there is a part one).

From the very beginning, it was evident that Beyoncé was the group's star, and not just because she just happened to be the manager's daughter. Knowles possessed in industrial amounts that ineffable quality known as star power. She was an absolute stunner with flawless skin, radiant eyes, a scorching figure, and the in-your-face sexuality of a young Tina Turner. For the first few years of her career Beyoncé threatened Britney Spears's popularity as pop music fans' jailbait fantasy of choice.

Destiny's Child wasted little time heading back into the studio to record a follow-up, 1999's *The Writing's on the Wall*. It was a monster smash that sold over eight million copies in the United States alone. The huge single "Bills, Bills, Bills" was a study in contradictions—a strong, empowered cry from a woman demanding her man take care of her financially. The number one hit "Say My Name," meanwhile, found the group triumphantly dressing down a cheating boyfriend and earned them a Grammy for Best R&B Performance by a Duo or Group with Vocals.

Roberson's and Luckett's dreams of pop stardom devolved into a nightmare when in 2000 they were suddenly and without warning replaced in the "Say My Name" video, and in the group itself, by newcomers Farrah Franklin and Michelle Williams. An ugly war of words ensued between the Knowles contingent and the group's disgruntled ex-members, both in the press and in court.

Knowles took on a much greater role writing and producing the group's next album, 2001's aptly named *Survivor*. By the time the ladies recorded the group's third album, they'd shrunk from a quartet to a trio. But lineup changes and public sniping did nothing to diminish their popularity. On the strength of the singles "Independent Women Part 1"—also a huge hit from the *Charlie's Angels* soundtrack—the title track, and "Bootylicious," the disc became the group's second quadruple-platinum-selling smash. Destiny's Child was now one of the top-selling girl groups of all time.

After venturing out on her own to much success, Knowles reunited with Destiny's Child in 2004 to release *Destiny Fulfilled*, a harder, more street album whose single "Soldier" paid homage to the commercial dominance of gritty southern hip-hop with guest appearances from T.I. and Lil Wayne. Though far from a flop, *Fulfilled* was a commercial disappointment compared to its predecessors and Knowles went solo again for 2006's humbly titled *B'Day*. Rowland and Williams also went on to release solo albums, as have other of the group's former members.

Which record label was the first to sign Destiny's Child?

   a. Arista Records

   b. Motown Records

   c. Elektra Records

   d. Columbia Records

POP quiz

On June 13, 2005, it was announced that DC would retire at the end of their world tour. In October of the same year, their greatest hits album, #1's, was released and eventually—as expected—reached platinum status. Destiny's Child had come a long way from living room rehearsals in Houston, Texas, to being one of the world's biggest-selling female groups of all time.

FAMILY AFFAIR: '90S R&B GROUPS

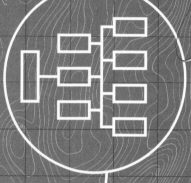

TOTAL SIGNED TO BAD BOY RECORDS, THE LABEL FOUNDED BY DIDDY, WHO WAS THE A&R FOR JODECI AT UPTOWN RECORDS.

BOTH DRU HILL AND DESTINY'S CHILD HAVE BLOND LEAD SINGERS WHO HAVE SUSTAINED SOLO CAREERS (SISQÓ AND BEYONCÉ).

JODECI WAS CREDITED AS PAVING THE WAY STYLISTICALLY AND VOCALLY FOR DRU HILL.

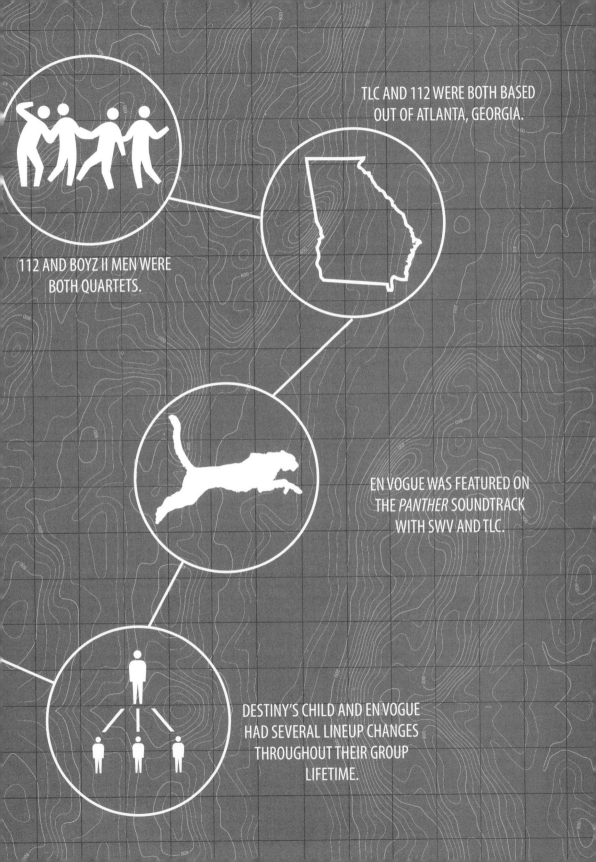

TLC AND 112 WERE BOTH BASED OUT OF ATLANTA, GEORGIA.

112 AND BOYZ II MEN WERE BOTH QUARTETS.

EN VOGUE WAS FEATURED ON THE *PANTHER* SOUNDTRACK WITH SWV AND TLC.

DESTINY'S CHILD AND EN VOGUE HAD SEVERAL LINEUP CHANGES THROUGHOUT THEIR GROUP LIFETIME.

CHAPTER 11

LADIES FIRST:

2000s FEMALE R&B

When Aaliyah declared that age ain't nothing but a number, it seems a lot of girls took that to heart. This decade's female vocalists are younger (and in some cases) more talented than their influences. Though sex sells more albums now than anything else, there's a good handful of incredibly talented female vocalists out there creating hit song after hit song. Beyoncé Knowles took her fame earned in Destiny's Child and turned it into a successful solo career (with a little help from Jay-Z), while youngsters Ciara and Amerie hooked up with hit-making producers and created some of the smoothest club jams ever heard. Club bangers aside, there's the other end of the spectrum with artists like Alicia Keys, who really take things back to the Motown era and release beautiful, and in her case, piano-based albums with no intention of killing subwoofers whatsoever. Like in decades past, R&B's subgenres span the board, all of it interesting in its own way.

Alicia Keys

Before her debut, 2001's *Songs in A Minor*, Alicia Keys was a household name. Which was exactly part of the well-executed and designed master plan. Under the tutelage of longtime record bigwig Clive Davis, the man who masterminded Whitney's debut, the barely-into-her-twenties Keys was hyped within an inch of her life and made her maiden national TV appearance on *Oprah*. Not too shabby. Of course, none of the maneuvering matters if the hype doesn't pay off, and in this case it did. Driven by the catchy, if not simplistic "Fallin'," and enough buzz to drown out a turbine engine ("She's young! She's gorgeous! She's biracial! She writes and plays the piano!"), *Songs in A Minor* hit number one and went multi-platinum, selling more than 50,000 copies on the first day in stores and settling comfortably in the number one spot. The CD also won an astounding five Grammys, including Best New Artist and Song of the Year. Keys created a solid CD that made everyone happy because it played it safe. And safe sells—especially to folks not used to picking up the hot new R&B CD.

Born Alicia Augello-Cook, Keys was a native New Yorker, a gifted student, and musician. Although she received a scholarship to attend Columbia University at sixteen, she decided instead to follow her musical aspirations. By her late teens she had appeared on several soundtracks, was signed and then dropped by a major label. Despite that setback, Alicia was getting noticed, and in 1998 she was the subject of a bidding war. The then head of Arista Records, Clive Davis, won that war, and after being ousted from Arista, he formed J Records and took Alicia with him.

Following *Songs in A Minor*, Alicia made her mark with showstopping TV appearances and then her sophomore CD, 2003's multiplatinum chart-topper *The Diary of Alicia Keys*. The LP featured the hits "You Don't Know My Name" (produced by Kanye West), "If I Ain't Got You," and "Diary."

The Diary too became a multiple Grammy winner in categories including Best R&B Song and Best R&B Album. In 2005 the R&B soul singer released the live CD/DVD *Unplugged*, and it too soared to the top of the charts and further cemented her golden-child status. Keys struck a chord with fans once again in 2007 with her third studio album, *As I Am*.

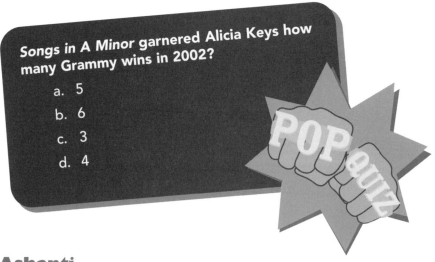

Songs in A Minor garnered Alicia Keys how many Grammy wins in 2002?

    a. 5

    b. 6

    c. 3

    d. 4

POP QUIZ

Ashanti

Pert, pretty, and polished, Ashanti was 2002's most popular and present R&B singer—whether it was as a featured artist or on her own. Guided—and possibly, some whispered, romanced—by Murder Inc. honcho Irv Gotti, the songbird excelled at the thug duet as well as her own airy brand of R&B, topping the charts with multiple singles at once.

A Strong Island native, former dancer, and sometime actress (2005's *Coach Carter*, 2006's *John Tucker Must Die*, and 2007's *Resident Evil:*

> "[ASHANTI] EXCELLED AT THE THUG DUET AS WELL AS HER OWN AIRY BRAND OF R&B, TOPPING THE CHARTS WITH MULTIPLE SINGLES AT ONCE."

Extinction), Ashanti was kicking around the industry when her combo of talent and good looks caught Gotti's attention, who thanks to the success of Ja Rule had started building his Murder Inc. empire. Soon Ashanti landed a song on *The Fast and the Furious* soundtrack and served as the "hook" girl on the late Big Pun's "How We Roll" (2001). The blend of her feminine charm and a rough-and-tumble hip-hop flow proved to be chart gold, and soon Ashanti worked in quick succession with Ja Rule (the number one "Always on Time"), Fat Joe ("What's Luv?"), and sampled the Notorious B.I.G. ("Unfoolish"). By mid-2002, she was the hottest singer in the game. The setup was perfect for her own debut, which came later in April of 2002. That self-titled CD topped the Billboard albums chart, her first debut solo single, "Foolish," did the same on the Hot 100, and *Ashanti* sold an eye-popping 503,000 copies in its first week—eventually also taking home the Grammy the next year for Best Contemporary R&B Album. Ashanti ruled.

She came back for more in 2003 with *Chapter II*, which also went to number one, propelled by the single "Rock Wit U (Awww Baby)." But the success was muted by an ongoing FBI investigation of Murder Inc. (if you don't want the feds all up in your face, don't name yourself after a convicted mob boss) and a then brewing war with G-Unit. Poor lil' Ashanti got caught in the crossfire—metaphorically speaking—and kept a somewhat lower profile, releasing a holiday CD late in '03 and *Concrete Rose* in 2004. In 2006 it was announced that Gotti, cleared of all charges brought against him by the government, was back in the mix and that Ashanti was reentering the studio. The R&B princess hooked up with her beau Nelly for "Switch," an ode to high heels off her fourth studio album *The Declaration*. She also appeared in the 2007 action blockbuster *Resident Evil: Extinction*, in which she kicked some serious ass.

Ciara

In 1992, Mary was anointed the Queen of Hip-Hop Soul. In 2005, Ciara also earned a title—the First Lady of Crunk & B—bestowed upon her by Lil Jon. The teenage Ciara stated her case with a look-but-don't-touch anthem, "Goodies," the first single from her huge-selling debut, *Goodies.*

Born in Austin, Texas, Ciara always wanted to be a singer. After her family moved to the ATL, she joined a girl group called Hearsay and practiced writing songs. After this she scored a publishing deal, and most significantly, joined up with producer Jazze Pha and songwriter Sean Garrett (Usher's "Yeah!"). With the team in place, Ciara co-wrote "Goodies," which caught the ears of starmaker Lil Jon. On the strength of her demo and looks, Ciara signed with LaFace Records, who released "Goodies" in the summer of 2004. The single exploded and that fall Ciara came through with her debut CD, which contained the hit singles "1, 2 Step" (featuring Missy Elliott) and "Oh" (featuring Ludacris). She toured with fellow teen sensations Chris Brown and Bow Wow—whom she dated for a minute. In the summer of 2006, Ciara released the hit "Get Up" (featuring Chamillionaire) and prepared for her sophomore CD, *Ciara: The Evolution*. The more mature and sexy CD got strong reviews and found Ciara dropping the crunk for a more '80s synth-funk sound, most notably in the sultry single "Promise."

Where was Ciara born?
a. Oakland, California
b. Chicago
c. Austin, Texas
d. Atlanta

POP quiz

Kelis

Harlem-bred Kelis Rogers (now Kelis Rogers-Jones, due to her marriage to Nas) got her name from the combination of her parents' first names, Kenneth and Eveliss. Her education was not from the streets, but from a private school and a school of the performing arts, and her first music business experience was with short-lived R&B group BLU (Black Ladies United). Post–high school graduation, Kelis hooked up with Chad Hugo and Pharrell Williams of the now famous Neptunes, and turned some heads after appearing on Ol' Dirty Bastard's "Got Your Money" from his second bizarre-fest, *Nigga Please*.

Teaming up with new friends The Neptunes for the entirety of her first solo record, *Kaleidoscope*, the album hit shelves in 1999 and broke the Billboard Top 200, but made more waves in the UK. The singles "Caught Out There," "Get Along with You," and "Good Stuff" blew up and helped to land her a Brit Award for "International Breakthrough Act," while "Caught Out There" peaked at number four on the UK singles chart.

Riding high on her success across the Atlantic, Kelis's sophomore album *Wanderland* was a UK, Asia, and South America–only release. In addition to this, the bigwigs at her then label, Virgin Records, pulled the ol' there's-not-a-huge-hit-on-this-record-so-we're-not-going-to-push-it trick, and sales subsequently floundered. Despite only one single seeing the light of day ("Young, Fresh N' New"), Kelis landed tours with U2 in Europe (which she now called her home) and Moby in the United States, and it was during this time that she met her now husband Nas.

Undeterred, Kelis shifted to Star Trak/Arista for her third release, *Tasty*, and found success with her Neptunes-produced lead single, "Milkshake," which has continued to shake club foundations since it hit shelves in December 2003 and landed at number three on the Billboard Hot 100.

2006 brought the release of *Kelis Was Here*; the first single, "Bossy," (featuring Too $hort) dominated airwaves despite its somewhat irritating (but infectious) chorus. But that wasn't enough to stop Jive Records from dropping her due to poor sales.

Despite an early-morning arrest on March 2, 2007, for disrupting police officers by screaming (she was charged with disorderly conduct and resisting arrest without violence), Kelis is in the midst of cementing herself as a female business mogul with a fashion line (Cake) and is writing a cookbook. In addition to those two interests, Kelis and Ashanti are collaborating on not a track, but a line of high-heeled shoes named KeShany.

Keyshia Cole

The tattoos. The Skittles-colored weave. The thick thighs poured into tight jeans stuffed into up-to-here boots. One look at Keyshia Cole and there was no mistaking that she pledged allegiance to the streets. Proof positive of Mary J. Blige's enduring influence, Keyshia Cole came out of Oakland, California, via Los Angeles and stormed up the charts with a 2005 debut that made fans and critics equally happy.

> "ONE LOOK AT **KEYSHIA COLE** AND THERE WAS NO MISTAKING THAT SHE PLEDGED **ALLEGIANCE** TO THE STREETS."

Keyshia recorded with Oaktown hero MC Hammer as a preteen. After Hammer, she worked with other local acts, but in 2001—after finding out her man had cheated—she headed to Los Angeles to seriously pursue music. In L.A. Keyshia met many industry insiders, among them president of A&M Records Ron Fair, who signed her. In 2005 Keyshia dropped *The Way It Is*, featuring production from the usual suspects, including Kanye West ("I Changed My Mind") and Polow Da Don ("Superstar"). The CD had fiery and yet still vulnerable songs and reached platinum status to become one of 2006's surprise hits. She followed up in 2007 with her sophomore album, *Just Like You*, featuring the smash single "Let It Go" with hitmakers Missy Elliott and Lil' Kim. Keysh was officially batting in the major leagues.

Amerie

If you think Beyoncé's "Crazy in Love" was producer Rich Harrison's breakthrough, think again. The beatmaker first got his shine with Amerie's "Why Don't We Fall in Love" (2002), which made Harrison and Amerie instant stars.

A former military brat, singing was always in Amerie's blood, but she deferred a career until after graduating from college at Georgetown University. While living in Washington, D.C., she met Harrison, a local resident, and the two teamed up to make demos. Amerie's girlish vocals and Harrison's go-go beats caught the attention of Columbia Records, who signed the singer in 2001. The next year, following the success of "Why Don't We Fall in Love," Amerie came through with *All I Have*. Three years later, in 2005, came the equally intoxicating *Touch*, which featured the banging hit "1 Thing," another Harrison production. In 2007, Amerie released her third LP, entitled *Because I Love It*, which saw distribution only in Europe. Noticeably absent from the album was her former mentor, Rich Harrison, but there were production appearances from The Buchanans and Bryan-Michael Cox.

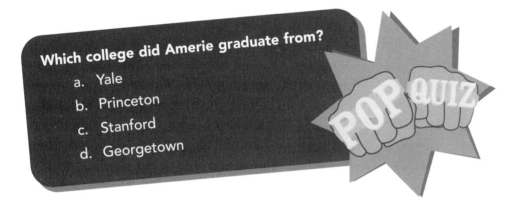

Which college did Amerie graduate from?

   a. Yale

   b. Princeton

   c. Stanford

   d. Georgetown

POP QUIZ

Rihanna

Not since Pink has the pop-meets-R&B world witnessed the evolution and transformation of an artist like Barbados-born beauty Rihanna. The then seventeen-year-old island girl gracefully brought her Caribbean flair and funky style to the forefront in 2005, with her rhythmic, reggae-flavored record, "Pon De Replay," on Def Jam. Hip-hugging jeans, midriff-baring tops, and long curls were standard wear for the newcomer, who filled the void where overprocessed singers stood before her. Rihanna's debut album, *Music of the Sun*, garnered a top ten Billboard chart position and secured a gold certification for its pop appeal.

Less than eight months after her breakthrough release, Rihanna scored again with a sophomore album—*A Girl Like Me*—and an infectious single—the dance-pop ditty "SOS," which exemplified the former island girl's quest to womanhood. Shedding her once casual getups, Rihanna donned designer gowns and sky-high heels for her return. Unlike her debut, *A Girl Like Me* brought three pop heavy, R&B inspired tracks into the spotlight: the Ne-Yo penned track "Unfaithful," "We Ride," and the Sean Paul–supported "Break It Off." A bevy of endorsement deals followed as a result of her sophomore success, including Nike, J.C. Penney, and Clinique. The chanteuse even landed a role in the movie *Bring It On: All or Nothing* and the soap opera *All My Children*.

In 2007, for her comeback, Rihanna shocked audiences by cutting off her curly tresses and sporting a black, blunt bob with bangs. *Good Girl Gone Bad*, a fitting title for her third album, showcased the sassy singer in her "baddest" state yet. Revealing more uptempo yet soulful tracks, her ubiquitous first single, "Umbrella," featuring Jay-Z, earned both U.S. and UK top chart positions. Her edgy look and shapely physique also garnered attention from Gilette, which gave her the title of the 2007 Venus Breeze "Celebrity Legs of a Goddess," thus prompting the bad girl to insure her legs for $1,000,000.

Beyoncé

Destiny's Child was one of the biggest girl groups of the '90s, but everyone knew—even if no one said it—that one day Beyoncé Knowles would go for self. After all, she was the hottest (sorry, Kelly), sang lead on most of the hits, and her dad was the group's manager. And so it came to be in 2001 that young B took baby steps toward solo stardom.

After racking up a few acting credits, Beyoncé recorded "Work It Out" (2002), off of the *Austin Powers in Goldmember* soundtrack, in which she had a key role. That same year, she cameoed on Jay-Z's "'03 Bonnie and Clyde." The song did two things. It gave Beyoncé a little 'hood cred and gave the public its first indication that Hov and B were more than just duet partners. Any doubts about the couple's status were dispelled in 2003 when Beyoncé Knowles (with Jigga by her side), dropped her last name and delivered a true modern classic, "Crazy in Love." Impossible to resist and even more difficult to avoid, "Crazy in Love" introduced her as the hip-hop generation's Tina Turner. The album *Dangerously in Love* firmly established Beyoncé as a star in her own right, even if going solo was part of a well-calculated Destiny's Child "hiatus." The disc spawned hits in the dancehall-flavored "Baby Boy," "Naughty Girl," and "Me, Myself and I," and also bagged B numerous Grammys, including Best R&B Song, Best Contemporary R&B Album, and Best Rap/Sung Collaboration.

In 2005, with DC winding down, for real, Beyoncé again made moves, first with "Check On It," featuring Slim Thug. She appeared in the film *The Pink Panther* from which the song spawned. Then in June of 2006, B returned again with "Déjà Vu," which reteamed her with her boo Jay. While "Déjà Vu" had its moments, it paled in comparison to "Crazy in Love." Likewise was the metallic "Ring the Alarm," a Swizz Beatz production. That said and discounting tepid reviews, Beyoncé's *B'Day* sold over 500,000 in its first week as B continued to grow and expand her horizons. Those horizons included the lead role in the much-hyped and well-received film *Dreamgirls*—whose story of iron-willed ambition, a guileful Svengali, and opportunistic lineup changes eerily echoes Destiny's Child's as well. But just as *B'Day* was floundering sales-wise, it roared back to the top, thanks to the edgy "Irreplaceable," which held down the number one spot for ten weeks in 2007, making it Beyoncé's most successful song of her solo career. A rereleased deluxe edition of the multiplatinum disc featured "Beautiful Liar," a sexy collaboration with Shakira.

Solo and with Destiny's Child, Beyoncé Knowles has seemingly accomplished just about everything she or her father ever dreamed about. But the scariest thing about the twenty-something mogul and international superstar is that her brightest, most commercially fruitful years could very well still be ahead of her.

Which is Beyoncé's longest-running number one single on the Billboard Hot 100 chart?

a. "Irreplaceable"

b. "Baby Boy"

c. "Crazy in Love"

d. "Check On It"

POP QUIZ

LADIES FIRST:
2000s FEMALE R&B

RIHANNA AND ASHANTI HAVE BOTH WON BEST R&B ACT AT THE UK'S MOBO AWARDS.

ASHANTI, ALICIA KEYS, AND KELIS WERE ALL BORN AND RAISED IN NEW YORK.

KELIS AND BEYONCÉ ARE ROMANTICALLY INVOLVED WITH TWO OF HIP-HOP'S INFLUENTIAL RAPPERS, NAS AND JAY-Z.

BEYONCÉ WORKED WITH THE PRODUCER KNOWN FOR HIS GO-GO SOUND, RICH HARRISON, WHO HELPED CRAFT AMERIE'S "1 THING."

AMERIE'S RECORD "TOUCH" WAS PRODUCED BY LIL JON, WHO ALSO PRODUCED CIARA'S "GOODIES."

CIARA AND KEYSHIA COLE WERE BOTH FEATURED ON DIDDY'S *PRESS PLAY* ALBUM.

CHAPTER 12

NEW JACKS:
2000s MALE R+B

It's more obvious than ever these days that Michael Jackson's influence will continue to work its magic for years to come. Listen to any of the artists in this chapter and you'll hear traces of the Gloved One's trademark R&B/soul/hip-hop fusion that has had dance floors quaking since his solo career got cooking with 1979's *Off the Wall*. Jackson has clearly seeped into the brains of everyone from boy-band survivor Justin Timberlake to *OC* guest star Chris Brown. Should any of the other men in this chapter claim that Jackson *isn't* an influence, it would just be an out-and-out lie, because what they're building upon wouldn't have a foundation without the moon-walking, controversy-creating, baby-dangling singer.

Akon

With the success of his 2004 debut *Trouble*, Akon became, as far as anyone can recall, the first African artist to hit the American R&B/hip-hop scene. Aliaune Thiam was born in St. Louis and raised in Senegal, and with a jazz-musician dad and a country steeped in rhythm, he grew up with the beat. A's musical inclination grew when the Thiams relocated to the United States, eventually settling in New Jersey. Once in the States, Akon got into hip-hop and something a little more dangerous—crime. He ended up doing time for armed robbery and drug distribution charges, but used that court-enforced hiatus to work on his music. When he got released Akon got down to business, recording and writing in a home studio. Some of his songs made their way to SRC/Universal, and soon later his debut, *Trouble*, hit shelves. The CD enjoyed a slow, steady rise to the top, thanks to introspective and soulful songs such as "Locked Up (Remix)," which featured Styles P, and "Lonely." In 2005 Akon gained even more popularity when he appeared on Young Jeezy's "Soul Survivor." He also became a hot producer and collaborator. In November of 2006, he dropped his sophomore CD, *Konvicted*, on his Konvict Muzik imprint, and eventually the CD reached double-platinum status. By the end of the year, Akon had three hits at the top of the Billboard Hot 100: "I Wanna Love You" featuring Snoop Dogg, "Smack That" featuring Eminem, and "Don't Matter." In 2007, Akon was accused of some R. Kelly action when he humped a fourteen-year-old girl on stage at a show in Trinidad. To his credit, the hitmaker didn't know the girl was underage. He addressed the controversy later that year with "Sorry, Blame It on Me," which shot right up the charts.

Chris Brown

What were you doing at sixteen? Studying for the SATs? Popping zits? Working at Mickey D's? Chris Brown was busy becoming one of R&Bs biggest rising stars. With the July 2005 release of the infectious single "Run It!" Chris owned the charts throughout most of 2005 and part of the following year too. He managed to straddle the line between semi-corny kid act and legit adult artist, thanks to hits like "Yo (Excuse Me Miss)" and "Gimme That." Born in Virginia, Brown soaked up classic soul and hip-hop and by his preteens was singing. Sensing he had real skills, he focused on making singing a career and within a few years' time had secured a recording contract with Jive Records. Chris worked with the best, including Jermaine Dupri, Sean Garrett, and Scott Storch. The payoff was his self-titled '05 debut, which was an instant top ten hit and kept selling far into 2006. It also helped Chris grab a Grammy nod for Best New Artist. Chris branched out into acting and made his big-screen debut in the box-office smash *Stomp the Yard*. Teenage female fans eagerly awaited his return to the R&B arena in 2007 with *Exclusive*.

In what movie did Chris Brown make his feature film debut?

a. This Christmas
b. You Got Served
c. Stomp the Yard
d. Roll Bounce

POP quiz

Ne-Yo

He was born Shaffer Smith, but R&B fans know him as Ne-Yo. The singer/songwriter went from behind-the-scenes utility player to a star in his own right, thanks to 2006's *In My Own Words*. The CD ended up at the top of the charts, pushed along by the number one ballad "So Sick."

Born in Arkansas to a musical family, Ne-Yo moved to Las Vegas and as a teen made his initial entry into the business as a songwriter, writing for, among others, rapper Cassidy and R&B/pop singer Christina Milian. His big break came in 2004 when he co-wrote Mario's "Let Me Love You," which became one of the most played songs that year on urban radio, as well as a number one on the Billboard Hot 100 for weeks. The success of the song led to Ne-Yo's own deal with Def Jam. At twenty-two, he was heralded as one of R&B's most promising newcomers. He kept up the side gigs, popping up on labelmate Ghostface Killah's *Fishscale* ("Back Like That"), penning Rihanna's top single "Unfaithful," and as one of the writers responsible for Beyoncé's hit "Irreplaceable." In 2007, he returned with his sophomore album, featuring the midtempo single "Because of You."

Mario

Baltimore homie Mario started his climb to the top by rocking out on the family's karaoke machine. By the time he was eleven, he had made his way from the living room to local talent shows, where he was discovered. Mario then headed to NYC, where he fell under the tutelage of industry starmaker Clive Davis, who helped shepherd his rise. After his contribution to the *Dr. Dolittle 2* soundtrack, Mario had his moment to shine when in 2002 he sang Stevie Wonder's "You and I" for an elite industry crowd at Davis's annual pre-Grammy party. It was clear Mario was ready for the next step, and in 2002, at fifteen years of age, he took that step with "Just a Friend." Based on old-school rapper Biz Markie's classic, Mario's song—with a video featuring the Biz—was huge for most of 2002. The single was followed up by the summer release of his self-titled CD, featuring contributions from labelmate (and comparatively older woman) Alicia Keys. Two years later, *Turning Point* indicated that the kid had grown up and had staying power. Featuring the massive "Let Me Love You" (co-written by Ne-Yo), *Turning Point* went platinum-plus. In '07 he earned good reviews with a role in the Hilary Swank film *Freedom Writers* and released his third album, *Go.*

John Legend

When you change your last name from Stephens to Legend, you're setting yourself up. Yet while he might not have all of the attributes the surname implies, there's no denying that John Legend has set himself apart from the pack.

Born John Stephens, he grew up in Ohio, where he began singing gospel in the church choir and took up the piano at the age of five. He wasn't only musically advanced—he was academically smart too, so much so that John entered college (the University of Pennsylvania) at sixteen. While there, he started playing gigs and attracted an audience as well as the attention of the music industry. Among the first to notice his talents was Lauryn Hill, who enlisted the then late teen to play piano on her 1998 hit "Everything Is Everything." John finished up college, got a job with Boston Consulting Group, and then moved to NYC and began to play around town, building up a dedicated fan base as well as releasing home-grown CDs that he sold at gigs. Session gigs followed, with Legend working with, among others Jay-Z, Alicia Keys, Janet Jackson, and Kanye West—who would sign him to his imprint G.O.O.D. Music.

Now known as Legend, John recorded his major-label breakthrough, *Get Lifted*. The CD dropped in late 2004 and received some buzz, thanks in some degree to the K. West connection. But soon folks began to figure out that there was more to Legend than just being a Kanye sidekick. With the smashes "Ordinary People" and "Used to Love U," *Get Lifted* was a critical and commercial triumph and would go on to earn an astounding eight Grammy nominations. Legend snagged Best New Artist, Best Male R&B Vocal Performance ("Ordinary People"), and Best R&B Album. *Get Lifted* went on to sell over three million copies.

In the fall of 2006, Legend returned with *Once Again*, which debuted at number three and showcased an even more focused and mature sound. Critics adored it, as did fans, and Legend had another R&B triumph.

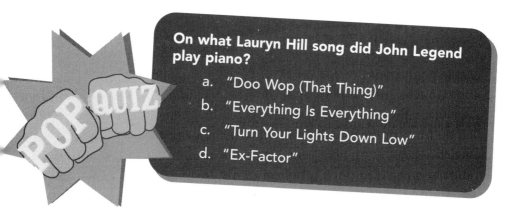

On what Lauryn Hill song did John Legend play piano?

   a. "Doo Wop (That Thing)"

   b. "Everything Is Everything"

   c. "Turn Your Lights Down Low"

   d. "Ex-Factor"

Justin Timberlake

Former 'N Syncer turned soul-lite crooner, Justin Timberlake showed that honkies could get down and top the R&B charts as well with '06's fantastic *FutureSex/LoveSounds*. Produced mainly by Timbaland and featuring the hits "SexyBack" and "My Love," JT's Prince-esque sound was critically acclaimed and commercially explosive, giving the Memphis-born former Mouseketeer, boy bander, and Britney boyfriend an even higher profile in urban music.

"JT'S PRINCE-ESQUE SOUND WAS CRITICALLY ACCLAIMED AND COMMERCIALLY EXPLOSIVE, GIVING THE MEMPHIS-BORN FORMER MOUSEKETEER, BOY BANDER, AND BRITNEY BOYFRIEND AN EVEN HIGHER PROFILE IN URBAN MUSIC."

That first hardcore taste of crossover appeal came following 'N Sync's last CD, 2001's *Celebrity*. 'N Sync was huge and popular among fans of all colors, in fact, but JT's ghetto pass would get validation with '02's *Justified*.

Working with Timbaland and Pharrell, JT made the album Michael Jackson hadn't in years, and hits like "Like I Love You," "Rock Your Body," and "Cry Me a River" blew up big time. *Justified* hit the number two spot on the Billboard 200 and JT also popped up on the Black Eyed Peas's breakthrough "Where Is the Love?" Justin hit a rough patch after his halftime show at Super Bowl XXXVIII, where he pulled off part of co-performer Janet Jackson's top (the infamous "wardrobe malfunction" incident) and then piggishly allowed Janet to take most of the heat and blame. But even that major goof couldn't slow Justin down. He won two Grammys and then came back stronger and more in control than ever with the multiplatinum and Grammy-nominated *FutureSex/LoveSounds*.

The album dropped in September of 2006 and debuted at the top of the charts, selling 684,000 copies in its first week of release. The first single, "SexyBack," became a summer anthem, prompting a response from Prince that sexy never left. Timbaland handled the bulk of production on the LP, while rappers T.I. ("My Love") and Three 6 Mafia ("Chop Me Up") made guest appearances. At the top of 2007, JT hit the road for his FutureSex/LoveShow tour.

NEW JACKS:
2000s MALE R&B

CHRIS BROWN AND NE-YO TOURED TOGETHER ON THE UP CLOSE & PERSONAL TOUR IN 2006.

NE-YO HELPED PEN MARIO'S "LET ME LOVE YOU."

MARIO AND JUSTIN TIMBERLAK HAVE BOTH WORKED WITH PRODUCER SCOTT STORCH.

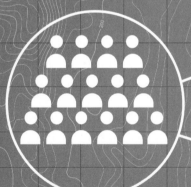

JUSTIN TIMBERLAKE AND JOHN LEGEND BOTH WON AWARDS AT THE 49TH ANNUAL GRAMMY AWARDS IN 2007.

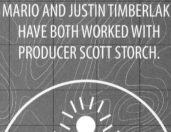

JOHN LEGEND DEBUTED HIS SOLO ALBUM, *GET LIFTED*, IN 2004, THE SAME YEAR AKON'S DEBUT, *TROUBLE*, WAS RELEASED.

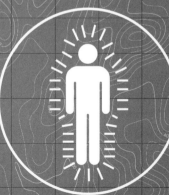

CHAPTER 13

YOU KNOW YOU'VE GOT SOUL:

NEO-SOUL

The neo-soul genre has come into its own as an amalgamation of all the influences soaked up by a younger generation, who have created a new subsect of soul, R&B, hip-hop, and jazz. The term, first introduced in the late '90s by Motown's Kedar Massenburg, has sometimes come under fire for being more of a marketing tool than anything else. Tell that to Erykah Badu, Lauryn Hill, and D'Angelo, who have created unclassifiable (and classic) records that can only really be labeled as neo-soul without relegating oneself to a long, confusing string of "sort of's" and "kind of like's." Since its inception, soul music has changed so much that it's only natural that neo-soul is an extension of that natural evolution.

Tony! Toni! Toné!

With its emphasis on an old soul vibe and live instruments over sequencers, neo-soul aimed to be more organic than its more polished cousin, R&B. The modern retro sound was jump-started in 1988 with Tony! Toni! Toné!'s self-titled debut.

Straight outta Sacramento, Tony! Toni! Toné! consisted of brothers D'Wayne and Charlie Ray Wiggins and cousin Timothy Christian. Unlike other R&B acts of the time, the Tonies wrote and produced and were an actual band. The trio dropped *The Revival* in 1990 and followed it in 1993 with their masterpiece *Sons of Soul*, which featured the hits "If I Had No Loot" and "Anniversary." A powerful live act, Tony! Toni! Toné! released their fourth album, *House of Music*, in the fall of 1996 and broke up soon afterward, with each member going on to pursue solo careers. The most notable post-TTT success story was Charlie, who changed his name to Raphael Saadiq and became a Grammy-winning producer/songwriter and a respected solo artist.

D'Angelo

Richmond, Virginia's Michael "D'Angelo" Archer was a self-taught pianist, good enough to win a talent competition at the Apollo Theater three weeks in a row. His first taste of fame came in 1994, when he helped write "U Will Know" for Black Men United. The track led to his songwriting deal with EMI. To construct *Brown Sugar*, D'Angelo gathered innovative players like A Tribe Called Quest's Ali Shaheed Muhammad, Raphael Saadiq, and Angie Stone. Stone was a former member of the '80s female rap trio the Sequence, mother of one of D'Angelo's kids, songwriter, and a superlative solo artist whose three solo CDs (*Black Diamond*, *Mahogany Soul*, and *Stone Love*) became cult and critical faves. The culmination of D's soulful think tank was a seductive hip-hop-flavored ode to women and weed, which quickly became the must-have album of 1995. Featuring hits like the title track and "Lady," *Brown Sugar* made the soft-spoken, laid-back D'Angelo a major musical force.

In early 2000, five years after the double-platinum *Brown Sugar*, D came back with *Voodoo*. The first single, "Untitled (How Does It Feel)," took over the R&B charts and won a Grammy for Best Male R&B Vocal Performance. It was promoted with an insanely sexual video, spotlighting a buffed-up and naked D'Angelo. Moody, vibey, and less structured than its predecessor, *Voodoo* came outta the box at number one, delighting the press and the public. Following an extensive tour, D'Angelo retreated. With few exceptions, the enigmatic D laid back in the cut, a position he maintains to this day—although rumor has it that he's working on a much-delayed third CD.

Which neo-soul singer did D'Angelo once date?
a. Erykah Badu
b. India.Arie
c. Angie Stone
d. Jill Scott

POP QUIZ

Erykah Badu

Her roots were in hip-hop, but thanks to a weedy, off-kilter (and more than often off-key) delivery, Erykah Badu drew comparisons to the late jazz legend Billie Holiday. She wasn't nearly the singer, but even Badu's detractors knew that her idiosyncratic style and sound helped usher in a new bohemian vibe.

Born Erica Wright in Dallas in 1971, Badu was a teacher and part-time singer who landed a gig opening up for D'Angelo in 1994. Impressed, D'Angelo's manager, former Motown executive Kedar Massenburg, signed her and produced her 1997 debut, *Baduizm*, which featured members of The Roots. *Baduizm*'s first single, "On & On," was a number one R&B hit. Beloved by devotees of R&B and hip-hop—in particular ex-boyfriend André 3000 (OutKast), with whom she had a son—Badu was a cult artist with mass appeal and commercial clout. Not only was her sound influential, but her edgy Afrocentric style (including a then signature sky-high head wrap) made her a fashion darling. Badu followed up *Baduizm* with *Live* later in '97, and in 2000 came back with the critically acclaimed, but less profitable *Mama's Gun*. The album spawned the top ten hit "Bag Lady," which sampled Dr. Dre's "Xplosive." In late 2002, Badu teamed up with then boyfriend Common for the Grammy-winning "Love of My Life (An Ode to Hip-Hop)," and four years later joined Dead Prez, Mos Def, Talib Kweli, The Roots, and Jill Scott in the documentary *Dave Chappelle's Block Party*.

Jill Scott

A powerful, emotional singer, and a songwriter whose (often naively) confessional lyrics have made her a sista-friend supreme, Jill Scott grew up in Philly and began her career as a spoken-word artist. It was there that she was "discovered" by The Roots' ?uestlove, who asked her to join the band in the studio. That collabo produced "You Got Me." Yet even though Scott wrote and sang on the original version, in 1999 when it was released as a single—The Roots' lone Top 40 pop hit—Scott was replaced by Erykah Badu, whom the label saw as being more commercial. She might have gotten the back of the hand, but the indie label Hidden Beach Recordings saw Jill's potential and released her debut, *Who Is Jill Scott? Words and Sounds Vol. 1*, in July 2000. *Experience: Jill Scott 826+* appeared the following year, featuring Jill's most successful single to date, "A Long Walk." Scott shined bright. She grabbed a Grammy nomination in early 2003 and followed that up with 2004's *Beautifully Human: Words and Sounds Vol. 2*. Jill won a Grammy in 2005 for Best Urban/Alternative Performance, and twelve months later added her dulcet tones to Lupe Fiasco's single "Daydreamin'." Jill returned in all her glory in 2007 with *The Real Thing*, proving that real talent never fades.

Lauryn Hill

Lauryn Hill got a lot of love and attention as one-third of The Fugees. So it was pretty much a foregone conclusion that, despite heated denials from The Fugees' camp, the New Jersey girl would go solo. She did so with 1998's *The Miseducation of Lauryn Hill*, which was a massive commercial and critical success, eventually earning a total of five Grammys (including Album of the Year and Best New Artist), an achievement that at the time was unheard of for a female rap artist.

Along with her vocal talents, the fact that the then twenty-three-year-old Hill had written and co-produced *Miseducation* made the album an event, as well as a fantastic CD. Ironically, Hill's solo venture made The Fugees future less viable as the focus honed in more and more on her, leaving Clef and especially Pras in the dust.

> **"IRONICALLY, [LAURYN] HILL'S SOLO VENTURE MADE THE FUGEES' FUTURE LESS VIABLE AS THE FOCUS HONED IN MORE AND MORE ON HER, LEAVING CLEF AND ESPECIALLY PRAS IN THE DUST."**

As the intense frenzy surrounding *Miseducation* slowly died down, Lauryn retreated further from the spotlight, concentrating on her four kids, spiritual pursuits, and self-examination. Adding to the mix was a lawsuit brought by two musicians claiming that they did not receive credit for their work on *Miseducation*. Hill settled the suit out of court for an undisclosed amount, and as quickly as she'd been championed as a soul savant, some began to question if much of the hype had been just that.

Soon rumors circulated that the once supremely self-assured and glamorous Miss Hill was acting strange and falling under the influence of quasi-religious/mystical teachings. That something wasn't quite right was obvious with 2002's *MTV Unplugged No. 2.0*. From the disjointed "songs" to Lauryn's often confused demeanor, it appeared the Hill had either suffered a breakdown or was on the verge of one. Even her most die-hard fans had a hard time supporting the disappointing two-CD set, and again Hill disappeared. In 2005 it was announced that the once feuding Fugees, with a reglammed Lauryn, were back in the studio. Yet outside of an advertisement for a wireless phone company and an incandescent guest spot on *Dave Chappelle's Block Party*, nothing's been heard.

India.Arie

The daughter of a singer and a former professional basketball player, India.Arie delved headfirst into the world of music while matriculating at the Savannah College of Art and Design. After landing a song on a local compilation, Arie performed on the second stage at Lilith Fair, a crunchy celebration of all things female, and eventually caught the attention of a Motown music scout.

Arie's 2001 debut, the thrillingly titled *Acoustic Soul*, generated gushing reviews for its warm, organic sound and the gently feminist bent of its lyrics. The album was a big commercial hit thanks to the single "Video" and was nominated for an astonishing seven Grammys—to the surprise of the music world, she ended up losing every category. *Voyage to India* followed a year later and finally snagged Arie Grammy wins for Best R&B Album and Best Urban/Alternative Performance for "Little Things." The album eventually also reached platinum status.

Arie was officially part of the pop music elite. She collaborated with everyone from Sergio Mendes to John Mellencamp to Stevie Wonder and in 2006 released *Testimony: Vol. 1, Life & Relationship*, a disc that lived up to its touchy-feely title by totally offering Arie's testimony on life and relationships. God only knows where Arie's reign of positivity and female empowerment will end, but an entire estrogen-fueled nation of wheatgrass-drinking, poetry-slam-attending, Maya Angelou devotees is happy to have her representing proudly for conscious sisters everywhere.

Which of the following artists has India.Arie not collaborated with?

a. Stevie Wonder

b. John Mellencamp

c. OutKast

d. Sergio Mendes

Anthony Hamilton

If Mary J. Blige is soul music's queen of pain, Anthony Hamilton is its king. The southern-fried soulster's gutbucket croon seems to emerge from somewhere deep and dark within his soul, dredging up a bottomless reservoir of hurt. Countless hip-hop artists have called upon Hamilton to deliver a chorus full of soulful suffering, but he's also emerged as one of neo-soul music's most refreshing solo artists.

After signing with Uptown Records in the early '90s, Hamilton released a debut album, *XTC*, in 1996. The album stiffed and Hamilton was dropped. He next popped up on the pop culture radar with his empathetic hook for Nappy Roots' Grammy-winning single "Po' Folks" in 2003. A slew of hip-hop collaborations followed, most notably the Jadakiss single "Why?," which generated controversy due to its assertion that President Bush had prior knowledge of the 9/11 attacks.

Hip-hop's passionate embrace of Hamilton's sweaty, blue-collar soul reignited the singer's solo career. In 2003, Jermaine Dupri's So So Def label released his masterful second album, *Comin' From Where I'm From*, which scored hits in the title track and "Charlene" and eventually went platinum. The year 2005 brought a follow-up, *Ain't Nobody Worryin'*, which generated strong reviews but failed to replicate its predecessor's commercial success. Hamilton has remained busy, however, and looks primed to exploit the strange absence of neo-soul peers like Lauryn Hill and D'Angelo from the recording scene. He scored hard-earned success after dispiriting early disappointments, but neo-soul music's quintessential workingman still has plenty of work left to do.

APHAEL SAADIQ (FORMERLY
TONY! TONE! TONÉ!)
RODUCED ON JOSS STONE'S
TRODUCING JOSS STONE,
HICH FEATURES LAURYN HILL
N THE TRACK "MUSIC."

YOU KNOW YOU'VE GOT SOUL:
NEO-SOUL

LAURYN HILL FEATURED
D'ANGELO ON HER SONG
"NOTHING EVEN MATTERS."

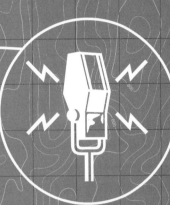

D'ANGELO IS A MEMBER OF THE
COLLECTIVE SOULQUARIANS WITH
ERYKAH BADU.

ERYKAH BADU AND JILL SCOTT
WERE BOTH ON DIFFERENT
VERSIONS OF "YOU GOT ME" BY THE
ROOTS (AND PERFORMED THE SONG
TOGETHER AT *DAVE CHAPPELLE'S
BLOCK PARTY* IN 2004).

JILL SCOTT AND INDIA.ARIE
WERE BOTH NOMINATED FOR
BEST NEW ARTIST AT THE 2001
BET AWARDS.

INDIA.ARIE AND ANTHONY
HAMILTON BOTH CITE STEVIE
WONDER AS A MUSICAL
INFLUENCE AND PERFORMED AT A
2005 GRAMMY TRIBUTE TO HIM.

CHAPTER 14

DROP THE BEAT:

PRODUCERS

Sure, Eric B., DJ Premier, and Dr. Dre are all classic artists, but where would they be without Rakim, Guru, and N.W.A.? Who knows? They might have found success, but speculation aside, beats have become big business. In some cases, the producer has gained more fame than the MC. Artists like The Neptunes and Lil Jon are able to release whole albums that feature just their own production, while producers like Just Blaze and Timbaland turn up on everything from Mariah Carey to Nelly Furtado tracks, raking in boatloads of money not only for their trademark style but their name in the credits.

Timbaland

Timothy Mosley a.k.a. Timbaland has created a forward-thinking electronic-blessed hip-hop/funk/pop sound that hardly ever—maybe never—uses sampling. That's rare. Whether working with Justin Timberlake, Missy Elliott, Jay-Z, or Nelly Furtado, Tim's steez is always adventurous.

He came up from Virginia and in the beginning worked almost exclusively with hometown girl Missy Elliott. Together they ruled as one of the hottest teams going, as well as maybe a handful—if that—of male/female songwriting/production crews. Missy's innovative "The Rain (Supa Dupa Fly)" set the ball in motion, and soon Tim was collaborating with the crème de la crème of rap artists, including LL Cool J, Nas, Snoop Dogg, and Ludacris.

Tim also lent his magic touch to smaller acts such including Petey Pablo, Kiley Dean, and Tweet. Soon Tim (and Missy) had their own artistic family that included, at various times, Ginuwine, rapper Magoo (with whom Tim recorded three CDs), and the late singer Aaliyah. Tim's production skills and success led to his inevitable own label, Beat Club. His signees included the other white rapper, Bubba Sparxxx, and flash-in-the-pan female MC Ms. Jade.

Timbaland continued to expand his sound, which many compared to an Americanized version of the British club groove drum-and-bass. Although he was most associated with "urban" artists, the musical community at large noticed Tim, and in late 2002 he showed he had real crossover power with Justin Timberlake's *Justified*.

Although he was never far from the charts, 2006 would prove to be the year of the Tim. His collabos with Nelly Furtado and Justin dominated radio and the charts. Icing the cake: JT's *FutureSex/LoveSounds*. With Tim providing the vast majority of the sounds, including singles "Sexy-Back" and "My Love," JT's CD landed on a ton of top ten lists. The album was also recognized by the industry and received several key Grammy nominations, including Album of the Year. Oddly, despite the love and the fact that Tim had produced the year's biggest, most interesting hits, Timbaland failed to get a Producer of the Year nod. So tight was the partnership between JT and Timbo that the former asked the latter to join him on tour. Timbaland released his own star-studded solo LP, *Timbaland Presents: Shock Value*, in April of 2007. The album was loaded with guest appearances from artists of all genres, including 50 Cent, Elton John, Nicole Scherzinger of the Pussycat Dolls, and Fall Out Boy.

HOT JOINTS

Missy Elliott—"The Rain (Supa Dupa Fly)" and "Work It"
Aaliyah—"If Your Girl Only Knew" and "Try Again"
Ginuwine—"Pony"
Jay-Z—"Big Pimpin'" and "Dirt Off Your Shoulder"
Justin Timberlake—"Cry Me A River" and FutureSex/LoveSounds
Nelly Furtado—"Promiscuous" and "Say It Right"

The Neptunes

Although The Neptunes are actually a duo, one-half of the team has basically overshadowed the accomplishments—or at least profile—of the other. The quieter Neptune is Chad Hugo, while the man-about-town, up in the videos, "singer," and "rapper" (although his awful CD would indicate otherwise) is of course Pharrell Williams, so ubiquitous that he gets to drop the surname.

Before Skateboard P was endorsing Louis Vuitton, dating models, creating skateboard teams, founding his flashy apparel line Billionaire Boys Club, hanging with BAPE's Nigo, and helping make that once exclusive label a must-have in the 'hood—before all that, The Neptunes were just a hot production duo.

The Virginia Beach tag team was one time protégés of megaproducer Teddy Riley a.k.a. the inventor of New Jack Swing. Chad and Pharrell began their climb to the top in the late '90s working with the late Ol' Dirty Bastard on his CD *Nigga Please*. Success in hip-hop would also help The Neptunes make the leap to pop, and by 2001 the guys were unstoppable: clearly the beat maestros to beat.

They also began their own rap-rock group, N.E.R.D. (No One Ever Really Dies), which expanded The Neptunes to a trio with childhood friend Shay now on board. N.E.R.D. dropped their debut, *In Search Of . . .* in 2002, and the singles "Lapdance" and "Rock Star" enjoyed some love. In 2004, they came back with *Fly or Die*. The Neptunes also formed Star Trak, whose roster included former hook singer Kelis (now married to Nas) and fellow Virginia homies the Clipse, whose "Grindin'" went platinum in 2002. Both artists appeared on *The Neptunes Present . . . Clones* (2003).

HOT JOINTS

Justin Timberlake—"Rock Your Body" and "Señorita"
Busta Rhymes—"Pass the Courvoisier, Part 2"
Nelly—"Hot in Herre"
Snoop Dogg—"Beautiful" and "Drop It Like It's Hot"
Ol' Dirty Bastard—"Got Your Money"
Pharrell—"Frontin'"
Gwen Stefani—"Hollaback Girl" and "Wind It Up"
Mystikal—"Shake Ya Ass"
Jay-Z—"I Just Wanna Love U (Give It 2 Me)" and
    "Change Clothes"
Britney Spears—"I'm a Slave 4 U"
LL Cool J—"Luv U Better"
Kelis—"Milkshake"
The Clipse—*Hell Hath No Fury*
Ludacris—"Money Maker"

Along with their side projects, The Neptunes continued to churn out hits and have remained—no matter what the prevailing trend—consistently in demand and on the cutting edge.

Scott Storch

Scott Storch started his career playing keyboards, contributing to home-town acts like OG Schoolly D and jam-bander G. Love & Special Sauce. Scott also linked up with a then underground group, The Roots, and went into the studio with them to record their indie debut, *Organix* (1993). The album helped The Roots get a major-label deal and also brought Scott's musical skills to the forefront.

After recording and touring with The Roots, Scott began to branch out into production, his big break coming when he laced Dr. Dre's "Still D.R.E." with its signature keyboard riff. He soon became part of Dre's crew and served as co-producer on many of the good doctor's projects, including a solo production stint on Snoop Dogg's *Tha Last Meal*. Along the way, Storch grew into one of the industry's go-to guys, scoring smashes in hip-hop, R&B, and pop—notably Justin Timberlake's "Cry Me a River." Although Timbaland is widely recognized as the hit's solo prod-

HOT JOINTS

Terror Squad—"Lean Back"
Mario—"Let Me Love You"
50 Cent—"Candy Shop"
Beyoncé—"Baby Boy" and "Naughty Girl"
Chris Brown—"Run It!"

ucer, Storch has often been quoted that the song's memorable keyboards were in fact his doing.

Jermaine Dupri

Jermaine Dupri's dad, Michael Mauldin, is a longtime music vet and former president of Columbia Records. It was at one of the shows his dad promoted in 1982 that JD first made his moves: getting onstage to dance. That led to gigs performing nationwide, and in the mid-'80s Dupri opened the New York Fresh Festival.

JD danced into production in 1987 when he was just fourteen. Two years later, he had formed So So Def Productions, and by '91 he found his kiddie rappers Kris Kross, who became teen sensations with catchy hits and their clothes on backward. When KK's fifteen minutes of fame ticked by, JD went back to the lab. Among the projects he worked on: TLC's first two CDs, *Oooooooohhh . . . On the TLC Tip* and *CrazySexyCool*.

Dupri added to his So So Def lineup with girl group Xscape and rapper Da Brat, both of whose debuts featured his production. Over the years, other So So Def acts would include Bow Wow, Jagged Edge, and Anthony Hamilton. Throughout the '90s JD worked with Mariah Carey, Run-D.M.C., and Whodini. In 1997 he stepped it up a notch when he handled production on Usher's sophomore CD, *My Way*, which became one of the biggest of that year.

Dupri made his own step into the spotlight when he released 1998's *Life in 1472*, and his second "solo" CD, *Instructions*, came in 2001. While the CD sold decently, JD's strong suit remained his production.

While JD continued to have big hits, his biggest moment came thanks to Mariah Carey's 2005 comeback *The Emancipation of Mimi*. Dupri handled most of the heavy lifting on the multiple-platinum chart-topper and helped make MC a star again. On the personal and professional side, he has been romantically involved with Janet Jackson for several years. As president of urban music at Virgin Records, he helped guide Janet's *20 Y.O.* The album was a major flop and helped lead to JD's dismissal (or quitting) from Virgin in late 2006. Not to worry. He landed on his feet and at Island Music as president of that label's urban music department.

HOT JOINTS
Usher—"You Make Me Wanna," "Confessions Part II," and "My Boo"
Jay-Z—"Money Ain't a Thang"
Mariah Carey—"We Belong Together" and "Always Be My Baby"
Bow Wow featuring Ciara—"Like You"
Nelly featuring Paul Wall, Ali & Gipp—"Grillz"

Swizz Beatz

Kaseem Dean (a.k.a. Swizz Beatz) was born in the Boogie Down and moved to Atlanta while a teen. It was there that he started DJing at parties and made the move to the big time when his relatives Chivon, Joaquin, and Darrin Dean formed Ruff Ryders. The NYC-based label/crew included among its family DMX, The Lox (Sheek Louch, Styles P, Jadakiss), and Eve. The elder Deans hired their sixteen-year-old nephew to do in-house production, and from the jump Swizz made an impact. Rather than relying on samples, like most hip-hop producers at the time, Swizz favored a synth/keyboard-heavy sound. Soon R&B acts caught wind of what the kid was laying down, but despite the credits, Swizz remained a bit on the DL. That changed when he dropped his solo CD, 2002's *G.H.E.T.T.O. Stories.* Swizzy had more people checking for him the second time around when his sophomore disc, *One Man Band Man*, dropped in 2007.

Rodney "Darkchild" Jerkins

Able to flip it between hip-hop, pop, gospel, and R&B, Rodney "Dark-child" Jerkins is one of the more prolific and versatile producers around, bringing a polished but never slick sound to a who's who of artists, among them Mary J. Blige, Whitney Houston, Brandy, Beyoncé, and Ciara.

Born to a minister dad and choir director mom, Rodney was raised near Atlantic City, New Jersey. Classically trained since he was a small fry, Rodney was also schooled in gospel, and as he matured he added other genres like R&B to the mix. He recorded rap demos for local talent and knew by the time he was in his teens that he wanted to become a producer. One of Rodney's homegrown demos came to the attention of Teddy Riley, who helped put the young'un on. At the age of fifteen, Rodney had written and produced his own gospel rap CD, *On the Move*.

Things began to pick up, and in 1997 Rodney produced five songs for Mary J. Blige's quadruple-platinum *Share My World*, including the single "I Can Love You" featuring Lil' Kim. Work kept coming in, and in 1999 he started Darkchild Productions, which eventually branched out into Dark-child Records.

Dallas Austin

Dallas Austin's been in the lab since he was a teenager. More importantly, Dallas has consistently put out bangers. He's able to flip it in every genre—rock, pop, hip-hop, R&B—and remains interesting.

Born in Columbus, Georgia, Dallas played guitar and keyboards as a kid, and his musical abilities would help make his production stand out. In 1986, he moved to Atlanta and played in various bands. He soon moved into production and in 1989 had his first Billboard chart success (Joyce Irby's "Mr. DJ"). In 1991, he went for the ultimate good look with Boyz II Men's high-profile debut *Cooleyhighharmony*. More hits followed: TLC's four-million-selling *Ooooooohhh . . . On the TLC Tip* (1992), as well as their double-platinum album *CrazySexyCool* (1994). Dallas branched into films when he executive-produced 2002's *Drumline*, which was partially based on his life, and 2006's *ATL*.

Dallas kept making hits with everyone from Michael Jackson to Lenny Kravitz and the Indigo Girls to Madonna. Yet in 2006, it was his life outside the studio that made headlines—though not the kind you'd wish for. En route to Dubai to attend Naomi Campbell's birthday party (already a red flag), Austin was detained by Dubai police and landed in prison for alleged drug possession. He spent several weeks in custody. Eventually with much wrangling and pressure from various lawyers, politicians, and industry figures (including Lionel Richie, Quincy Jones, and Utah Republican senator Orrin Hatch), Austin was pardoned after pleading guilty to possession of cocaine and ecstasy. The deal allowed him to avoid a potential four-year jail sentence.

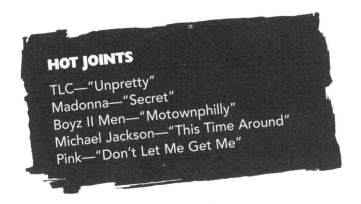

HOT JOINTS

TLC—"Unpretty"
Madonna—"Secret"
Boyz II Men—"Motownphilly"
Michael Jackson—"This Time Around"
Pink—"Don't Let Me Get Me"

Just Blaze

One of hip-hop's hottest, Just Blaze (born Justin Smith) first got his shine in the early 2000s. Back then, he was down with Roc-A-Fella Records, fashioning anthems like Cam'ron's "Oh Boy," Jay-Z's "Girls, Girls, Girls," and Beanie Sigel and Freeway's "Roc the Mic." While at the Roc, Just spent quality studio time with the label's other in-house producer, Kanye West. Like K. West, his signature sonics involved utilizing old-school soul samples and tweaking them in standout ways in order to cook up killer hooks and punchy choruses. That way of mixing the tried and true with the new and innovative helped to make Just Blaze a sure shot and another in a lengthy line of blazing East Coast producers and DJs.

Jimmy Jam and Terry Lewis

From the late '80s through the mid-'90s, it was damn near impossible to not hear a song produced and/or written by Jimmy Jam and Terry Lewis. Along with the now disbanded production/writing team Antonio "LA" Reid and Kenneth "Babyface" Edmonds a.k.a. LaFace, Jam and Lewis's melodic, hook-heavy, and often groundbreaking style defined black pop and R&B. They've been making hits for two decades and their impact is undeniable. These guys are the shit.

James Harris III met Terry Lewis while both were high school kids in Minneapolis. The guys formed Flyte Tyme, which in 1981 mutated into the Time, a group fronted by Prince protégé Morris Day. Along with Prince (the area's leading star), the Time helped to shape and popularize what became known as the Minneapolis Sound, a synth-drenched sexy fusion of funk, rock, and R&B. Soon after the Prince-produced *The Time* debut, Jam and Lewis formed Flyte Tyme Productions. In 1983, while on tour with the Time, Jam and Lewis used their off time to go to Atlanta and produce some tracks for the S.O.S. Band. The guys became stranded in Georgia due to bad weather and were forced to miss a show, and the notoriously controlling Prince canned Jimmy and Terry on the spot. Luckily for the guys, the S.O.S. Band's "Just Be Good to Me" exploded and Jimmy and Terry were suddenly on the map.

In 1985 the guys' lives and careers went into high gear when they worked on Janet Jackson's third album. *Control* made Janet a superstar and contained the hits "What Have You Done for Me Lately," "Nasty," "When I Think of You," "Let's Wait Awhile," and the title track. Along with the sales, *Control* earned Jam and Lewis a Grammy award for Producer of the Year (Non-Classical). Jimmy and Terry reteamed with Janet in '89 for *Rhythm Nation 1814*, which was bigger than *Control* and also produced a barrage of smashes, among them "Miss You Much" and "Black Cat." Over the years J&L would produce nearly every major R&B act, but it was their hugely successful and often amazing contributions to every one of Janet's albums—continuing all the way to 2006's *20 Y.O.*—that brought them the most acclaim and helped make them true starmakers.

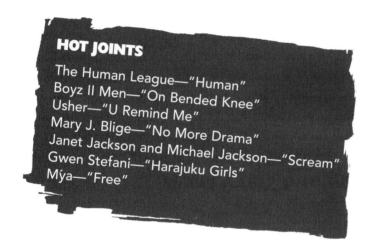

HOT JOINTS

The Human League—"Human"
Boyz II Men—"On Bended Knee"
Usher—"U Remind Me"
Mary J. Blige—"No More Drama"
Janet Jackson and Michael Jackson—"Scream"
Gwen Stefani—"Harajuku Girls"
Mýa—"Free"

DROP THE BEAT: PRODUCERS

JUST BLAZE PRODUCED SAIGON'S SINGLE "C'MON BABY," WHICH FEATURED SWIZZ BEATZ.

SWIZZ BEATZ AND JIMMY JAM AND TERRY LEWIS WERE ALL FEATURED PRODUCERS ON MAR J. BLIGE'S *NO MORE DRAMA.*

JIMMY JAM AND TERRY LEWIS PRODUCED *CONTROL*, THE BREAKTHROUGH ALBUM BY JANET JACKSON, WHO JERMAINE DUPRI IS CURRENTLY DATING.

TIMBALAND HAS BEEF WITH
IANO MAN SCOTT STORCH, THE
PRODUCER HE WORKED
ALONGSIDE ON JUSTIN
MBERLAKE'S "CRY ME A RIVER."

THE NEPTUNES' ROOTS TRACE
BACK TO VIRGINIA, WHICH IS
THE SAME STATE TIMBALAND
HAILS FROM.

JERMAINE DUPRI, DALLAS AUSTIN,
AND RODNEY JERKINS ALL BOAST
PRODUCTION CREDITS FOR R&B
SINGER MONICA.

RODNEY JERKINS AND THE NEPTUNES
BOTH CAME UP UNDER THE GUIDANCE
OF PRODUCER TEDDY RILEY, OF GUY
AND BLACKSTREET FAME.

CHAPTER 15

IT'S ALL ABOUT THE BENJAMINS:

MOGULS

For obvious reasons, the music industry has always been focused on the people who make the music, and with very, very few exceptions, such as the late Ahmet Ertegün, founder of Atlantic Records, the legendary Clive Davis, founder of Arista and J Records, and Motown's Berry Gordy, nobody could name a record company chief.

Hip-hop changed all that. Suddenly, not only did fans know who the executives behind the scenes were, but the executives behind the scenes weren't behind the scenes any longer. The guys signing the checks inexplicably showed up in the videos (à la former Roc-A-Fella co-founder and CEO Damon Dash), or in lyrics (Dash again). Most of us can't even name our senator, but we do know The Inc.'s Irv Gotti, former Untertainment head Lance

"Un" Rivera, or Violator's Chris Lighty. Possibly the most you-must-be-freaking-kidding-me example of misplaced visibility is Andre Harrell. The former head of Uptown Records and one-half of the marginal hip-hop duo Dr. Jekkel & Mr. Hyde actually appeared in billboards and promotional posters plastered throughout L.A. and NYC to announce his appointment as the head of Motown Records back in the mid-'90s. Oh, and Harrell's gig lasted like three minutes.

Russell Simmons

Probably the first celeb exec is Russell Simmons. The former co-founder and head of the seminal Def Jam Records, Simmons started his climb to the lifestyles of the rich and famous department in Hollis, Queens. As a young mogul-to-be, Russell (nicknamed Rush) did a little time on the hustle and then enrolled in college. In 1978, he began to promote block parties and hip-hop shows in Harlem and Queens, often with an old pal, Curtis Walker. Walker would morph into Kurtis Blow, one of rap music's earliest breakout solo stars, whose biggest hits were "The Breaks" and "If I Ruled the World." Simmons became Blow's manager and also co-wrote Blow's '79 single "Christmas Rappin'."

Flush with Blow's success, Simmons quit college and formed Rush Productions. In 1982, he added to his client roster when he took on his kid brother Joe's rap trio, dubbed them Run-D.M.C., and over the years that followed guided them to the hip-hop-and-beyond promised land. Around the same time, Russell met Rick Rubin, at the time a punk rock fan, college student, and fledgling producer, who like Simmons dug hardcore hip-hop. Pooling their meager resources, Rubin and Simmons founded Def Jam Records in 1984, which pretty much from the jump established itself as the hip-hop label to beat. Over time, Def Jam would not only be rap's home away from home, but one of the most influential and commercially successful music labels around. One look at the Def Jam logo signaled straight-up hip-hop hooray, beginning with its first single, LL Cool J's "I Need a Beat."

In the early days, Def Jam's roster included Slick Rick, Public Enemy, the Beastie Boys, EPMD, 3rd Bass, and Onyx. In 1985, Russell flipped Def Jam's saga into the fictionalized *Krush Groove*, starring a very young Blair Underwood as Simmons and featuring Rubin and Run-D.M.C. as themselves. Three years later Rubin departed from the label, but no tears: he'd go on to become a very big dog working with, among others, the late Johnny Cash, Dixie Chicks, Shakira, and Jay-Z ("99 Problems"). In 1998 there was also Run-D.M.C.'s movie *Tougher Than Leather*, which stunk up the place, but signaled that Simmons was aiming to make Def Jam a hip-hop-influenced entertainment company.

"POOLING THEIR MEAGER RESOURCES, RUBIN AND SIMMONS FOUNDED DEF JAM RECORDS IN 1984, WHICH PRETTY MUCH FROM THE JUMP ESTABLISHED ITSELF AS THE HIP-HOP LABEL TO BEAT."

In 1991 Simmons produced the groundbreaking HBO series *Russell Simmons' Def Comedy Jam*, which helped kick-start the careers of basically every hot young black comic, including Martin Lawrence, Chris Rock, Jamie Foxx, Bernie Mac, and Chris Tucker.

And he didn't stop. In 1992 Simmons shifted his considerable energies (animated doesn't begin to describe the dude) into fashion, launching Phat Farm. The natty men's line would soon expand into female apparel with Baby Phat, overseen by Simmons's then girlfriend (the infamous playboy got hitched in '99), now ex-wife, former model Kimora Lee. Both lines became huge successes. Simmons came back to the big screen producing 1996's hit comedy *The Nutty Professor*, which marked Eddie Murphy's (a.k.a. Golden Globe winner for *Dreamgirls*) comeback. The same year came urban magazine *One World*, which begat a syndicated TV show hosted by Kimora. More films followed—1997's *Gridlock'd* (starring Tupac Shakur) and *How to Be a Player*. Def Jam Records, which had slipped a bit during the dominance of West Coast rap, also came back strong with a beefed-up roster that included Redman, Method Man, DMX, and Ja Rule, among others.

Simmons sold the remainder of his forty percent share of his label to the conglomerate Universal Music Group for a reported 100 mil, but stayed on as a chairman in pretty much name only. But he kept going, returning to HBO in 2001 with *Russell Simmons' Def Poetry Jam*, hosted by Mos Def. A theatrical piece inspired by the show would also end up on Broadway and prove to be a big, Tony-winning achievement. Yet along with stacking chips, Simmons, who was by now a devout yogini and vegan, increasingly used his clout to make the world a better place. He did that through charities and political activism, including lobbying against New York's repressive drug laws, speaking out against intolerance, and creating the Hip-Hop Summit Action Network (HHSAN), a nonprofit that came out of an industry sitdown concerning hip-hop's direction and social role. HHSAN worked on voter registration, no doubt an influence on Puff's flashier "Vote or Die" campaign. In 2003, Simmons called for a boycott of Pepsi when the soda company cut Def Jam's Ludacris as its spokesman after right-wing blowhard Bill O'Reilly bugged. Not shabby for a dude who got his break promoting dope parties. No wonder every other hip-hop CEO who followed acknowledges Russell as the Godfather.

In what year did Russell Simmons found Def Jam?

a. 1985
b. 1987
c. 1983
d. 1984

POP QUIZ

Diddy

Sean, Puffy, Diddy, whatever you want to call him, Combs has been an artist and a producer, responsible for over $100 million in record sales, ASCAP's 1996 Songwriter of the Year, a fashion designer, executive, movie star, Broadway actor, and celebrity. Never you mind that he's a mediocre rapper at best (to paraphrase one of his hits, "Don't worry if I write rhymes/I write checks"), or that, well, you don't think he's actually designing those fly coats himself, do you? Or that maybe he doesn't do *all* the production on those club bangers. Don't matter. Puffy's talent has always been his ambition, and it's made him rich, bitch.

Born in Harlem, Sean grew up in nearby Mount Vernon, New York. He attended D.C.'s Howard University and shuttled back and forth to NYC to throw parties, sometimes with childhood pal Heavy D, who helped Combs land an internship at Uptown Records. Tragically, one of Puff's parties held at New York's City College ended in chaos when nine people were trampled to death because the event was oversold. Both Puffy and Heavy would settle out of court with the families, and rumors were rampant that as the chaos was unfolding, Diddy secured the cashbox rather than deal with the emergency. Regardless, the incident didn't impede Puffy's climb and soon the intern was an A&R dude, executive-producing Father MC (not worth worrying about), Mary J. Blige's *What's the 411?*, and Heavy D & the Boyz's *Blue Funk*. Yet after some internal skirmishes, Combs was gone by 1993.

During his break, Puff did some remixes and then set up Bad Boy Entertainment. After grinding for twelve months, he signed EPMD's ex-roadie Craig Mack and Brooklyn underground king the Notorious B.I.G. Mack hit in '94 when "Flava in Ya Ear (Remix)" featuring LL Cool J, Busta Rhymes, Rampage, and B.I.G. went top ten and became Bad Boy's first million-seller. To kick off 1995, Biggie got his label's second platinum disc with "Big Poppa." Bad Boy was in full effect.

Puff added more acts to the roster and also did more outside production. But the good stuff was being overshadowed by the bad stuff, namely Combs and Biggie's public feud with Death Row's Suge Knight and Tupac Shakur. The issues were personal (Knight believed Combs was involved in

Tupac's shooting outside a Manhattan studio) and professional (Bad Boy and Death Row were considered the preeminent labels of their respective coasts). Everything ended very badly. In September of '96, Pac was gunned down and killed, and then six months later in 1997, Biggie met the same fate. And just like that Combs had suffered the loss not only of his top-selling, most revered artist, but one of his best friends.

After taking a hiatus to mourn, Combs came roaring back in the spring of 1997 with "Can't Nobody Hold Me Down," which was number one for six weeks. Still grieving over Big, Combs took his understandable sadness to a whole new level by releasing "I'll Be Missing You." The track sampled the Police's "Every Breath You Take" and featured the Bad Boy fam, including Big's estranged widow, Faith Evans. The combo of maudlin, melody, and Puffy's undeniable, flamboyant showmanship propelled the homage to number one, where it stayed for quite some time. Puff and crew (with Sting) would later offer a respectfully over-the-top rendition of the song on that year's MTV Video Music Awards. "I'll Be Missing You" and Puff's number one album *No Way Out* (also featuring the gigantic hit "Mo' Money Mo' Problems") would win 1998's Grammys for Best Rap Performance by a Duo or Group and Best Rap Album respectively. Equally massive were the videos, which featured Puff and sidekick Ma$e in their shiny-suited regalia, accompanied by flash pots and pyro. Subtle Combs was not, and the hits and clips, while widely popular, were also ridiculed for their ultra-flashy and somewhat shallow images. Tossing dollar bills in the air, parading around in white, hiring a guy to shade him from the St. Tropez sun with a personalized umbrella, throwing parties with dress codes and captains of industry as guests—Puffy was both the biggest rap artist/mogul in the game and an embarrassment. Not that he let it bother him.

In '98 Puff inaugurated his clothing line Sean John. It was an unqualified triumph artistically and financially. The next year came his second CD, *Forever*, but it failed to excite fans or critics. Yet Puff did cause some excitement, the bad kind. That year he appeared in the video for Nas's "Hate Me Now." In one scene, both rappers were portrayed as Christ figures nailed to the cross. Shock of shock, the imagery caused an uproar, and Puff, who claimed he thought the scenes would be edited out, was also angry. It all culminated in Puff being accused of severely striking (with

"TOSSING DOLLAR BILLS IN THE AIR, PARADING AROUND IN WHITE, HIRING A GUY TO SHADE HIM FROM THE ST. TROPEZ SUN WITH A PERSONALIZED UMBRELLA, THROWING PARTIES WITH DRESS CODES AND CAPTAINS OF INDUSTRY AS GUESTS—PUFFY WAS BOTH THE BIGGEST RAP ARTIST/MOGUL IN THE GAME AND AN EMBARRASSMENT."

a champagne bottle allegedly) Nas's then manager and former Interscope exec, Steve Stoute. Puffy pleaded guilty to second-degree harassment and did some time in anger management.

P's proclivity for being in the wrong place at the wrong time became an issue again when his high-profile relationship with Jennifer Lopez hit a major snag. Right before New Year's in NYC, Puff and Lopez (along with Puff's new star Shyne) were "involved" in a shooting at a midtown nightclub. Both Combs and Lopez were brought in for questioning, and while Lopez was released, Puffy was indicted on weapons charges and then later an additional bribing-a-witness charge. Shyne was indicted on various charges including attempted murder. The drama piled up. In 2000, Puff's driver on that infamous night sued for $3 million (personal injury and stress), and then the club owner also filed suit. If that wasn't bad enough, Jenny from the Block decided she'd stood by her man long enough, ending the relationship on Valentine's Day 2001. Oh snap!

Puff's planned gospel CD took a backseat as his world seemed on the brink of collapse. But by March of 2001, it seemed that there might be some glimmer of light. After a high-profile trial, Puffy was acquitted of every charge, which effectively deaded the civil suits. Fans were delighted, but P's detractors became convinced that once again Combs had wiggled his way out of a bad situation and that someone else—in this case Shyne, who got a ten-year bid—had taken the fall. Puffy marked his acquittal with another "look at me" move by publicly changing his nickname to P. Diddy. The change meant to signal a new direction.

Combs took a major hit in 2002 when Bad Boy's longtime distributor, Arista, cut ties and took Faith Evans. The Arista/Bad Boy swan song was the compilation *We Invented the Remix*. To add more fuel to the fire engulfing Diddy's career, 112 also tried to bolt, but a restraining order slowed their plans of freedom down. Diddy secured a new home for his label, celebrating his deal with Universal with 2004's *Bad Boy's 10th Anniversary . . . The Hits*. The CD sold well but Bad Boy was coasting on fumes until Diddy revitalized the label in the summer of '06 with Yung Joc and the blockbuster "Me & U" from "singer" Cassie. In addition, Danity Kane (from the third edition of Puff and MTV's *Making the Band*) debuted at number one. That achievement bested the fate of the show's previous winning rappers, Da Band. You remember them, right? Those are the clowns Puffy ordered to march across the Brooklyn Bridge to fetch him some cheesecake—a skill all aspiring rappers need.

With hot new CDs putting Bad Boy back in play, the stage was set for Diddy's *Press Play* in 2006. The CD marked a more musically adventurous sound and included numerous guest stars, but while it did well, it didn't do amazing. Diddy's brand got bigger in late December 2006 when he became a daddy again as he and longtime (and -suffering) girlfriend Kim Porter celebrated the birth of twin girls. The Bad Boy had some bad girls and his eye was once again on the prize.

In what video did Diddy appear dressed in a "shiny suit"?

    a. "Hypnotize"

    b. "Mo' Money Mo' Problems"

    c. "Bad Boy for Life"

    d. "Can't Nobody Hold Me Down"

POP QUIZ

CHAPTER 16

FROM HOLLIS
TO HOLLYWOOD:

HIP-HOP & HOLLYWOOD

C ommonplace as it is these days, hip-hop's visibility in mainstream films—or any films, for that matter—was once nonexistent. Following the trailblazing *Style Wars* (1983), *Beat Street* and *Breakin'* (both released in 1984) continued hip-hop's infiltration of mainstream America via movie screens, and paved the way for films like 2005's *Hustle & Flow* to take home an Oscar via Three 6 Mafia's "It's Hard Out Here for a Pimp," and for Will Smith (a.k.a. the Fresh Prince) to become the first MC turned Academy Award nominee.

Films and Television

Style Wars

Released in 1983, *Style Wars*, aside from being an early film about hip-hop culture, was unique in its main focus on graffiti, with less emphasis placed on break dancing and music. Rather than portraying the kids in the film as lawbreakers and hoodlums, directors Henry Chalfant and Tony Silver depicted the youngsters for what they really were: artists. Although what they did was illegal, it was clear through *Style Wars* that graffiti was just as real an art form as any other, more "legitimate" form.

In addition to being an excellent documentary on a specific area of hip-hop culture, *Style Wars* serves as a perfectly preserved time capsule from late-'70s and early-'80s New York City, with then mayor Ed Koch cracking down on graffiti artists who straddled the line between illegality and fine art.

Breakin'

Aside from being Ice-T's film debut (as a club's MC, T would later become a Hollywood staple), this 1984 break-dancing-based film introduced a new style of dancing to the mainstream. With disco on the outs, its straightforward drumbeats giving way to more complex and electronic-based ones (whatever dances coked-up white people did to disco were left as a confused and unique form of dance) break dancing evolved right along with every other aspect of hip-hop, becoming more intense and complex as it grew older. Now a solid piece of Americana, break dancing owes a huge debt to *Breakin'*.

Beat Street

Also released in 1984, *Beat Street* looked to *Style Wars* for inspiration and found it in the story of young aspiring artists looking to break into the next level. This movie was classic not only for the break-dancing battles (which featured the now famous Rock Steady Crew and New York City

Breakers), but for appearances from such hip-hop luminaries as Grandmaster Flash and the Furious Five, the Treacherous Three, and Doug E. Fresh.

Krush Goove

A thinly disguised story about what is clearly Russell Simmons and his growing Def Jam empire, *Krush Groove* focused on Russell Walker (Blair Underwood) and his Krush Groove record label. When Krush Groove act Run-D.M.C. scores a hit and Walker can't keep up with demand, he turns to a shady character (not Eminem) to borrow funds. At the same time, we have the obligatory love story, which involves Walker and (Reverend) Run vying for Sheila E., who plays herself, along with LL Cool J, the Fat Boys, the Beastie Boys, and New Edition.

House Party

Nineteen ninety's *House Party* starred rappers Kid 'N Play, who are less remembered as MCs and more as those two guys who were in *House Party*. The clichéd plot revolves around a house party (duh) thrown by Play, who has invited his boy Kid (despite Kid's being grounded) and the wacky trials and tribulations that come along with being a teenager and sneaking around on your parents. Aside from being little more than a goof, *House Party* is one of—if not *the*—earliest examples of rappers turned comedians committed to film.

The Fresh Prince of Bel-Air

Debuting in 1990, this classic show starred Will Smith in his first breakout performance that wasn't on wax. Starring as a troublemaking teen from Philly sent to live with his rich aunt and uncle in Bel-Air (we all know the theme song), six seasons' worth of wackiness ensued. Well written, the show still airs in syndication, and if you're lucky you'll see Smith's DJ Jazzy Jeff (as Jazz) get tossed out the front door by Uncle Phil after overstaying his welcome.

New Jack City

Released in early 1991, *New Jack City* was rapper Ice-T's stepping-stone to the big leagues of film, portraying an undercover New York City cop trying to bring down the city's big-deal drug kingpin, Nino Brown. Gritty and brutal, Ice-T also appeared on the soundtrack with his "New Jack Hustler."

Boyz N the Hood

The other hip-hop-related film released in 1991, this bleak urban tale featured a film-stealing Ice Cube in all of his Jheri-curled glory as Doughboy, the bad-influence older brother to Cuba Gooding Jr.'s character, who's set to head to college on a football scholarship. Fairly depressing in tone, *Boyz N the Hood* was the first glimpse the rest of America had into South Central Los Angeles, where gunplay and drugs were everyday occurrences. Unlike for Mario Van Peebles with *New Jack City*, writer/director John Singleton was nominated for an Oscar, a doubly impressive feat considering *Boyz* was his first feature film.

Poetic Justice

Despite 1992's *Juice* being Tupac Shakur's first starring role, it was *Poetic Justice* that helped propel his acting career into the spotlight. He portrayed postal worker Lucky, who, in typical Hollywood fashion, finds love with Justice (Janet Jackson) despite their surface dissimilarities.

Friday, Next Friday, and Friday After Next

Can you believe it's been over a decade since *Friday* hit theaters? Written by Ice Cube and DJ Pooh, this day-in-the-life comedy has become a cult classic since its 1995 release, solidifying Ice Cube as a comedic actor as well as a big-screen badass. *Friday*'s two sequels may lack the freshness of the O.G., but both proved successful at the box office, if nothing else.

Don't Be a Menace to South Central While Drinking Your Juice in the Hood

Quite possibly the best Wayans-related project since *In Living Color*, this 'hood-movie spoof relies heavily on *Boyz N the Hood* and *Poetic Justice* for material, but succeeds wildly in the process. Though it doesn't seem like it would be easy to find the humor in gang violence, escaping the 'hood, and teen pregnancy, *Don't Be a Menace* somehow finds a way and keeps the laughs coming constantly.

Belly

Starring both Nas and DMX as ex-cons, the film featured the duo dealing with conflict in their relationship when one goes straight and the other participates in a drug deal. In addition to starring two hip-hop giants, the 1998 film was shot by acclaimed music video director Hype Williams and features supporting roles by Method Man and T-Boz (TLC).

Baby Boy

The lead role was written with Tupac in mind, but the rapper's untimely death put Tyrese Gibson in the lead role instead, opposite Snoop Dogg as his girlfriend's ex, a gangbanger looking to beef with Tyrese's character. The 2001 film was directed by John Singleton.

How High

Best pals Method Man and Redman got silly on film in this 2001 weed-based picture, which sees the duo take their on-record chemistry to the big screen for the first time. A stoner cult classic, *How High* finds Meth and Red at Harvard after smoking some sort of magic weed and scoring perfectly on their college entrance exams. As you can imagine, humor ensues, but it definitely helps if you're, to put it bluntly . . . never mind.

BarberShop

Another notch in Ice Cube's belt is this 2002 Chicago-set film, which sees the more-actor-less-rapper Cube taking on both a dramatic and comedic role as the proprietor of a local (you guessed it) barbershop that's subject to removal in favor of a new strip club (maybe Cube's character from *The Player's Club* could manage it!). Not only does Cube succeed wildly in his role as a father figure, but *BarberShop* saw female MC Eve emerge as a natural actress.

Scratch

A fairly recent film, this 2001 documentary focused on the MC's best friend, the DJ. Tracing scratching and DJing from its roots with Grand Wizard Theodore up to the present day, as displayed by turntable maniacs like DJ Swamp and DJ Q-Bert, *Scratch* is as detailed of a look as you're going to get behind the decks of hip-hop's most well-respected turntablists.

8 Mile

Like *Krush Groove* before it, *8 Mile* is the loosely disguised story of Eminem's rise from struggling Detroit rapper to successful MC. Though the film's outcome was pretty obvious, Em turned in a great performance as himself, essentially, showing that he has more sides than his violent and maniacal on-record Slim Shady character. The picture scored Em an Oscar for Best Original Song.

You Got Served

In an interesting coincidence, this 2004 film starred Omarion (B2K) and Marques Houston, who not only was in boy band Immature (later IMx), but appeared in *House Party 3*. *You Got Served*, though, revolves not around a party, but dance battles akin to '80s break-dancing battles seen in films like *Beat Street*. When the characters get entangled in drug dealing, their antics eventually lead up to a major dance battle, somehow guest-officiated by female MC Lil' Kim.

Fade to Black

After announcing his "retirement," Jay-Z released this, a concert film that also served as a farewell and retrospective of his illustrious career. The film featured cameos from everyone imaginable, including Common, Diddy, Slick Rick, Ghostface Killah, Kanye West, and about a million more.

Get Rich or Die Tryin'

Riding high on the success of his album of the same name and labelmate Eminem's *8 Mile*, 50 Cent turned in this 2005 performance as, you guessed it . . . a struggling drug dealer who gets shot up and eventually makes it as a dad and a rapper.

Hustle & Flow

More notable for what the soundtrack achieved than anything else, 2005's *Hustle & Flow* saw Three 6 Mafia take home an Academy Award in the Best Original Song category for their contribution "It's Hard Out Here for a Pimp." Finally taking hip-hop-related cinema past the nominations level, Three 6 Mafia broke new ground for the genre, reinvigorating the hope that someday a rapper can grab an Oscar for acting or directing.

ATL

The 2006 film starred T.I. and Big Boi (OutKast), with T.I. as the fresh high school graduate trying to find himself, and Big Boi as the local drug dealer who ropes in T.I.'s little brother. In your typical coming-of-age-after-high-school flick, T.I. and Big Boi both delivered memorable performances despite the film's predictable format.

Idlewild

Another 2006 release, *Idlewild* marked the big move from record to cinema for Atlanta rap duo OutKast. A natural step from their ambitious *Speakerboxxx/The Love Below* double album, *Idlewild* is a musical set in the Prohibition era, and revolves mostly around insane dance sequences.

Grand in scope, the film was criticized for lack of focus, but accomplished what it most likely set out to do: give OutKast some Hollywood clout.

Actors

Will Smith

Easily the largest rapper turned actor, Smith first broke onto the scene with 1990's *The Fresh Prince of Bel-Air*, a fish-out-of-water comedy that saw Smith leap into homes for six seasons straight. Using the television as a stepping-stone to bigger and better things, Smith broke away from the feel-good *Fresh Prince* to star alongside Martin Lawrence in 1995's *Bad Boys*, playing a fast-talking detective. Following the success of *Bad Boys*, the floodgates opened for Smith, who landed roles in back-to-back blockbusters *Independence Day* and *Men in Black*.

The turn of the century saw Smith's acting career take a turn for the serious with roles in *The Legend of Bagger Vance* and 2001's *Ali*. Returning to the *Bad Boys* and *Men in Black* franchises for sequels, Smith has since branched out into everything from science-fiction thrillers (*I, Robot*) to animated features (*Shark Tale*). Most recently, he appeared alongside his real-life son Jaden in 2006's tale of perseverance, *The Pursuit of Happyness*.

Ice Cube

Breaking onto the film scene with little subtlety as Doughboy in 1991's *Boyz N the Hood*, former N.W.A. member Ice Cube has played every part imaginable since his debut. From slacker good-guy in the *Friday* films to a snake-fighter in *Anaconda* to a military man in *Three Kings* to wacky kid-wrangler in *Are We There Yet?*, Cube has proven himself not only as an actor but as a writer, with co-writing film credits on all three *Friday* movies and writer/director credits for *The Player's Club*.

Ice-T

Though it's incredibly ironic that the man responsible for "Cop Killer" has played mostly cops in his acting career, Ice-T happens to play them really well. From his hard-nosed appearance in *New Jack City* to the present day on TV's *Law & Order: Special Victims Unit*, T has appeared in countless straight-to-DVD titles (*Leprechaun in the Hood*, anyone?), as a voice in *Grand Theft Auto: San Andreas*, and, well, a bunch more movies you've never heard of. *Point Doom? Air Rage? Out Kold?* Point is, Ice-T has made the leap from gangsta rapper into legitimate actor by using his street knowledge and hustler's ambition.

Queen Latifah

Understated, but no less accomplished than her male counterparts, hip-hop's Queen has appeared in more notable films than one might suspect. She's appeared alongside Kid 'N Play in *House Party 2*, with Will Smith on *The Fresh Prince of Bel-Air*, with Tupac in *Juice*, in a voice-only role in *Bringing Out the Dead*, and as a main character on TV's *Living Single*. Small parts and cameos aside, Latifah really caught everyone's attention with an Oscar-nominated role in 2002's *Chicago* as well as *BarberShop 2: Back in Business* and the subsequent spin-off, *Beauty Shop*.

Ludacris

Just beginning his screen legacy, Chris "Ludacris" Bridges turned heads in 2004's *Crash* as well as 2005's *Hustle & Flow*. Aside from these two roles, Luda has seen mainly one-off appearances on *Law & Order: Special Victims Unit* and a few small parts in *2 Fast 2 Furious* and *The Wash* remake.

DMX

Though his filmography is still limited, DMX has channeled his lyrical anger into action roles opposite Steven Seagal (*Exit Wounds*) and twice with kung-fu genius Jet Li in *Romeo Must Die* (also with the late Aaliyah) and *Cradle 2 the Grave*. DMX also starred in his own reality show, *DMX: Soul of a Man*, on BET in 2006.

Jamie Foxx

When this *In Living Color* alumni first started on the big screen, it was with movies like *Booty Call* and *The Great White Hype*. After hooking up with Kanye West, though, Foxx's profile rose, and he's since landed acclaimed roles in *Dreamgirls* and *Miami Vice* as well as winning an Oscar for Best Actor for his work as Ray Charles in the 2004 biopic *Ray*.

Mos Def

Known mostly as an MC with incredible lyrics, Mos Def has appeared as an actor in a million TV roles, including the universally loved *Chappelle's Show*, *The Boondocks*, *NYPD Blue*, and *The Wayne Brady Show*. Outside of a TV setting, Mos turned up in *The Hitchhiker's Guide to the Galaxy* as well as alongside Bruce Willis in the action/thriller *16 Blocks*. With no less than seven projects in the pipeline during 2007, the future looks anything but dull for Mos.

Beyoncé Knowles

Using her success with Destiny's Child as a jump-off point, Beyoncé turned up first in the comedies *Austin Powers in Goldmember* and *The Pink Panther*, as well as the "hip-hopera" *Carmen*, alongside Mos Def. In 2006 Beyoncé showed up in the acclaimed *Dreamgirls*, although her excellent performance seems to have been overshadowed by Chicagoan Jennifer Hudson. We will most definitely be hearing more from Knowles in the future, though.

Eve

Following her initial appearance in *BarberShop*, Eve reprised her role in *BarberShop 2: Back in Business*, and with female rapper and trailblazer Queen Latifah in *The Cookout*. She also held down the role as Shelly Williams in her own television sitcom, *Eve*. Taking a turn for the more serious, Eve is slated to appear in *Ego*, a police drama slated for release in 2008.

Brandy

Aside from TV's *Moesha* (where Onyx's Fredo Starr, Master P, and Russell Simmons also appeared from time to time), Brandy has only been seen in a handful of features: 1990's spider-based fright fest *Arachnophobia*, slasher flick *I Still Know What You Did Last Summer*, and animated feature *Osmosis Jones*. She's turned up more on TV, though, with guest spots on *Sabrina, the Teenage Witch*, *Reba*, and *One on One*.

LL Cool J

One of the most classic MCs ever, LL Cool J has appeared in mostly less-than-serious films, including remakes of *Rollerball* and *SWAT*, but has really shone on TV's small screen. Turning up on HBO's *Oz*, the brilliant comedy *30 Rock* (as big-time rapper Ridikolus), and holding the lead in the sitcom *In the House*, LL's appearances in any of these releases are more memorable than his emergence in 1986's football comedy *Wildcats*, where he's credited way below Nipsey Russell and Wesley Snipes as "rapper."

Master P

Capitalizing on the declining cost of digital equipment and DVD mass production, P took his hip-hop wealth and broke onto the straight-to-DVD scene with such 'hood classics as *I'm Bout It* and *I Got the Hook Up*. Master P has appeared on the MC-friendly *Oz*, as well as *CSI: NY*. In addition to those roles, he has been involved with a number of relatively unknown projects like *Uncle P* and *Don't Be Scared*.

André 3000

The half of OutKast that seems more interested in Hollywood than making records, André 3000 made his first notable roles in 2005's *Be Cool* and *Four Brothers*, a John Singleton film. Appearing alongside his partner Big Boi in the OutKast-scored *Idlewild*, André has since premiered his own cartoon, the semi autobiographical *Class of 3000*, and played the voice of a crow in the half-animated film *Charlotte's Web*.

TIMELINE

1983: *Wild Style* is released.

1984: *Breakin'*, *Breakin' 2: Electric Boogaloo*, and *Beat Street* are released.

1985: *Krush Groove* is released.

1990: *The Fresh Prince of Bel-Air* debuts, *House Party* is released.

1991: *Boyz N the Hood*, *New Jack City*, and *House Party 2* are released.

1992: *Boyz N the Hood* director John Singleton is nominated for an Academy Award; *Juice* and *Poetic Justice* are released; Tupac Shakur is arrested for attacking Allen Hughes on the set of *Menace II Society*.

1993: *Menace II Society* is released.

1994: Snoop Dogg's short film/EP *Murder Was the Case* is released, *House Party 3* is released.

1995: Ol' Dirty Bastard appears on MTV picking up food stamps in a limo; *Bad Boys* and *Friday* are released.

1996: *Don't Be a Menace to South Central While Drinking Your Juice in the Hood* and *Independence Day* are released.

1997: *Men in Black* is released.

1998: *Belly* and *I Got the Hook Up* are released.

2001: *Baby Boy*, *How High,* and *Scratch* are released; burgeoning actress Aaliyah dies in a plane crash.

2002: Will Smith is nominated for an Oscar for Best Actor for *Ali*; *8 Mile* and *BarberShop* are released.

2003: Eminem wins Oscar for Best Original Song for *8 Mile*'s "Lose Yourself"; Queen Latifah is nominated for Best Supporting Actress Oscar for *Chicago*.

2004: *You Got Served, Fade to Black, Crash,* and *BarberShop 2: Back in Business* are released.

2005: Jamie Foxx wins Oscar for Best Actor for *Ray*; *Get Rich or Die Tryin'* and *Hustle & Flow* are released.

2006: Three 6 Mafia wins Oscar for Best Original Song in *Hustle & Flow*; *Idlewild* and *ATL* are released.

2007: Will Smith is nominated for a second Oscar for Best Actor for *The Pursuit of Happyness*.

Answer Key

16: c. LL Cool J's "I Need a Beat"
18: a. King Asiatic Nobody's Equal
21: b. Al B. Sure!
26: d. Salt-N-Pepa
29: b. *Ali*

35: b. "Whatta Man"
39: c. *Back from Hell*
43: d. Jive Records
48: b. 5

56: a. Brooklyn
61: c. "Mo' Money Mo' Problems"
65: b. Ciara
72: a. 5
79: d. *The Rugrats Movie*
85: a. *Turn It Up*
89: b. Brooklyn
91: c. Jay-Z—"Moment of Clarity"
94: d. "Fresh 40"
102: b. Kimberly Jones
105: c. DMX
109: a. Sista
115: b. Jay-Z
120: c. *Represent*
128: b. Columbia Records
135: d. T-Mobile

141: c. Lollapalooza
145: a. *Southernplayalisticadillacmuzik*
148: b. Macy Gray
153: d. Bizzy Bone
159: a. *Saturday Night Live*

166: b. Architectural drafting
170: d. Def Jam
178: a. Harlem, New York

184: d. 9
188: b. MTV's European Music Awards
191: c. "What More Can I Say"
196: b. Basketball

217: c. "Be Without You"
221: b. "We Belong Together"
226: d. *Aaliyah*
228: a. *The Rugrats Movie*

235: d. *R.*
238: b. Eric Clapton

244: c. *Cooleyhighharmony*
247: d. Teddy Riley
249: b. "Creep"
254: c. Elektra Records

260: a. 5
262: c. Austin, Texas
265: d. Georgetown
267: a. "Irreplaceable"

271: c. *Stomp the Yard*
273: b. "Everything Is Everything"

279: c. Angie Stone
283: c. OutKast

303: d. 1984
307: b. "Mo' Money Mo' Problems"

INDEX

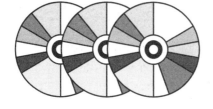